Wallace Wang

John Wiley & Sons, Inc.

Beginning Programming For Dummies®, 4th Edition

Published by
John Wiley & Sons, Inc.
111 River Street
Hoboken, NJ 07030-5774
www.wiley.com

Published by John Wiley & Sons, Inc., Hoboken, New Jersey

Published simultaneously in Canada

For general information on our other products and services, please contact our Customer Care Department within the U.S. at 877-762-2974, outside the U.S. at 317-572-3993, or fax 317-572-4002.

For technical support, please visit www.wiley.com/techsupport.

Wiley publishes in a variety of print and electronic formats and by print-on-demand. Some material included with standard print versions of this book may not be included in e-books or in print-on-demand. If this book refers to media such as a CD or DVD that is not included in the version you purchased, you may download this material at http://booksupport.wiley.com. For more information about Wiley products, visit www.wiley.com.

Library of Congress Control Number: 2006932692

ISBN 978-1-119-17380-9

About the Author

Wallace Wang is one of many carbon-based life forms currently populating the planet Earth. He began his working career by going to college and getting a "good" job — only to find that a college education never guaranteed you a "good" job and most "good" jobs actually stink.

So faced with the prospect of spending the rest of his waking life in a caffeine-induced stupor coupled with shots of alcohol and gambling to dull the frustration of a dead-end job, he decided to pursue one of many dreams by becoming a writer. First starting out writing magazine articles for a local San Diego computer magazine, he soon graduated to writing for national publications and book publishers as well.

After nearly 20 years of writing full-time, he's still pursuing a variety of different dreams besides continuing book and magazine writing. He's still bouncing around comedy clubs around Michigan, Las Vegas, and San Diego, performing stand-up comedy to anyone sober enough to listen.

He's also branched away from computer books by teaming up with coauthors to write non-computer related books, most notably *Breaking Into Acting For Dummies* with Larry Garrison. (Thanks go to Ben Affleck for carrying around a copy and getting his picture taken with the book, which appeared in many major magazines including *People Magazine* and *The New York Post.*)

In his latest mad venture to avoid having to work in an ordinary 9–5 job, he's also teamed up with three other comedians (Rick Gene, Wes Sample, and Justin Davis) to create, produce, and host a radio show called "Keeping It Weird," currently (at least at the time of this writing) airing on 103.7 Free FM in San Diego.

By the time you read this, the author may be off pursuing something entirely different. Whatever he may be doing at the time, it should at least make for interesting stories to tell his grandchildren about one day.

Dedication

This book is dedicated to all the wonderful people I've met along the path of life, including . . .

Cassandra (my wife), Jordan (my son), and Bo, Scraps, Tasha, and Nuit (our cats).

Lily Carnie, the only person I know who can truly see both sides of the story.

All the friendly folks I've met while performing at the Riviera Comedy Club, located at the Riviera Hotel & Casino in Las Vegas: Steve Schirripa (who also appears on the HBO show, *The Sopranos*, which you can read about at `www.hbo.com/sopranos`), Don Learned, Bob Zany, Gerry Bednob, Bruce Clark, Darrell Joyce, and Kip Addotta. The next time you're visiting Las Vegas, drop by the Riviera and watch a comedy show. Then dump some money in a slot machine on the way out to ensure that the Riviera Hotel & Casino continues making enough money to keep its comedy club open.

Thanks also go to Roger Feeny at the Ann Arbor Comedy Showcase in Ann Arbor, Michigan; Russ Rivas at Laff's in Albuquerque, New Mexico; Pat Wilson at Mesquite, Nevada; and Joe Jarred at Primm and Pahrump, Nevada for running some of the friendliest comedy clubs around the country.

Final thanks must also go to Leo (the man, the myth, the legend) Fontaine, Chris (the Zooman) Clobber, Rick Gene, Wes Sample, Justin Davis, and Dante (who gets excited just to see his name in a book).

Author's Acknowledgments

If it wasn't for Bill Gladstone at Waterside Productions, I might still be staring off into space in a cubicle somewhere, working in a dead-end job, wondering what could have been.

Additional thanks go to Allen Wyatt for making sure that everything in this book is accurate, along with Rebecca Senninger and Virginia Sanders for making the process of writing a book always painless, easy, and often fun.

Final acknowledgements go to Cassandra (my wife) for putting up with multiple computers that (from her point of view) seem to spontaneously appear and disappear around the house at random. Each time a computer disappears, a more advanced model appears that promises more speed and hard drive space, but still never seems to have more speed or as much room as the previous computer model that it replaced.

Publisher's Acknowledgments

We're proud of this book; please send us your comments through our online registration form located at `http://dummies.custhelp.com`.

Some of the people who helped bring this book to market include the following:

Acquisitions, Editorial, and Vertical Websites

Project Editor: Rebecca Senninger

(Previous Edition: Andrea C. Boucher)

Acquisitions Editor: Katie Feltman

Copy Editor: Virginia Sanders

Technical Editor: Allen Wyatt

Editorial Manager: Leah Cameron

Vertical Websites Specialists: Angela Denny, Kate Jenkins, Steven Kudirka, Kit Malone

Vertical Websites Coordinator: Laura Atkinson

Vertical Websites Project Supervisor: Laura Moss

Vertical Websites Manager: Laura VanWinkle

Editorial Assistant: Amanda Foxworth

Sr. Editorial Assistant: Cherie Case

Cartoons: Rich Tennant (`www.the5thwave.com`)

Composition Services

Project Coordinator: Michael Kruzil

Layout and Graphics: Claudia Bell, Carl Byers, Brooke Graczyk, Denny Hager, Joyce Haughey, Stephanie D. Jumper, Barbara Moore, Barry Offringa, Laura Pence, Alicia South

Proofreaders: Laura Albert, Aptara

Indexer: Steve Rath

Publishing and Editorial for Technology Dummies

Richard Swadley, Vice President and Executive Group Publisher

Andy Cummings, Vice President and Publisher

Mary Bednarek, Executive Acquisitions Director

Mary C. Corder, Editorial Director

Publishing for Consumer Dummies

Kathleen Nebenhaus, Vice President and Executive Publisher

Composition Services

Debbie Stailey, Director of Composition Services

Contents at a Glance

Table of Contents

Part III: Advanced Programming Topics 213

Introduction

Anyone can learn to program a computer. Computer programming doesn't require a high IQ or an innate proficiency in advanced mathematics. Computer programming just requires a desire to learn and the patience never to give up.

Programming is a skill like rock climbing, tap dancing, and pole vaulting. Some people are naturally better than others, but anyone can get better with regular practice. That's why so many kids become programming wizards at such an early age. These kids aren't necessarily brilliant; they're just willing to put in the time to learn a new skill, and they're not afraid of failing because they know that failure is nothing more than a part of learning.

If you ever dreamed about writing your own programs, rest assured that you can. Programming can be lots of fun, but it can also be frustrating, annoying, and time-consuming. That's why Wiley publishes this particular book — to help you discover how to program a computer with minimum inconvenience and maximum enjoyment.

Whether you want to pick up computer programming for fun, to start a new career, or to help make your current job easier, consider this book your personal guide through the sometimes scary — and initially intimidating — world of computer programming.

Although this book won't turn you into a programming wizard overnight, it can teach you enough about programming to help you understand how programming works, what the strengths and weaknesses of different programming languages are, and how you can get started writing programs all by yourself.

Who Should Buy This Book

You should buy this book if you want to learn how computer programming works without getting bogged down in the technical details of a particular programming language. When you understand how computer programming works, you'll better understand how to use a specific programming language with cryptic names like C++ or Java. But you should buy this book if you especially want to know any of the following:

- How computer programs work
- The common parts of every computer programming language
- How to write programs for multiple platforms such as Windows, Mac OS X, or Linux
- Whether to write your next computer program by using Visual Basic, C++, Perl, SmallTalk, C#, or some other programming language

Like any skill, you can learn programming only by practicing it. To help you get hands-on experience, the CD enclosed with this book includes trial versions of four language compilers so you can practice writing programs on any computer that runs Windows, Mac OS X, or Linux.

The three main languages you learn in this book are BASIC, C++, and a scripting language called Revolution.

BASIC is specially designed to introduce beginners to programming, so you can practice writing BASIC programs in two programming languages: Liberty BASIC and REALbasic.

Liberty BASIC represents the BASIC language in its purest and simplest form so you can understand the concepts of programming without getting lost in the technical details. When you understand how BASIC works, you can study REALbasic to see a version of the BASIC language that includes advanced programming features similar to more powerful languages such as C++.

This book also provides examples in C++, which is the most popular programming language in use today. If you want to write programs professionally, you must at least become familiar with the way C++ works.

You also learn a nontraditional programming language called Revolution, which uses English-like sentences to control your computer. Scripting languages like Revolution are designed to be easy to write and understand. They also provide commands capable of solving complicated problems more easily than traditional programming languages like BASIC or C++.

In addition, the Revolution programming language is based on AppleScript, which is a programming language used to automate a Mac OS X computer, so after you're familiar with Revolution, you also know most of the AppleScript programming language.

By learning BASIC, C++, and Revolution, you're exposed to three different programming languages, styles, and approaches to solving problems so you can better understand the advantages and limitations of any programming language. Then you can choose the best programming language for your needs.

How This Book Is Organized

To help you find what you need quickly, this book consists of five parts, and each part covers a certain topic about computer programming. Whenever you need help, just flip through the book, find the part that covers the topic you're looking for, and then keep the book at your side as you get back to work.

Part I: Programming a Computer

If computer programming seems a mysterious arcane science, relax. This part of the book demystifies all the common myths about computer programming, shows you exactly how computer programs work, and explains why programming isn't as difficult as many people think.

This part also shows you how programming has evolved, why so many different programming languages exist, and how programming follows easy-to-remember principles so you can start programming your own computer right away.

Part II: The Building Blocks of Programming

Although literally thousands of different programming languages are available for you to learn, every programming language tends to work in similar ways. So in this part of the book, you learn the basic building blocks of writing and creating a program regardless of the particular programming language you use.

To help you understand the building blocks of programming, each chapter provides plenty of examples in different programming languages so you can see how they accomplish the same task. You can also try out the examples on your own computer.

Part III: Advanced Programming Topics

After you master the basics of writing a program, you need to worry about making your program work efficiently, eliminating problems, and designing a user interface so other people will know how to use it. In this part of the book, you learn how programmers fine-tune their software (and what the consequences might be if they don't).

Part IV: Internet Programming

The Internet is fast becoming an integral part of the computer world, so this part of the book introduces you to the basics of various Internet languages, including HTML (which designs the appearance of Web pages), JavaScript, and Java.

In this part, you also see how other people create cool Web pages that look good and can display forms and respond to users. You can use this information to create Web sites that interact with users.

Part V: The Part of Tens

To help gently guide you toward writing your own programs for money, this part of the book provides information about programming jobs you might want to pursue and how to find more tools and source code to help you learn more about programming all by yourself.

How to Use This Book

This book is meant to show you the basics of computer programming without bogging you down with the technical details of any particular programming language. Typed code often looks like chicken scratches or the random characters that a monkey might type if left alone with a keyboard. So you can use this book as a tutorial (to show you how programming works) and as a reference (to help refresh your memory for understanding different programming techniques).

Ideally, you want to use this book along with your computer. Read some of the book and then try what you just read on your computer so that you can see with your own eyes how programming works.

Foolish assumptions

To get the most out of this book, you need access to a computer (because trying to understand computer programming without a computer is like trying to learn to drive without a car). To take full advantage of this book, you need a computer running Microsoft Windows, Mac OS X, or Linux.

Icons used in this book

Icons highlight useful tips, important information to remember, or technical explanations that can amuse you for a moment before you forget all about them. Keep an eye open for the following icons throughout the book:

This icon highlights useful information that can save you time (as long as you remember it, of course).

This icon reminds you to do something or emphasizes an important point that you don't want to forget.

Watch out! This icon tells you how to avoid potential headaches and trouble.

This icon identifies the name of a particular file on the CD that contains a sample program printed in the book. By loading the sample program off the CD, you don't have to type the program yourself.

This icon highlights information that's nice to know but which you can safely ignore if you choose. (If you want to become a real programmer, however, you need to cram your brain with as much technical information as possible so that you can fit in with the rest of the programmers in the world.)

Part I

Programming a Computer

In this part . . .

Figuring out how to program a computer may seem intimidating, so this part of the book gently guides you through the wonderful world of computer programming. First, you see exactly what programs do and how professionals write programs.

Next, you discover why so many different programming languages exist and why some are more popular than others. You get to know the different tools that programmers use to create, edit, and distribute a program from start to finish.

Finally, this part shows you what to consider if you decide to write a program. You see the pros and cons of using different programming languages. You also find out how people can write programs even if they possess very little programming experience.

By the time that you finish this part of the book, you'll have a better idea of how to write a program, what steps to follow, and how to convert your idea for a program into an actual working product that you can sell or give away for others to use. Who knows? With a little bit of imagination and a lot of persistence, you may create the next program that makes so much money that you can start your own software company and make a million bucks.

Chapter 1

Learning Computer Programming for the First Time

In This Chapter

- Learning computer programming
- Understanding how a computer program works
- Knowing how to program a computer

Despite what you may have heard, programming a computer isn't difficult. Computer programming is a skill that anyone can pick up, given enough practice, patience, and caffeinated beverages.

Although computers may seem like tremendously complex electronic beasts, relax. Few people know how internal-combustion engines work, yet people can still figure out how to drive a car. Similarly, anyone can pick up programming skills without worrying (too much) about the specific details that make a computer work.

Why Learn Computer Programming?

The first question that you (or your friends, co-workers, and relatives) may ask is, "Why bother learning to program a computer?" The answer depends on your ultimate goals, but the following list offers some common answers to consider:

- **For fun:** People learn skiing, dancing, gardening, scuba diving, and painting because they enjoy the experience. They may never become professionals or experts in their chosen hobbies, but they enjoy fiddling around nevertheless. Similarly, programming a computer can prove fun because you might design a simple program that displays your boss's ugly face on the computer. More complex programs may make you a million dollars so that you never again need to work for a boss with an ugly face. Figure 1-1 shows a program known as *Comic Life,* which can turn any photograph into a comic book. This program was written in a programming language called Objective-C on a Macintosh.

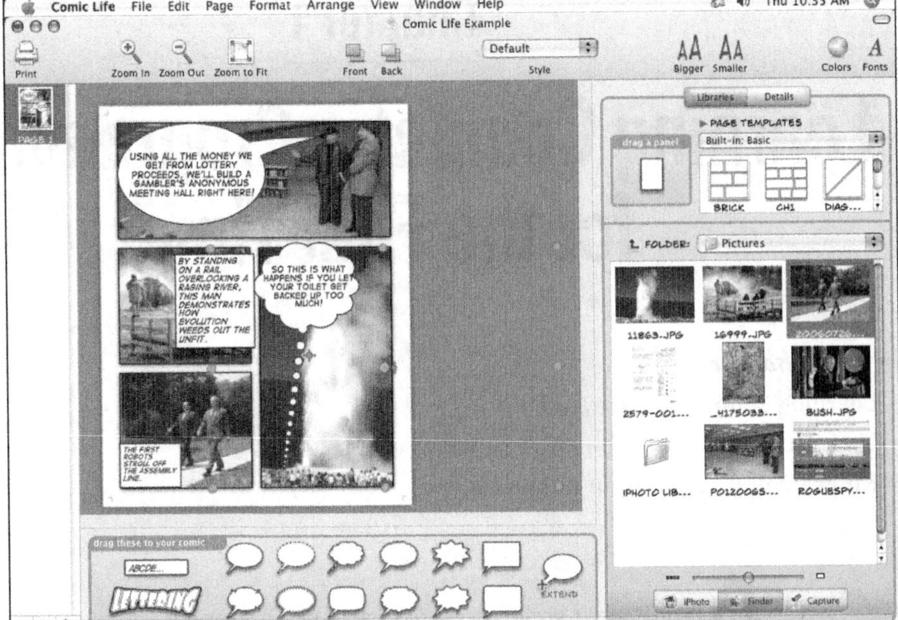

Figure 1-1: Comic Life is a program that can turn any picture into a comic book cartoon.

- **To fill a need:** Many people learn programming with no intention of becoming full-time, professional programmers. They just want a program that solves a particular problem, but they can't find a program that does it, so they write the program themselves. A man once needed a program to help him file his taxes, for example, but he couldn't find one, so he taught himself programming and wound up creating TurboTax, one of the most popular tax-preparation programs in the country. Similarly, a freelance writer got frustrated with trying to write a novel with an ordinary word processor, so he created a word processor, specially designed to organize a story, called Z-Write, as shown in Figure 1-2. Z-Write was written by using a program called REALbasic. Whatever your interests, you can write a program to solve a specific problem that others may find useful as well.
- **For a new or second career:** With computers taking over the world, you're never unemployed for long if you know how to program a computer. Companies are always looking to create new programs, but you also find a growing market for programmers who can maintain and modify the millions of existing programs that do everything from storing hotel reservations to transferring bank deposits electronically. If you know how to program a computer, you're in a much better position to

earn a lot of money and live wherever you want. You may still want to keep your current job, but programming gives you a new way to expand and share your knowledge. A group of alternative healthcare practitioners, for example, wrote *IBIS,* a program that provides information for treating a variety of ailments by using acupuncture, massage, diet, and homeopathy (see Figure 1-3). They wrote IBIS by using a program known as Revolution.

- **As an intellectual challenge:** Many people find the sheer complexity of computers as fascinating as studying a mathematical puzzle. Not surprisingly, computers tend to attract people of above-average intelligence who enjoy programming a computer to pry into the thought processes of their own minds. To help turn a computer into a thinking tool, one programmer created the *Axon Idea Processor* (see Figure 1-4) by using Prolog, a popular programming language used for researching artificial intelligence. The goal was to create a program to help people manipulate ideas, concepts, and facts so that they can devise a variety of possible solutions while better understanding their own ways of thinking in the process. If using a computer normally seems boring, try writing your own program to help you use your brain more effectively.

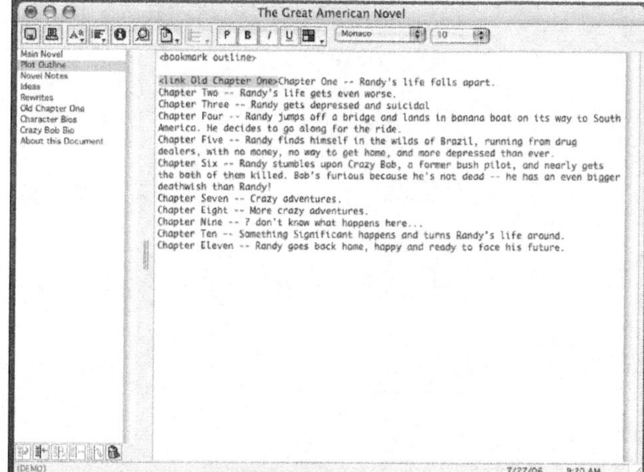

Figure 1-2: Z-Write can help you organize and write a novel or short story.

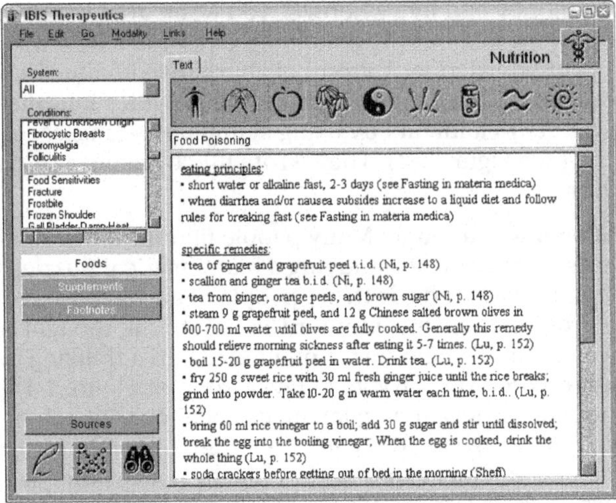

Figure 1-3: IBIS harnesses computer power to help healthcare workers find a variety of alternative healthcare procedures.

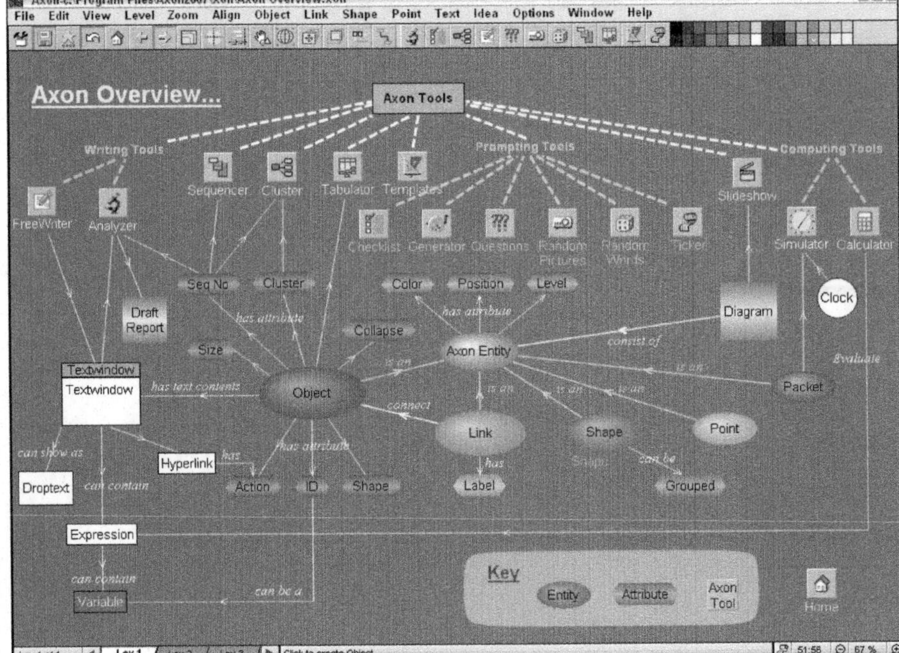

Figure 1-4: The Axon Idea Processor turns your computer screen into a canvas for organizing and manipulating ideas.

As you can see from these four examples, the programming language you use doesn't matter as much as what you want to make your computer do. The magic of computer programming doesn't come from using any particular tool, computer, or language. The real magic of programming comes from applying your own imagination and using programming as a means to achieve whatever you want to create.

Although you can make a decent living programming computers, you can also make a decent living selling paper clips, fixing leaky toilets, or raising farm animals. If you aren't doing what you truly enjoy, all the money in the world isn't going to make you happy. Choose to learn programming because you want to — not because you think that it's going to make you rich.

How Does a Computer Program Work?

Computers don't do anything without someone telling them what to do, much like the average teenager. To make the computer do something useful, you must give it instructions in either of the following two ways:

- **Write a program** that tells a computer what to do, step by step, much as you write out a recipe.
- **Buy a program** that someone else has already written that tells the computer what to do.

Ultimately, to get a computer to do something useful, you (or somebody else) must write a program.

A program does nothing more than tell the computer how to accept some type of input, manipulate that input, and spit it back out again in some form that humans find useful. Table 1-1 lists some common types of programs, the types of input that they accept, and the output that they produce.

Table 1-1 Input and Output for Various Programs

Type of Program	*Input*	*What the Program Does*	*Output*
Word processor	Characters you type from the keyboard	Formats the text; corrects spelling	Displays and prints neatly organized text
Game	Keystrokes or joystick movements	Calculates how fast and far to move a cartoon figure on-screen	Moves a cartoon figure on-screen

(continued)

Table 1-1 *(continued)*

Type of Program	*Input*	*What the Program Does*	*Output*
Stock-market predictor	Current and past prices for stocks	Tries to recognize trends in a stock's price fluctuations	Predicts the future price of a stock
Missile guidance program	Current location of the missile and the target	Calculates how to make the missile's location and the target's location coincide	Corrects the trajectory so that it stays aimed at the target
Optical character recognition (OCR)	Text from a scanner	Recognizes shapes of characters	Converts scanned text into a text file that a word processor can edit
Web browser	HyperText Markup Language (HTML) codes on other computers	Converts the HTML codes into text and graphics	Displays Web pages on-screen

Programming is problem-solving

Essentially, a program tells the computer how to solve a specific problem. Because the world is full of problems, the number and variety of programs that people can write for computers is practically endless.

But to tell a computer how to solve one big problem, you usually must tell the computer how to solve a bunch of little problems that make up the bigger problem. If you want to make your own video game, for example, you need to solve some of the following problems:

- Determine how far to move a cartoon figure (such as a car, a spaceship, or a man) on-screen as the user moves a joystick.
- Detect whether the cartoon figure bumps into a wall, falls off a cliff, or runs into another cartoon figure on-screen.
- Make sure that the cartoon figure doesn't make any illegal moves, such as walking through a wall.

- Draw the terrain surrounding the cartoon figure and make sure that if the cartoon figure walks behind an object such as a tree, the tree realistically blocks the figure from sight.
- Determine whether bullets that another cartoon figure fires are hitting the player's cartoon figure. If so, determine the amount of damage, how it affects the movement of the damaged cartoon figure, and how the damage appears on-screen.

The simpler the problem is that you need to solve, the more easily you can write a program that tells the computer how to work. A program that displays a simple Ping-Pong game with two stick paddles and a ball is much easier to write than a program that displays World War II fighter airplanes firing machine guns and dropping bombs on moving tanks while dodging anti-aircraft fire.

Programming isn't difficult; it's just time-consuming

Programming really isn't that difficult or mysterious. If you can write step-by-step instructions directing someone to your house, you can write a program.

The hardest part about programming is identifying all the little problems that make up the big problem that you're trying to solve. Because computers are completely stupid, you need to tell them how to do everything.

If you're giving a friend instructions to get to your house, for example, you may write down the following information:

1. Go south on Highway I-5.
2. Get off at the Sweetwater Road exit.
3. Turn right at the light.
4. Turn left into the second driveway.

Of course, if you try giving these instructions to a computer, the computer will get confused and wants to know the following additional information:

1. Where do I start and exactly how far south do I drive down Highway I-5?
2. How do I recognize the Sweetwater Road exit, and how do I get off at this exit?
3. After I turn right at the light, how far to the right do I turn, and do you mean the traffic light or the streetlight on the corner?

4. After I turn left into the second driveway, what do I do next? Park the car? Honk the horn? Gun the engine and accelerate through your garage door?

You need to tell computers how to do everything, which can make giving them instructions as aggravating and frustrating as telling children what to do. Unless you specify everything that you want the computer to do and exactly how to do it, the computer just plain won't do what you want it to do.

Sometimes programs never work

After spending years writing a program, people sometimes find that throwing away the whole thing and starting over is easier (and cheaper) than trying to figure out why the current program isn't working in the first place.

Back in the mid-1980s, for example, the United States government had the bright idea to develop a self-propelled, anti-aircraft weapon nicknamed *Sergeant York.* The purpose of the Sergeant York weapon was simple: Find an enemy aircraft and shoot it down.

Unfortunately, the program controlling Sergeant York never quite worked correctly. After spending millions of dollars and countless hours rewriting the program, testing it, and rewriting it again, the programmers thought that they'd finally gotten the program to work right.

To celebrate their achievement, the company that made the Sergeant York weapon staged a demonstration for the top Pentagon generals and officials. They put Sergeant York in a field, sat all the people from the Pentagon in a nearby grandstand, and flew a remote-controlled drone overhead to demonstrate Sergeant York's capability to track and shoot down an enemy airplane.

But instead of aiming at the overhead target, rumor has it that Sergeant York leveled its twin 40-mm cannons toward the ground and swiveled its guns until they pointed directly at the grandstand where all the Pentagon officials were sitting.

Needless to say, the Pentagon officials created quite a commotion as they scrambled to get out of the line of fire. Fortunately, Sergeant York didn't fire its cannons into the grandstand, but after this disastrous demonstration, the Pentagon cancelled further development and scrapped the entire Sergeant York project.

So if you ever start writing a program and feel like giving up before it ever works, you're in good company along with the Pentagon, military contractors, Fortune 500 corporations, the FBI, and practically everyone else in the world.

What Do I Need to Know to Program a Computer?

If you're the type who finds the idea of making a program (such as a video game) just as exciting as actually using it, you already have everything you need to program a computer. If you want to learn computer programming, you need a healthy dose of the following three qualities:

- **Desire:** If you want something badly enough, you tend to get it (although you may serve time in prison afterward if you do something illegal to get it). If you have the desire to learn how to program a computer, your desire helps you learn programming, no matter what obstacles may get in your way.
- **Curiosity:** A healthy dose of curiosity can encourage you to experiment and continue learning about programming long after you finish reading this book. With curiosity behind you, learning to program seems less a chore and more fun. And as long as you're having fun, you tend to learn faster and retain more information than does someone without any curiosity whatsoever (such as your boss).
- **Imagination:** Computer programming is a skill, but imagination can give your skill direction and guidance. A mediocre programmer with lots of imagination always creates more interesting and useful programs than a great programmer with no imagination. If you don't know what to do with your programming skill, your talent goes to waste. You need imagination prodding you onward.

Desire, curiosity, and imagination are three crucial ingredients that every programmer needs. If you possess these qualities, you can worry about trivial details such as learning a specific programming language (such as C++), studying advanced math, or attending a university where you can buy a college degree that you can just as easily make with your computer and a desktop-publishing program instead.

Learning to program a computer may (initially) seem an impossible task, but don't worry. Even the best programmers in the world were beginners once. Computer programming is actually simple to understand; everything just tends to fall apart when you write and put a program into actual use.

Chapter 2

All about Programming Languages

In This Chapter

- Understanding the need for different programming languages
- Knowing the differences between programming languages
- Choosing a programming language

Programming is nothing more than writing step-by-step instructions telling the computer exactly what you want it to do. Because computers are stupid, they require exact instructions, and this limitation is what makes programming so time-consuming.

Computers don't understand English (or French, Chinese, Arabic, Spanish, or any other language that human beings use). Because computers are functionally brain-dead, people must write instructions for a computer by using a language that the computer can understand. Hence, the term *programming language* came into being.

A collection of instructions that tell the computer what to do is known as a *program*. The instructions, written in a specific programming language, are known as the *source code*.

Why So Many Different Programming Languages?

You have many programming languages to choose among because each language serves a specific purpose, and people are always creating new languages to solve different types of problems.

Ultimately, computers understand only one language, which consists of zeroes and ones, also known as *machine language* or *machine code*. A typical machine-language program might look something like the following example:

```
0010 1010 0001 1101
0011 1100 1010 1111
0101 0110 1101 0101
1101 1111 0010 1001
```

Writing a program directly in machine language can create the smallest and fastest programs possible, but it has the following three major drawbacks:

- You can easily mistype a 0 (zero) or 1 by mistake, thereby preventing you from giving the computer the correct instructions.
- Programs written in machine language cannot be transferred to run on other processors. If you write a machine-language program to run on a PowerPC processor, you have to rewrite the whole thing completely to run on an Intel processor (and vice versa).
- Machine language takes a long time to write (and an even longer time to understand what the language is actually telling the computer to do).

Because of these two huge problems, almost nobody writes programs in machine language. To make writing a program easier, programmers quickly invented a simpler programming language known as *assembly language*.

The joy of assembly language

The whole purpose of any programming language is to make programming easier. So rather than force programmers to write cryptic programs with the 0s and 1s of machine language, assembly language uses short, easy-to-remember (to programmers, that is) commands with names such as JMP, MOV, and ADD. A single assembly-language command is a shortcut for typing multiple machine-language commands in much the same way that typing an abbreviation like LOL is a shortcut for writing out the phrase "Laughing Out Loud."

As a result, assembly-language source code is not only shorter and easier to write than machine code, but also easier to read and modify. A typical assembly-language program looks like the following example:

```
title Nap Program
; This program displays "Take a nap!" on the screen
dosseg
.model small
.stack 100h
.data
```

```
my_message db 'Take a nap!',0dh,0ah,'$'
.code
main    proc
        mov ax,@data
        mov ds,ax
        mov ah,9
        mov dx,offset my_message
        int 21h
        mov ax,4C00h
        int 21h
        main endp
end main
```

Making programs easy to read and modify is crucial because most programs don't work right the first time you use them. If you can't understand how a program works, you won't be able to fix any problems with it.

Because computers understand only machine language, programmers have written special programs that translate and convert assembly-language commands into their equivalent machine-language commands. These special programs are known as *assemblers*. If you give your computer an assembly-language program, it won't know how to follow your instructions until you feed your program to an assembler. The assembler translates your assembly-language program into machine code.

Assembly language offers the following two distinct advantages over machine language:

- **Easier reading:** Assembly-language programs are much easier to read than machine-language programs.
- **Easier writing:** Assembly-language programs are much easier to write (and modify) than machine-language programs.

Of course, assembly language has the following disadvantages:

- **Large, slow programs:** Programs that you create by using assembly language run slower and gobble up more space (both physical hard drive space and memory) than equivalent programs that you may create with machine language.
- **Limited portability:** You can't easily transfer (or, to use programming lingo, *port*) an assembly-language program from one computer to another computer.
- **Frustration factor:** Writing a program in assembly language can prove extremely tedious, time-consuming, and complicated. That's why few people bother to write large programs in assembly language.

In general, the easier the programming language is to read and write, the slower and larger are the programs it creates. The three main goals of computer programming are to create programs that are easy to write and modify, that run as fast as possible, and that take up as little space as possible.

C: The portable assembler

Writing assembly-language programs is often difficult and time-consuming, and the programs are difficult to modify and impossible to port from one computer to another. To combat this situation, programmers created a wide variety of different programming languages with names such as COBOL and FORTRAN. (See the following section, "High-level programming languages," to find out more about the advantages and disadvantages of these types of programming languages.)

But some programmers felt that they needed a language that offers the power to access hardware (like assembly language) but is easier to read, write, and modify (like COBOL and FORTRAN). Eventually, they invented a programming language known simply as *C*.

Programmers based the C programming language on an early programming language by the name of B (although no programming language known as A ever existed).

Programmers wanted to make programming as easy as possible for themselves, so they made the C programming language look more like actual words that people can understand, as the following example demonstrates:

```
main()
{
    printf ("Take a nap!\n");
}
```

This C program is equivalent to the assembly-language program found in the preceding section of this chapter. Both programs display "Take a nap!" onscreen. Comparing the two, you can see that the C language source code is smaller and easier to read than the equivalent assembly-language source code.

To run a program written in assembly language, you need to convert the assembly-language commands into equivalent machine-language commands. Similarly, to run a program written in any other language, such as C (or BASIC, FORTRAN, Pascal, and so on), you must translate your commands into equivalent machine-language commands, which you do by using a special program called a *compiler*.

The programmers who created the C programming language had the following three main goals:

- To create a language that's easier to read and write than assembly language.
- To offer programmers the capability to access all the parts of the computer just as they can by using assembly language.
- To provide a small, simple language that you can easily port from one computer to another. Programs that you write in C can run on different computers without massive rewriting, which is the main drawback with assembly- and machine-language programs.

The third goal may look strange, so here's the rationale behind it: Computers don't understand C any better than they understand assembly language. (Computers are notorious for not understanding much of anything, which is why programming must be so precise.) If you write an entire program in C, your computer doesn't have the slightest clue how to read your instructions.

To make a computer read and understand instructions written in C, you must convert your C program into equivalent machine-language instructions. Programmers created special programs, known as *compilers,* to do this conversion for them. A compiler takes your C program and converts it into machine language, which is like translating a Jules Verne novel from French into English.

As is true of translations between human languages, the simpler the programming language, the easier the translation. Translating a children's book from French into Japanese is much easier than translating a mathematics dissertation from French into Japanese, mainly because a children's book uses simple words, whereas a mathematics dissertation uses more complicated words. Similarly, translating C into machine-language code is more difficult than translating assembly-language code into machine-language code.

So the only way that you can run a C program on another computer is if someone has already written a C compiler for that other computer. Because C is a simple language, writing C compilers for different computers is relatively easy.

Because C compilers are fairly easy to write, you can find C compilers for almost every computer in the world. Theoretically, you can write a C program for the Macintosh, copy it to a computer running Windows, recompile it, and run the program with just minor modifications.

Although, in theory, C programs can run on different computers without modification, the reality is that you almost always must modify a C program slightly or drastically to get it to run on a different computer. Modifying a C program, however, is still much easier than rewriting an entire assembly- or machine-language program to run on different computers.

Given its power and portability, C has quickly become one of the most popular programming languages in the world. The majority of all programs are written in C although most newer programs are now written in a C derivative language called C++. Some of the more famous (or infamous) programs that have been written in C or C++ include operating systems such as Microsoft Windows, UNIX, and Linux, as well as major commercial programs such as Quicken, Photoshop, and Microsoft Word.

Although C is popular, it has its share of flaws:

- **Large, slow programs:** C creates larger and slower programs than equivalent assembly- or machine-language programs.
- **Danger to computer memory:** The C language gives programmers access to all parts of a computer, including the capability to manipulate the computer's memory. Unfortunately, all this power can prove as dangerous as giving a hyperactive monkey a chain saw and a hand grenade. If you don't write your C programs carefully, they can accidentally wreck your computer's memory, causing your program to crash your computer.

In a desperate attempt to make C programming more reliable, programmers developed languages similar to C, such as *C++, Java, Perl, Python,* and *C#.* All these C-derived languages try to protect programmers from writing programs that can mess up the computer's memory, as C programs can do, which increases the chance of writing a program that won't crash an entire computer.

High-level programming languages

Because writing machine- or assembly-language programs was so difficult and confusing, people developed additional languages that look more like human languages, with names such as *FORTRAN, COBOL, BASIC,* and *Pascal.* Programming languages that resemble written human languages are called *high-level languages.* The main goal of high-level languages is to make programs easier to write and modify later on.

One of the first high-level languages was FORTRAN (which stands for FORmula TRANslator). FORTRAN was designed specifically for mathematical calculations. Another early high-level language was COBOL (COmmon Business-Oriented Language), which was designed for business data processing.

Because each language has a specialized purpose, most people don't use FORTRAN or COBOL to write video games, operating systems, or word processors (although you can still do so if you really want to try).

Beginners could start learning to program by using C, but the complexities of C often discouraged people too soon. (It was sort of like trying to learn how to ride a bicycle by hopping on a motorcycle in the middle of rush-hour traffic.) Because programming was still too difficult for many people, computer scientists soon created both Pascal and BASIC to teach people programming. BASIC (Beginner's All-purpose Symbolic Instruction Code) was designed to teach complete novices how to program.

The main advantage of BASIC is its simplicity. To print the words "Take a nap!" on-screen, you need only the following command:

```
PRINT "Take a nap!"
```

If you compare it with the equivalent C or assembly-language source code, BASIC source code enables you to focus on the task that you want to accomplish instead of worrying about the cryptic commands of a specific programming language.

Pascal (named after the French philosopher, Blaise Pascal) is another language designed to help beginners learn how to program. The main difference between BASIC and Pascal is that Pascal encourages you to write well-structured programs that you can easily read, understand, and modify at a later date. The following Pascal program displays "Take a nap!" on-screen:

```
Program Message (Input, Output);
Begin
  Writeln ('Take a nap!');
End.
```

Compared with Pascal, BASIC is much less structured, which makes writing a BASIC program easy but makes reading and understanding large BASIC programs much more difficult. Pascal is more structured and forces you to plan your program before you write it. This planning may take longer, but your program will be more organized than if you rush into writing the program right away, which BASIC programmers often do because BASIC doesn't require any planning whatsoever.

BASIC is such a popular language that programmers have combined the structured features of Pascal with the simplicity of BASIC to create various dialects of BASIC. Two popular dialects of BASIC are Liberty BASIC and REALbasic. (The next section discusses REALbasic.) Liberty BASIC represents the simplicity of the original BASIC language, whereas REALbasic represents a more structured version of the BASIC language.

High-level programming languages such as Pascal, BASIC, FORTRAN, and COBOL offer the following advantages over C, assembly language, or machine language:

- **Speedy writing:** You can write programs much faster in a high-level programming language than you can in assembly language or machine language. (You can write a program in C in roughly the same amount of time as you can in a high-level language such as Pascal.)
- **Easy learning curve:** Learning and mastering a high-level programming language often takes less time than learning and mastering machine language, assembly language, or C programming.
- **Stability:** Because high-level programming languages shield you from accessing all parts of a computer, they protect you from writing programs that accidentally mess up the computer, causing it to crash.
- **Easy reading and modifying:** Reading and modifying a program written in a high-level language is much easier than reading and modifying an equivalent program written in C, assembly language, or machine language.
- **Portability:** Programs written in high-level languages can run on a variety of computers as long as the other computer has a compiler for that particular programming language. If you write a program in a high-level language, you can (theoretically) port that program to run on a different computer.

Naturally, high-level languages have their own share of problems that include the following:

- **Complexity issues:** Programs written in high-level languages are more complicated to translate into machine code, which means that a program written in FORTRAN or COBOL will likely run much slower and require more memory and hard drive space than a similar program written in C, assembly, or machine language.
- **Compiler woes:** Creating a compiler for a high-level language is much harder than creating one for C. As a result, not all computers have compilers available for every high-level language. So if you write a program in Liberty BASIC, you may find it nearly impossible to port your program to another computer or operating system.

Rapid application development (RAD) programming languages

Most programming languages were designed back in the days when computer screens displayed nothing but text. The screen didn't show graphics, mouse pointers, buttons, or windows.

Because computer screens could display only text, languages such as C++, BASIC, and Pascal had simple commands to display information, such as the following BASIC command:

```
PRINT "This sentence appears on-screen."
```

After computers developed fancy graphical user interfaces with windows, scroll bars, and toolbars, people began demanding programs that included all these fancy graphical features. To help programmers create programs with graphical user interfaces, many companies developed special dialects of existing languages, which they dubbed *rapid application development (RAD)* languages.

RAD languages enable programmers to design the way that they want their programs to look (the user interface) and then write source code to make that user interface actually do something useful, such as display information in a window. Figure 2-1 shows such an interface in REALbasic.

Some popular RAD languages are *Visual Basic* and *REALbasic* (based on BASIC), *Delphi* and *Kylix* (based on Pascal), and *Visual C#* (based on C#).

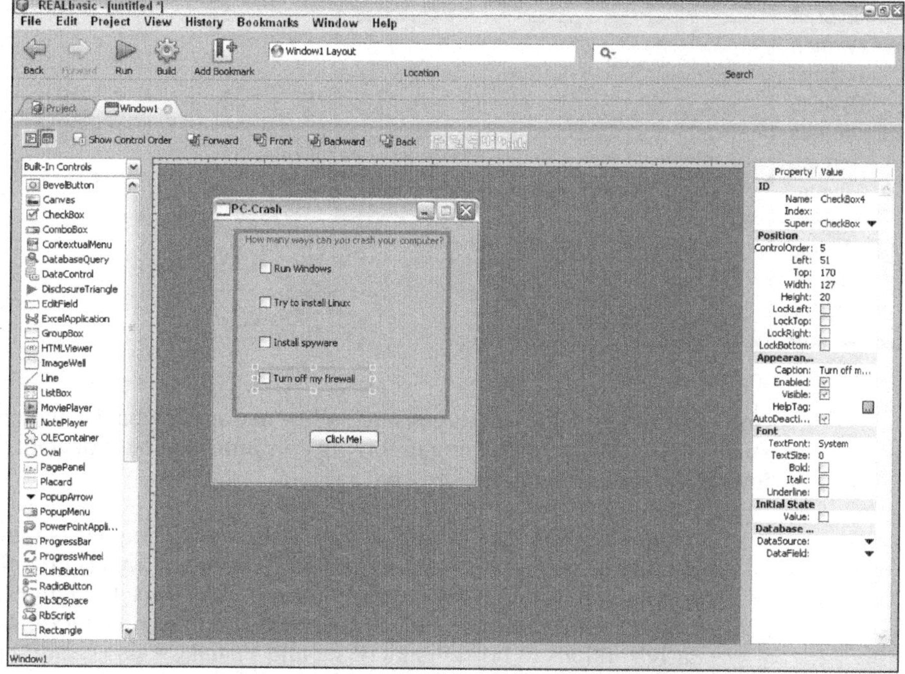

Figure 2-1: REALbasic enables you to create a user interface and then write BASIC commands to make that user interface do something useful.

RAD languages offer the following benefits:

- **Speedy writing:** You can write programs with graphical user interfaces much faster by using RAD than you can by using ordinary C++, BASIC, or Pascal. Figure 2-2 shows StoryCraft, a story-creating program that two professional fiction writers developed to help people create original stories for novels, short stories, plays, or screenplays.
- **Less work:** RAD languages simplify the process of creating user interfaces so that you can focus on getting the rest of your program to work. Without a RAD language, you'd need to write instructions to make the user interface work and then write additional instructions to make the rest of the program work as well, essentially doubling your work and the chance of making a mistake.
- **Similarity to other languages:** Because RAD languages derive from existing high-level languages (BASIC and Pascal), you can learn and start programming in a RAD language right away if you already know BASIC or Pascal.

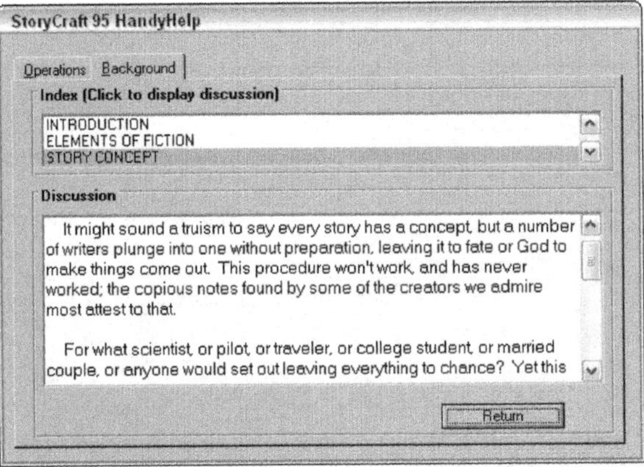

Figure 2-2: StoryCraft was written in Visual Basic to help writers create better stories, novels, and screenplays.

Not surprisingly, RAD languages have a few major drawbacks, which shouldn't surprise you because nothing involving computers is ever perfect. The following list describes these drawbacks:

- **Low portability:** Programs that you write in RAD languages may not be portable between different computers. Delphi and Kylix can only create programs that run on Microsoft Windows and Linux, but can never create programs that run on the Macintosh without extensive modification. (Early versions of both Visual Basic and Visual C# also created programs that could only run on Windows, but newer versions promise to run on other operating systems as well. However, note the word "promise." If you need to create a program that runs on Windows, Linux, and Mac OS X right now, a "promise" for tomorrow isn't going to help you today.)

- **Large, slow programs:** RAD languages create larger and slower programs than the equivalent programs written in pure BASIC or Pascal. A RAD language may help you create programs faster, but you sacrifice speed and program size.

Database programming languages

Programming languages such as C++, BASIC, and Pascal were designed as general-purpose languages, which means that you can use them to write practically anything, such as a flight simulator, an accounting program, a voice-recognition program, or a word processor.

Microsoft Windows is written in C/C++, whereas the original Macintosh operating system was written in Pascal. The latest version of the Macintosh operating system, Mac OS X, is written in a programming language called Objective-C, which looks similar to C and C++.

One of the most popular uses for computers, however, is storing and retrieving information, such as names, addresses, phone numbers, prison records, credit history, and past job experience. Computers store such information in *databases.*

Almost every business relies on databases to store information about customers, inventories, and employees, so nearly every company uses a database program.

Unfortunately, most people don't want to know the strange and often bizarre commands necessary to store, retrieve, or print information from a database. To make databases easier to use, most databases include a programming language.

Most popular database programs, such as FileMaker and Microsoft Access, offer their own special programming languages. For manipulating large amounts of data such as what's stored on big mainframe computers, database programs tend to use a language known as *SQL* (which stands for Structured Query Language). The following SQL code displays the message "Take a nap!"

```
select 'Take a nap!' from dual;
```

Database programming languages can fill the following specific needs:

- **Speedy writing:** If you're writing a program that stores huge chunks of information, you can write it much faster by using a database programming language than by using a general-purpose language such as C++ or Pascal.

- **Compact and understandable:** A program written in a database language is much smaller and easier to understand than an equivalent program written in C++ or Pascal.
- **Big bucks:** Database programming is a lucrative field. If you know how to create customized databases, you almost never need to worry about being unemployed or not making enough money.

Of course, database programming languages aren't for everybody. They have several crucial limitations, as the following list describes:

- **Program specificity:** Database programs are often tied to a specific computer. If you write a custom database by using FileMaker, for example, you can run your program only on any computer that can also run the FileMaker program. Because FileMaker is currently limited to the Macintosh and Windows operating systems, you can't run a FileMaker program on a computer that uses Linux.
- **Limited uses:** Database programming languages are great for making custom databases but lousy for making anything else, such as video games, word processors, or utility programs (such as antivirus utilities). If you need to create a variety of programs, you can't rely on a database programming language by itself.

Scripting programming languages

Writing a program from scratch gives you the most flexibility but can take a really long time and drive you nuts in the process. Suppose, for example, that you want to write a word processor specifically for creating screenplays.

If you decide to use a general-purpose language such as C++ or Pascal, you first need to write instructions that create a simple word processor; you then need to write additional instructions to give the word processor the features necessary to create and format screenplays.

As an alternative to going mad by writing everything yourself, many programs offer their own scripting languages. Instead of writing an entire word processor from scratch, you can buy an existing word processor (such as WordPerfect or Microsoft Word) and then use that word processor's scripting language to make the word processor do what you want it to do (such as create and format screenplays). A scripting language enables you to focus on the task that you want to accomplish without worrying about irrelevant details.

Most Microsoft programs, such as Word, Excel, PowerPoint, and Access, offer a scripting language known as *Visual Basic for Applications (VBA),* which is nearly identical to Visual Basic. The Macintosh operating system also includes a scripting language, known as *AppleScript,* so you can write programs to automate your Macintosh (to a limited extent). The following code shows how to use AppleScript to display the "Take a nap!" message on-screen:

```
on DisplayMessage()
 display dialog "Take a nap!" buttons {"OK"}
end DisplayMessage
DisplayMessage()
```

Scripting programming languages can come in handy in the following ways:

- **Modification fun:** A scripting language enables you to modify an existing program, such as a word processor or spreadsheet. That way, you can create sophisticated programs quickly with very little programming.
- **Easy learning curve:** Scripting languages are generally easier to learn than more powerful programming languages, such as C++. As a result, you can learn and start writing programs faster.

But before you jump wholeheartedly into learning and using a scripting language, beware of the following problems:

- **Specificity:** Scripting languages are tied to a specific program. If you customize a word processor by using a scripting language, your program runs only on computers that run that particular word processor. If you customize Microsoft Word, your program works only on computers that can run Microsoft Word, such as Windows and Macintosh computers.
- **Limited marketability:** Selling and distributing your programs is much more difficult. To use your program, people must buy or already own the program (word processor, spreadsheet, and so on) that you customize. So if you create a custom program for WordPerfect, Microsoft Word users can't use it.
- **Limited flexibility:** A scripting language provides much less flexibility than does a general-purpose programming language such as C++. Make sure that the trade-off of convenience and ease of programming is worth the limitations of using a scripting language.

In this book, you learn a scripting language called Revolution, which you use to control a program called Revolution. Because Revolution runs on Windows, Macintosh, and Linux computers, the Revolution scripting language can create programs that run on multiple computers with little or no modification.

Most programs are designed to run only on a single operating system or platform. If a program can run on different operating systems (also called *platforms*), it's called *cross-platform.*

Web page programming languages

In the early days of the Internet, people communicated through plain old text without the fancy graphics, animation, or forms that make up today's Web pages. Although people have been reading text for years, it can get boring and difficult to read if you view it on a computer screen that requires constant scrolling to view an entire document.

To remedy this problem and spruce up the appearance of text, programmers created *HyperText Markup Language (HTML),* which defines the graphical appearance of Web pages. Figure 2-3 shows a typical Web page as its HTML code defines it.

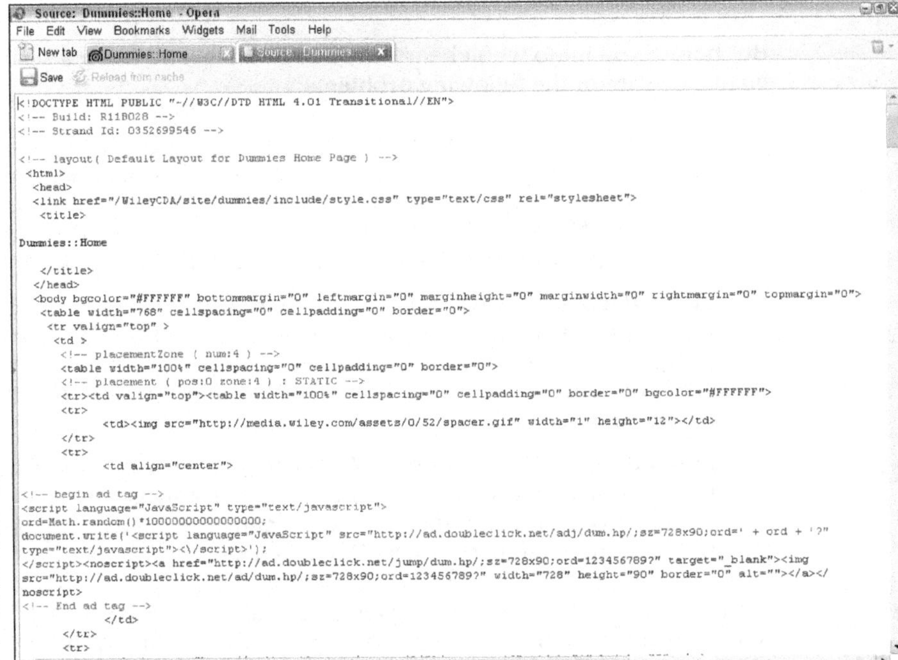

Figure 2-3: HTML code can look messy and unreadable.

HTML codes tell a browser how to display a page. So whenever you use a browser to view a Web page (such as `www.dummies.com`), your browser automatically converts the HTML code into the fancy graphics, as shown in Figure 2-4.

Figure 2-4: The cryptic HTML code from Figure 2-3 actually defines the appearance of the *For Dummies* Web site.

After a while, people got tired of plain ol' HTML Web pages that resemble billboards that you view through your computer screen. To make Web pages capable of interacting with the user (for playing games, filling out forms, and so on), programmers created special Web page programming languages such as *Java, JavaScript,* and *Ajax (Asynchronous JavaScript and XML).*

Java can create two types of programs: standalone applications (such as games or word processors) and smaller programs designed to run inside a Web browser known as an *applet.* The following code shows how a Java application can display the "Take a nap!" message on-screen:

```
public class DisplayMessage {
  public static void main (String args[]) {
system.out.println ("Take a nap!");
  }
}
```

Web page programming languages offer the following advantages:

- **Increased viewer interest:** You can create interactive Web pages to make your site more interesting to look at and to encourage viewers to stay on your site longer.
- **Easy learning curve:** The language is easy to learn and enables you to create programs that anyone around the world with Internet access can use.

Then again, Web page programming languages are very limited in their capabilities, as the following list describes:

- **Limited browser support:** Not all browsers support all features of Web page languages such as JavaScript. As a result, users of older browsers can't run programs that you create by using Web page languages. Even newer browsers often have trouble with Web pages that were designed and tested only in a popular browser like Internet Explorer.
- **Slow Web access, slow program:** For Internet users saddled with slow access (such as through a 28.8 baud modem), programs that you create in a Web page language (such as JavaScript) can run slowly, discouraging visitors from visiting your Web site.
- **Limited audience:** Only people with Internet access can run programs that you create with a Web page language (except for Java). If you want to sell a program to others, you don't want to use a Web page language.

So What's the Best Programming Language to Learn?

No single "best" programming language exists. If you want to write programs professionally, you want to learn at least one high-level language (most likely C++ because it's the most popular of the high-level languages) and one database programming language (such as SQL). You can't go wrong learning C++. With so many companies writing programs in C++, people with C++ programming experience can get a job almost anywhere.

Even if you can't find a job programming in C++, you can often find a job programming in a similar language, such as C, C#, Perl, Python, or Java, all of which resemble C++ to a large extent.

If you prefer to work for yourself, one of the most lucrative markets is writing custom databases for companies. To get into this field, you obviously must know a database programming language, such as SQL. If you plan to create Web pages, you need to know HTML and gain some familiarity with Java, JavaScript, Ajax, and the other Internet programming languages. Ultimately, the best programming language to know is the one that enables you to accomplish a task as quickly and easily as possible, whether that language is C++, BASIC, Java, SQL, or assembly language.

For a quick introduction to the way different programming languages solve the same problem, visit the Hello World! Web site at `www.latech.edu/~acm/HelloWorld.shtml`. This Web site provides sample programs, written in a variety of programming languages, that tell the computer to display the words "Hello World!" on-screen.

The programming language "religious" wars

Ask ten different programmers the best language to learn and you'll likely get ten different answers from ten passionate programmers who can cite endless studies, reports, and other empirical evidence on why their particular favorite programming language is the "best" language to learn and use.

Even worse, many programming language fanatics go so far as to claim that a program written in one language is actually inferior to an equivalent program written in a different language.

The truth is that no single language is best for all possible tasks, and the language you use to write a program doesn't determine the quality of your program any more than the paper you use determines the quality of a written report. The main reason why people defend their chosen programming language and attack the other languages is because they want to feel "right" about their decision to use a particular programming language.

So if you want to learn C++, do it because you want to and not because you think it will make you "cool" or more computer savvy. Knowing C++ won't make you any more knowledgeable about computers than knowing French will make you more knowledgeable about French cooking.

A programming language is nothing but a tool for expressing ideas. A great BASIC programmer will always be more productive than a mediocre C++ programmer.

So the next time you hear programmers argue about which language is superior, walk away and do something more productive with your time (like mastering your favorite language). Or watch and listen to these meaningless programming language arguments that are about as useful as arguing whether the color red is superior to the color purple, or whether zinc is a better mineral than iodine. The quality of a program is a direct reflection of the quality of the programmer; the language will always be secondary.

Chapter 3

How to Write a Program

In This Chapter

- Preparing to write your program
- Understanding the technical details
- Defining how the program should work
- Knowing the life cycle of a typical program

Although you can sit down at your computer and start writing a program right now without any planning whatsoever, the result would likely prove as messy as trying to bake a cake by throwing all the ingredients together without following a recipe.

You can write a simple program that displays your cat's name on-screen without much planning, but for anything more complex, you want to take time to design your program on paper before you even touch a computer. After you're sure that you know what you want your program to do and how you want it to look on-screen, you can worry about writing a program that actually accomplishes its task.

Before You Write Your Program

Design your program before you start writing it. That way you don't waste time writing a program that doesn't work or that solves the wrong problem and isn't worth trying to salvage afterward. By planning ahead of time, you increase the odds that your program actually works and performs the task that you want.

The following four items are crucial to consider in designing any program:

- **The problem:** What problem does your program solve? If you can't clearly state what your program does, you won't know how to design it.
- **The user:** Who's going to use your program?

- **The target computer:** Which computer do people need to run your program? Is it a Windows computer, a Macintosh, a mainframe, a computer running Linux, a handheld Palm or Pocket PC, or a supercomputer?
- **You:** Are you going to write the entire thing yourself or get help from others? If you're going to get others to help you, which parts of the program are they going to write?

The problem

Every program solves a problem. A tax return program solves the problem of organizing and filing your taxes. A word processor solves the problem of writing, editing, formatting, and printing text. Even a video game solves the problem of keeping people amused.

A program is only as useful as the problem it solves. Most programs simplify and automate an existing problem, such as a money management program that simplifies organizing and paying bills instead of using paper and an adding machine. The goal of any program is to make a specific task faster, easier, and more convenient. The only way reach that goal is to identify what task your program is trying to solve in the first place.

The program's users

If you're the only person who's going to use your program, you can pretty much make your program look and act any way you want, just as long as you know how to make it work. But if you plan to give or sell your program to others, you need to know who's going to use it.

Knowing your program's typical user is critical. If users don't like your program for any reason, they're unlikely to use it. Whether the program actually works is often irrelevant.

By designing your program with the user in mind, you increase the odds that people use your program and (you hope) buy a copy for themselves.

Even if you write a program that works perfectly, users still may ignore it because they don't like the way it looks, they don't understand how to give it commands, it doesn't work the same way as the old program they currently use, the colors don't look right to them, and so on. The goal is to make your program meet your users' needs, no matter how weird, bizarre, or illogical they may seem (the needs — not the users).

Portability and cross-platform issues

Rather than pick a single computer, many programmers try to write programs that can run on a variety of operating systems, such as the Macintosh and Windows. Any program that can run on two or more different types of operating systems is *cross-platform*. Microsoft Word is a cross-platform program because you can buy separate versions that run in the Macintosh and Windows environments.

A program that can run on multiple computers increases your number of potential customers, but it also increases the number of potential problems that you must face. Some of the problems include offering customer support for each program version and trying to make each version work the same although they may run on completely different operating systems and computers with totally different capabilities.

Programming tools like REALbasic, Revolution, and Java claim that you can write a program once and run it on multiple computers (in theory). In reality, you always need to modify the program slightly to run under the quirks of each individual operating system, although modifying a program a little is still better than rewriting the whole thing from scratch.

The target computer

After you identify the user, you need to know what type of computer the user intends to run the program on. The type of computer that your program runs on can determine which computer languages you can use, the hardware that your program can expect to find, and even the maximum size of your program.

If you're writing a program to run on a Macintosh, for example, your program can take advantage of sound, color graphics, a large hard drive, and plenty of memory. You may need to rewrite that same program drastically, however, to run it on a smart phone with its limited sound capability, much simpler color graphics, and limited amount of memory and storage space.

If you can copy and run your program on another computer with little or no modification, your program is considered *portable*. The computer language that you use to write your program can determine its portability. That's why so many people use C/C++ — C and C++ programs tend to be more portable than other programming languages.

Your programming skill

When designing any program, consider your programming skill. You may get a great idea for a program, but if you're a beginner with little experience, writing your program may take a long time — if you don't give up out of frustration first.

Your programming skill and experience also determine the programming language that you choose. Experienced programmers may think nothing about writing entire programs in C or C++. But novices may need to spend a long time studying C and C++ before writing their programs, or they may choose an easier programming language, such as BASIC.

Some novices take the time to learn difficult languages, such as C/C++, and then go off and write their program. Others take an easier approach and choose a simpler language such as Visual Basic so they can create (and market) their programs right away. Don't be afraid to tackle a heavy-duty language such as C/C++, but don't be afraid to use a simpler language such as Visual Basic either. The important goal is to finish your program so you can start using it and (possibly) start selling it to others.

Many programmers create their programs by using a language such as Visual Basic and then later hire more experienced programmers to rewrite their programs in a more complex language such as C/C++, which can make the program faster and more efficient.

The Technical Details of Writing a Program

Few people create programs overnight. Instead, most programs evolve over time. Because the process of actually typing programming commands can prove so tedious, time-consuming, and error-prone, programmers try to avoid actually writing their programs until they're absolutely sure that they know what they're doing.

Prototyping

To make sure that they don't spend months (or years) writing a program that doesn't work right or that solves the wrong problem, programmers often *prototype* their programs first. Just as architects often build cardboard or plastic models of skyscrapers before a construction crew starts welding I-beams together, programmers create mock-ups (prototypes) of their programs first.

A prototype usually shows the user interface of the program, such as windows, pull-down menus, and dialog boxes. The prototype may look like an actual program, but clicking menus doesn't do anything. The whole idea of the prototype is to show what the program looks like and how it acts, without taking the time to write commands to make the program actually work.

Beware of the golden handcuffs

Rather than learn programming themselves, many people hire someone to write programs for them. But take care! Freelance programmers sometimes live by a rule known as the *golden handcuffs,* which means that they get the gold and you get the handcuffs.

Here's how the golden handcuffs work: You hire someone to write your program, and the programmer takes your money. Then that person writes a program that doesn't work quite the way that you want. Rather than lose the money you already invested in developing the program, you pay the programmer more money, and then this programmer develops a new version of your program that doesn't quite work either.

At this point, you're handcuffed. Do you keep paying money to a programmer who never completely finishes the job, or do you give up altogether? What's worse, you can't hire a new programmer to work on the same program because the original programmer owns your program's source code, so nobody else can modify it. Thus the only way that you can modify the program is to hire the original programmer again and again and again and. . . .

After the programmer is happy with the way the prototype looks, he or she can proceed, using the prototype as a guideline toward completing the final program.

Many programmers use RAD languages like Visual Basic to create prototypes quickly. After you use Visual Basic to create a prototype that shows how your user interface works, you can start adding actual commands to later turn your prototype into an honest-to-goodness working program.

Choosing a programming language

After you refine your prototype until it shows you exactly how your program will look and act, the next step is choosing a programming language to use.

You can write any program by using any programming language. The trick is that some languages make writing certain types of programs easier than others.

The choice of a programming language to use can pit people against one another in much the same way that religion and politics do. Although you can't find a single "perfect" programming language to use for all occasions, you may want to consider a variety of programming languages. Ultimately, no one cares what language you use as long as your program works. (See Chapter 2 for more information about the pros and cons of different programming languages.)

General-purpose versus specialized programming languages

General-purpose programming languages, such as C/C++, BASIC, Pascal, assembly language, and so on, give you the ability to create practically anything you want, but you may take a longer time to do so. To make programming faster and easier, many people have developed specialized programming languages for solving specific types of problems.

For example, SNOBOL is a little-known language specifically designed for manipulating text. If that's what you need, writing a program in SNOBOL can be much quicker than using C/C++. Of course, if you want to do something else besides text manipulation, programming in SNOBOL is likely a horrible choice.

Similarly, programmers often use LISP and Prolog to create artificially intelligent programs because both LISP and Prolog include commands for decision-making. Although you could create an artificially intelligent program by using FORTRAN, C/C++, COBOL, or BASIC, you might have to write twice as many instructions to accomplish what a single LISP or Prolog command can accomplish.

So the moral of the story is that you can make programming a lot easier if you just choose the right programming language to help you solve the right problem.

Defining how the program should work

After choosing a specific programming language, don't start typing commands into your computer just yet. Just as programmers create mock-ups (prototypes) of their program's user interface, they often create mock-up instructions that describe exactly how a program works. These mock-up instructions are known as *pseudocode.*

If you need to write a program that guides a nuclear missile to another city to wipe out all signs of life within a 100-mile radius, your pseudocode may look as follows:

```
1. Get the target's coordinates.
2. Get the missile's current coordinates.
3. Calculate a trajectory so the missile hits the target.
4. Detonate the nuclear warhead.
```

By using pseudocode, you can detect flaws in your logic before you start writing your program — places where the logic behind your program gets buried beneath the complexity of a specific programming language's syntax.

In the preceding example, you can see that each pseudocode instruction needs further refining before you can start writing your program. You can't just tell a computer, "Get the target's coordinates," because the computer wants to know, "Exactly how do I get the target's coordinates?" So rewriting the preceding pseudocode may look as follows:

```
1. Get the target's coordinates.
          a. Have a missile technician type the target
         coordinates.
          b. Make sure that the target coordinates are
         valid.
          c. Store the target coordinates in memory.
2. Get the missile's current coordinates.
3. Calculate a trajectory so the missile hits the target.
4. Detonate the nuclear warhead.
```

Using multiple programming languages

Instead of writing an entire program in one programming language (such as C++), some compilers can convert source code into a special file known as an *object file.* The purpose of object files is to allow one programmer to write a program in C++, another in assembly language, and still a third in Pascal. Each programmer writes a portion of the program in his or her favorite language and stores it in a separate object file. Then the programmers connect (or link) all these object files together to create one big program. The program that converts multiple object files into an executable program is known as a *linker.*

In the world of Microsoft Windows, another way to write a program by using multiple languages is to use *dynamic link libraries (DLLs),* which are special programs that don't have a user interface. One programmer can use C, another can use Java, and a third can use COBOL to create three separate DLL files. Then a fourth programmer can write a program using another language such as Visual Basic, which creates the user interface and uses the commands that each separate DLL file stores.

A third way to write a program is to use your favorite language (such as Pascal) and then write assembly-language instructions directly in parts of your program. (Just be aware that not all compilers enable you to switch between different languages within the same program.)

Finally, Microsoft offers a programming framework known as .NET. By using the .NET framework, one programmer can program in C#, another can program in FORTRAN, and still another can program in BASIC. Then their different programs can share data and communicate with other programs through the .NET framework and create a single user interface that unifies these separate programs. The whole point to all these different methods is that by using different programming languages, you can take advantage of each language's strengths while minimizing its weaknesses.

You can refine the instructions even further to specify how the computer works in more detail, as follows:

```
1. Get the target's coordinates.
        a. Have a missile technician type the target
       coordinates.
        b. Make sure that the target coordinates are
       valid.
            1) Make sure that the target coordinates
       are complete.
            2) Check to make sure that the target
       coordinates are within the missile's range.
            3) Make sure that the target coordinates
       don't accidentally aim the missile at friendly
       territories.
        c. Store the target coordinates in memory.
2. Get the missile's current coordinates.
3. Calculate a trajectory so the missile hits the target.
4. Detonate the nuclear warhead.
```

When programmers define the general tasks that a program needs to accomplish and then refine each step in greater detail, they say that they're doing a *top-down design.* In other words, they start at the top (with the general tasks that the program needs to do) and then work their way down, defining each task in greater detail until the pseudocode describes every possible step that the computer must go through.

Writing pseudocode can prove to be time-consuming. But the alternative is to start writing a program with no planning whatsoever, which is like hopping in your car and driving north and then wondering why you never seem to wind up in Florida.

Pseudocode is a tool that you can use to outline the structure of your program so that you can see all the possible data that the computer needs to accomplish a given task. The idea is to use English (or whatever language you understand best) to describe the computer's step-by-step actions so that you can use the pseudocode as a map for writing the actual program in whatever language (C/C++, FORTRAN, Pascal, Java, and so on) that you choose.

The Life Cycle of a Typical Program

Few programs are written, released, and left alone. Instead, programs tend to go through various cycles where they get updated continuously so companies can sell the newer versions to new and existing customers.

Generally, a typical program goes through a development cycle (where you first create and release it); a maintenance cycle (where you eliminate any glaring bugs as quickly as possible); and an upgrade cycle (where you give the program new features to justify selling the same thing all over again).

The development cycle

Every program begins as a blank screen on somebody's computer. During the development cycle, you nurture a program from an idea to an actual working program. The following steps make up the development cycle:

1. **Come up with an idea for a program.**
2. **Decide the probable identity of the typical user of the program.**
3. **Decide which computer the program is to run on.**
4. **Pick one or more computer language(s) to use.**
5. **Design the program by using pseudocode or any other tool to outline the structure of the program.**
6. **Write the program.**
7. **Test the program.**

   Step 7 is known as *alpha testing.*
8. **Fix any problems that you discover during alpha testing.**

   Repeat Steps 7 and 8 as often as possible.
9. **Give out copies of the program to other people to test.**

   Step 9 is known as *beta testing.* The idea is to let total strangers use your program so they can tell you what they like and dislike. If you give your program to your friends or relatives to test, they might overlook problems because they don't want to hurt your feelings. Strangers are likely more objective in evaluating a program.
10. **Fix any problems that people discover during beta testing.**

    Repeat Steps 9 and 10 as often as possible.
11. **Release the program to the unsuspecting public and pray that it works as advertised.**

The maintenance cycle

Most programmers prefer creating new programs to maintaining and modifying existing ones, which can prove as unappealing as cleaning up somebody else's mess in an apartment. But the number of new programs that programmers create every year is far less than the number of existing programs, so at some point in your life, you're likely to maintain and update a program that either you or somebody else wrote months, years, or even decades ago.

The following list describes typical steps that you may need to follow to maintain an existing program:

1. **Verify all reports of problems (or *bugs*) and determine what part of the program may be causing the bug to appear.**
2. **Fix the bug.**
3. **Test the program to make sure that the bug is really gone and that any changes you make to the program don't introduce any new bugs.**
4. **Fix any problems that occur during testing.**
5. **Repeat Steps 1 through 4 for each bug that someone reports in the program.**

   Given the buggy nature of software, these steps may go on continuously for years.
6. **Release a software *patch,* which users can add to an existing version of the program to incorporate corrections that you make to "patch up" the problems.**

The upgrade cycle

Companies don't make money fixing software and making it more stable, reliable, and dependable. Instead, companies make money by selling new versions of their programs that offer additional features and options that most people probably don't use, need, or even want in the first place.

Still, because so many programs undergo modification to take advantage of new hardware or software, you may find yourself occasionally upgrading a program by adding new features to it. The following steps make up the upgrade cycle:

1. **Determine what new feature you want to add to the program.**
2. **Plan how this new feature is to work (by using pseudocode or another tool to help structure your ideas).**

3. **Modify the program to add this new feature.**
4. **Test this new feature (by using alpha testing) to make sure that it works and doesn't introduce new bugs into the program.**
5. **Fix any problems that occur during alpha testing.**
6. **Give out copies of the program to other people to beta test.**
7. **Fix any problems that the beta testers report.**
8. **Repeat Steps 1 through 7 for each new feature that you need to add to the program.**
9. **Release the program as a new version and wait for the public to start reporting bugs that keep the program from working correctly so that you can start the maintenance cycle all over again.**

Despite all the university courses and such important-sounding titles as "software engineer," programming is still less of a science and more of an art. Writing, modifying, and updating software doesn't require a high IQ or an advanced mathematics degree as much as it requires creativity, determination, and plenty of imagination. You can write a program any way that you want, but the best way to prevent possible problems later on is to be organized and methodical in your approach.

Chapter 4

The Tools of a Computer Programmer

In This Chapter

- Using an editor to write programs
- Creating a program with compilers and interpreters
- Exterminating bugs with a debugger
- Creating a Help file
- Building an installation program

To make computer programming easier, programmers use a variety of tools. Just as a hammer, screwdriver, and hacksaw have special purposes for building furniture, so do programming tools have specific purposes for writing a program.

A program consists of one or more instructions that tell the computer what to do. The instructions that make up a program are known as the program's *source code.*

The only two crucial tools you absolutely must have to write a program are

- **An editor** (so that you can type and save your source code).
- **A compiler,** which converts your source code into machine language so that the computer knows what you want it to do. Instead of using a compiler, some programming languages use an *interpreter.* The main difference between the two is that an interpreter converts your instructions into machine language and stores them in memory each time you run the program, whereas a compiler converts your instructions into machine language once and saves those instructions in a file often called an EXE or executable file.

Linux and the open-source movement

In the early days of computers, programmers freely created and shared the source code for their programs. The idea was that, if enough people voluntarily worked together on a single program, the chances were good that the program would actually work.

Then programmers decided that they should get paid for their hard work, so they started keeping the source code for their programs to themselves, which helped to spawn the software industry as we know it today (with all its missed deadlines, unreliable programs, and horribly written software manuals).

But now the idea of sharing the source code (often known as the *open-source movement*) has resurfaced with the emergence of the Linux operating system. Users can again peek at the source code without paying for it.

Having access to the source code gives you the option of modifying the program if you want or (more likely) hiring someone else to modify it for you. In any event, access to the source code prevents you from being at the mercy of companies that refuse to reveal their source code so that they can force you to pay for program upgrades that still may not fix or add the features that you want.

You may want to use the following additional tools in writing a program:

- **A debugger** (which helps identify problems or bugs in your program)
- **A Help-file-authoring program** (so that your program can provide help on-screen instead of needing to supply the user with a decent manual)
- **An installation program** (to copy your program to the user's computer)

Many language compilers, such as Visual Basic, Visual C#, and REALbasic, include a combination editor, compiler, and debugger, called an *integrated development environment* (IDE). If you have an IDE, you just need to buy a separate Help-file-authoring program and an installation program.

Writing Programs in an Editor

An editor acts like a simple word processor where you can type the commands you want your computer to follow. When you save your commands, you save them in a text (or *ASCII*) file. Although you can use a word processor to create a text file, a word processor offers fancy formatting features (such as changing fonts or underlining text), which you don't need to write a program.

An ASCII file consists of nothing but characters that you can type from a keyboard. ASCII stands for American Standard Code for Information Interchange, which is simply a universal file format that any computer can use.

An editor looks like a word processor but may offer special features to make programming easier, such as automatically formatting your source code, offering shortcuts for editing your source code, or providing pop-up help as you're typing program commands, as shown in Figure 4-1. Anytime that you need to write or modify the source code of a program, you must use an editor.

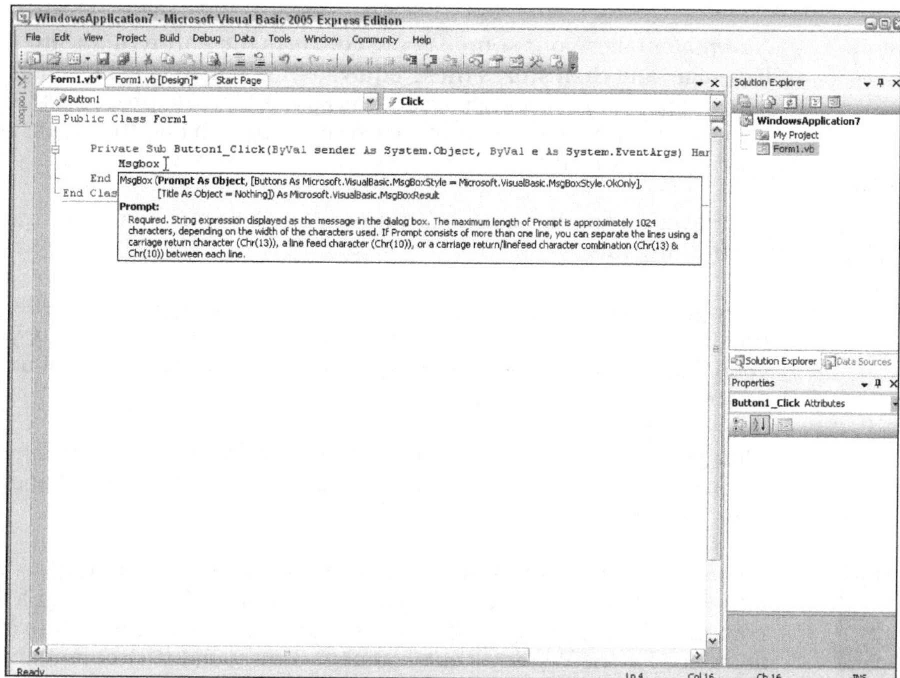

Figure 4-1: The Visual Basic editor shows you the correct syntax for a command.

Using a Compiler or an Interpreter

After you type your instructions in an editor by using a programming language such as C++ or Java, guess what? The computer doesn't have the slightest idea what you just created. Computers understand only machine language, so you need to use another special program to convert your source code (the instructions that you write in C++ or Java) into machine language.

You can use either of the following two types of programs to convert source code into machine language:

- A compiler
- An interpreter
- A combination compiler/interpreter (p-code)

Compilers

A *compiler* takes your source code, converts the entire thing into machine language, and then stores these equivalent machine-language instructions in a separate file, often known as an *executable file*. The process is like having a translator study an entire novel written in Spanish and then translate and rewrite it into Arabic.

Whenever a compiler converts source code into machine language, it's *compiling* a program.

After you compile a program, you can just give away copies of the executable (machine-language) version of your program without giving away your source code. Most commercial programs (such as Microsoft PowerPoint and Quicken) are compiled, but you never see the source code.

After you use a compiler to convert source code into machine language, you never need to use the compiler again (unless you make changes to your source code).

A compiler creates machine language for a specific microprocessor. If you write a program in BASIC and want to run it on a Macintosh and a Windows computer, you need to compile your program twice: once for the Macintosh and once for the Windows environment. However, many compilers, such as REALbasic, let you compile for multiple platforms at the same time. So if you wrote a program in REALbasic and compiled it for Windows and Macintosh, you'd wind up with a compiled executable file for Windows and a second compiled executable file for Macintosh.

Not all compilers are equal. Given identical C++ source code, one C++ compiler may create a program that runs quickly, whereas a second C++ compiler may create a smaller file that runs much slower, yet both programs may look and work exactly alike.

"Bootstrapping" a compiler

A compiler is nothing more than a program. So if you want to create a compiler, guess what? To write any type of a program, you need a compiler (or an assembler, which is just a special compiler for converting assembly language into machine language). So here's the dilemma. How did computer scientists create the first compiler?

To create the first compiler, computer scientists used a technique called *bootstrapping*, derived from the phrase "pulling yourself up by the bootstraps." First, they wrote the bare bones of the compiler in machine language, which the computer can understand without any translation whatsoever. Then they used this bare bones compiler to create an assembler so they could write more of the compiler in assembly language. Finally, when enough of the compiler had been built from a small base of machine-language code and a larger base of assembly-language code, they used the compiler itself to write additional instructions in a higher-level programming language (such as C) to build the rest of the compiler.

Nearly every language compiler is written partially or entirely in another programming language. Microsoft wrote the original Visual Basic compiler in assembly language but wrote later versions in C++. Shoptalk Systems wrote its Liberty BASIC compiler in a language called SmallTalk. So if you want to create a compiler for a brand-new programming language, you have to start creating that compiler by using an existing programming language.

Your program is at the mercy of the compiler you use. Many Macintosh programs were created by using a compiler called CodeWarrior, but when Apple switched from PowerPC to Intel processors, guess what? CodeWarrior wouldn't compile C++ source code for the new Intel Macs. So everyone (including Microsoft and Adobe) who had written C++ programs with CodeWarrior had to rewrite their C++ programs and compile them with Apple's C++ compiler instead. Switching compilers and rewriting programs to run under a different compiler is rarely easy, so not only is it important to choose the right programming language, but also the right compiler.

Interpreters

A second, but less popular, way to convert source code into machine language is to use an *interpreter*. An interpreter converts each line of your source code into machine language, one line at a time. The process is like giving a speech in English and having someone translate your sentences, one at a time, into another language (such as French).

Whereas a compiler stores machine code in a separate file, an interpreter converts source code into machine language but stores the machine code in the computer's memory. Every time that you turn off the computer, you lose the machine-language version of your program. Each time you want to run the program, you must feed the source code into the interpreter again.

If anyone wants to run your program, that person needs both an interpreter and the source code for your program. Because your source code enables everyone to see how you wrote your program (and gives others a chance to copy or modify your program without your permission), few commercial programs use an interpreter.

Interpreters are often used for Web page programming languages, such as JavaScript. Because different computers can view Web pages, you can't compile programs that you write in JavaScript into machine language because people with different computers may visit your Web site. Instead, your computer's browser uses an interpreter to run a JavaScript program.

In the old days, when computers were slow and lacking in sufficient memory and storage space, interpreters were popular because they gave you instant feedback. The moment you typed an instruction into the computer, the interpreter told you whether that instruction would work and even showed you the results. With an interpreter, you could write and test your program at the same time. Now, computers are so fast that most programmers use compilers rather than interpreters, although a handful of languages like LISP still rely on interpreters.

P-code: A combination compiler and interpreter

Getting a program to run on different types of computers is a big pain in the neck. Even though Macintosh and Windows programs use pull-down menus and dialog boxes, programs often need to write one set of commands to create Macintosh pull-down menus and a second set of commands to create the identical menus in Windows.

Because one program almost never runs on multiple computers without extensive modification, programmers combined the features of a compiler with an interpreter to create something called *p-code*.

Instead of compiling source code directly into machine language, you compile the source code into a special intermediate file format (called *p-code* or *byte code*).

To run a program compiled into p-code, you need a special p-code or byte code interpreter, often called a *run-time file.* To run a p-code file on a Macintosh, your computer needs a Macintosh p-code run-time file. To run that same p-code file on Windows, your computer needs a Windows p-code run-time file. Instead of creating compilers for multiple computers, it's often easier just to create different run-time files for multiple computers.

Java is the most popular programming language that uses p-code. After you compile a Java program into p-code, you can copy that p-code to a Macintosh, a Windows computer, or a Linux computer. As long as that computer uses a Java p-code interpreter, you can run the Java program on that computer without modification.

Best of all, programs that you compile into p-code can run without the original source code, which means that you can protect your source code and still give your program away to others.

Naturally, p-code has its own disadvantages. Programs stored as p-code tend to run much slower than programs that compiled directly into machine language. Although p-code programs can run without a copy of the original source code that you use to create them, you can also *decompile* p-code programs.

Decompiling a p-code program can reveal the original source code that the programmer used to create the program. So if you write a program in Java and compile it into p-code, a rival can decompile your p-code program and see your original Java source code. Your rival then ends up with a nearly identical copy of your source code, which gives him the opportunity to steal your program.

You can actually decompile any program, including programs that you compile into machine language. But unlike with decompiling p-code programs, decompiling a machine-language version of a program never gets you the original high-level language source code that the programmer used to write the program. If you compile a program into machine language, the original source code can be written in C++, COBOL, FORTRAN, BASIC, Ada, LISP, Pascal, or any other programming language in the world. Because the decompiler has no idea what language the original source code was written in, it can decompile a machine-language version of a program only into equivalent assembly language. After you decompile a program into assembly-language source code, you can rewrite or modify that source code. Decompiling effectively allows you to steal the ideas of others, but it's often used to dissect computer viruses and worms to understand how they work (and how to defend against them).

So what do I use?

If you want to write programs to sell, use a compiler, which protects your original source code. If you want to write a program to run on your Web page, you can use either an interpreter or p-code. If you want to write a program that can run on different types of computers, p-code may prove your only choice. As a safer but more cumbersome alternative, you can also use multiple compilers and modify your program to run on each different computer.

The language that you choose can determine whether you can use a compiler, an interpreter, or p-code. You often convert Java programs into p-code, for example, although you can also compile them directly into machine language. On the other hand, you usually compile C++ and rarely interpret or convert C++ programs into p-code.

Squashing Bugs with a Debugger

No computer program works 100 percent correctly, which explains why computers crash, lose airline reservations, or just act erratically at times. Mathematically, writing a program that works 100 percent correctly every time is impossible because testing a program for all possible types of computers, hardware, and additional software that may interfere with the way your program runs is impossible.

The .NET framework

If you try running a program written in Visual Basic, it won't run unless it finds a copy of its run-time file on your computer, which usually has an odd name like `VBRUN300.DLL` or `MSVBVM60.DLL`. With the latest version of Visual Basic, Microsoft has replaced the Visual Basic run-time file with a whole bunch of files that make up something called the *.NET framework*.

Unlike the old Visual Basic run-time files that could run only Visual Basic programs, the .NET framework is designed to run any programs that have been compiled to p-code for the .NET framework. So instead of requiring a separate run-time file for a Visual Basic program and second run-time file for a Visual C# program, computers now just need a single copy of the .NET framework.

By porting the .NET framework to other operating systems, such as Linux or the Macintosh, it's (theoretically) possible to run Visual Basic and Visual C# programs on other types of computers. Until this happens though, Visual Basic and Visual C# programs run only on computers that can install the .NET framework, which currently limits Visual Basic and Visual C# programs to any computer that uses Windows.

A problem that keeps a program from working correctly is known as a *bug.*

In the early days, computers used mechanical relays and vacuum tubes rather than circuit boards and microprocessors. One day, the computer failed to work correctly. The scientists examined their program; it should have worked. So they next examined the computer itself and found that a moth had gotten smashed in a mechanical relay, preventing it from closing and thus keeping the computer from working correctly. From that point on, problems in computers have been called bugs. So it's a good thing that a dog never got trapped in a mechanical relay because then computer problems might be called *Chihuahuas.*

Because writing a program that works 100 percent correctly all the time is impossible, operating systems (such as Windows XP) unavoidably contain bugs that keep them from working correctly. When you convert your source code into machine language, you must use a compiler or interpreter, which also contain bugs. Finally, your program may contain bugs of its own. With so many places for bugs to creep in, you shouldn't be surprised that bugs infest computer programs the way cockroaches infest cheap apartment complexes.

Although you can do little about bugs in other people's programs (except not buy their programs), you can reduce (but not completely eliminate) bugs in your own program by using a *debugger.* A debugger is a special program (which may also contain bugs) that can help you track down and wipe out bugs in programs that you write.

A debugger provides several ways to track down bugs in your program:

- **Stepping:** The debugger runs your program, line by line, so that you can see exactly which line may contain the bug. This process is like rereading written instructions to get to another person's house if you're lost. By going over these instructions, one by one, you can find out where you made a wrong turn.
- **Breakpoints:** Rather than force you to step through an entire program, line by line, *breakpoints* enable you to specify where you want to start examining your program line by line. So if you were lost, instead of rereading the instructions to get to another person's house from start to finish, you skip those instructions that you know you followed correctly and examine only the remaining instructions that you aren't sure that you followed correctly. Similarly, by using breakpoints, you can selectively examine only parts of your program, line by line, and skip over the parts that you know already work.

- **Watching:** Watching enables you to see your program storing data in memory and to determine what that data may be. If your program stores incorrect data (such as saving a name instead of a telephone number), you know exactly where in your program the bug is occurring.

  Figure 4-2 shows a sample debugger at work that highlights a specific instruction in your program and displays a window that shows the value of specific data. Each time you examine a line in your program, the debugger shows you how that particular line affects the value you're watching. As soon as you see the value change, the debugger shows you exactly which line in your program caused that change. This process is like having someone tell you to drive ten miles south down a certain road after turning right. The moment that you exceed ten miles, a *watchpoint* alerts you so that you know exactly where you almost made a mistake and got lost.

Chapter 15 explains more about how to debug a program.

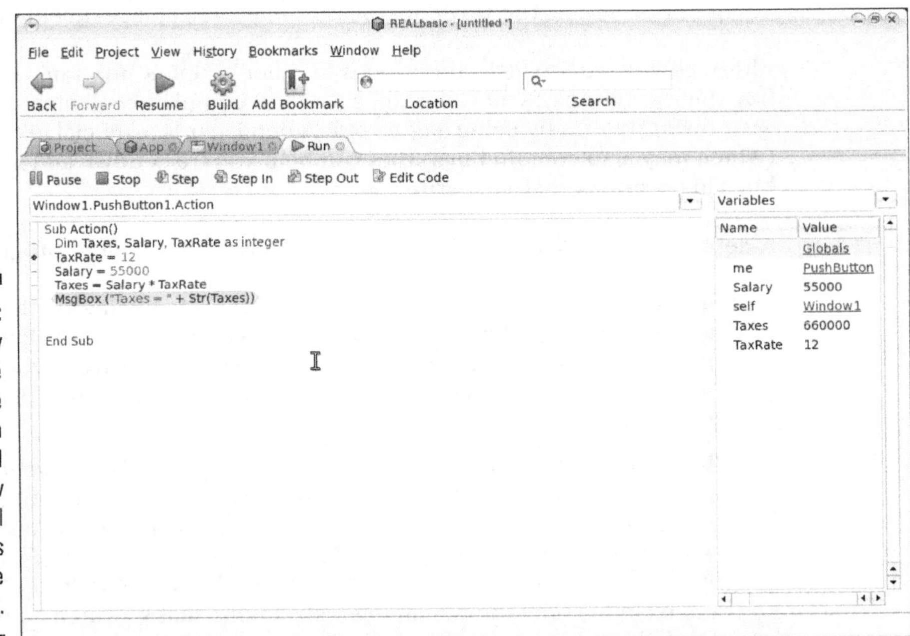

Figure 4-2: One window displays the source code, and a second window shows all the values you're watching.

A debugger essentially shows you exactly how a computer is going to interpret the instructions in your program. That way you can see where you need to modify your instructions so that the bug doesn't occur anymore. Of course, if you fix one bug, you may introduce several new ones. That's why writing bug-free programs is impossible.

Writing a Help File

Few people have trouble using a doorknob, a toaster, or a microwave oven, but many more people still complain that computers and video recorders are too hard to use.

The problem with video recorders lies in the cryptic controls that aren't easy to figure out just by looking at them. Similarly, the problem with computer programs is that programs are too complex to use at first glance. If you can make a program that's easy to use, people can actually use it.

Because computer programs are still being designed for programmers by other programmers, computers still mystify the average user. To help the poor befuddled user, most programs now offer Help files.

A Help file provides instructions and explanations on-screen. Theoretically, if the user experiences trouble with the program, he or she can browse through the Help file (as shown in Figure 4-3), find an explanation or step-by-step instructions, and continue using the program.

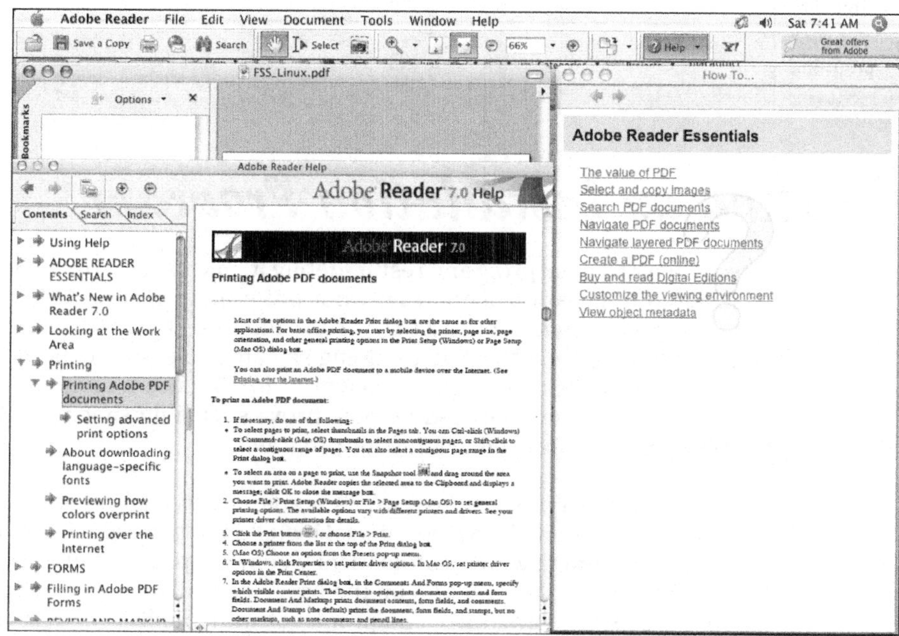

Figure 4-3: Many programs provide Help screens to give you the information that you need.

Although Help files still can't substitute for designing a program that's easy to use in the first place, most programs offer Help files anyway. To keep your program modern and up-to-date, include a Help file with it.

To create a Help file, you can use a special Help-file-authoring program, which simplifies the process of creating and organizing topics for your Help file, as shown in Figure 4-4.

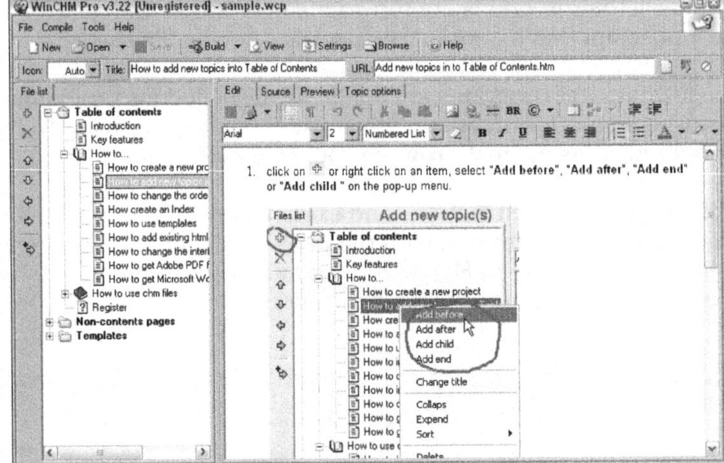

Figure 4-4: Help-file-creation programs simplify the process of making a Help file for your program.

Creating an Installation Program

After you write your program, test it, debug it, and write a Help file for it, the final step is to give or sell copies of your program to others. Although you can copy your program onto a CD or DVD and force buyers to manually copy your program to their hard drive, doing so can cause problems. Users may not copy all the files correctly. Even worse, forcing users to manually copy your program to their hard drives may prove such a nuisance that most people won't bother even using your program.

To make copying a program to a user's hard drive as easy as possible, most commercial programs include a special installation program. Users run this installation program, which automatically copies a program and all necessary files to the appropriate location on the user's hard drive. By making the installation of a program practically foolproof, software publishers make sure that users install the programs correctly.

So the final step to distributing your program to others is to use a special installation-creation program, which can smash all your program files into a single file that can automatically install itself on another computer.

Installation programs offer the following features for distributing programs to others:

- **File compression:** Most programs are fairly large, which means that they can't always fit on a single CD. Rather than store your program on multiple CDs, an installation program can smash your files so that they can fit on a single disc.
- **Display graphics and play sounds:** Installing a program usually takes a few minutes while the computer copies files from the CD to its hard drive. Rather than force the user to stare into space, an installation program can display advertisements or messages to make the installation process mildly interesting. Other uses for graphics include displaying an hourglass icon or a status bar that shows how far the installation is complete, such as 54 percent complete. That way, users know how much longer they need to wait.
- **Simplify the copying process:** Most important, an installation program simplifies copying your program to the user's hard drive, making the entire process accurate, fast, and foolproof.

The first impression that people get from your program is through its installation process, so an installation program helps give your program a professional appearance.

Of course, you need to make sure that your installation program installs your program correctly, or the first impression that users get from your program will be a highly negative one.

Armed with all these different tools (editor, compiler, debugger, Help file creator, and installation program), you're ready to write, test, and distribute your programs. Who knows? You just might wind up writing a new category of software that nobody ever thought of before, like 19-year-old, college dropout Shawn Fanning did when he created Napster, which revolutionized the way the world distributes music and video files.

If a kid who didn't even finish college can change the world by writing a single computer program, just think what you can do with your imagination.

Part II

The Building Blocks of Programming

In this part . . .

Although you have literally millions of different ways to write the same program with different instructions or programming languages, the general principles of programming consist of three buildings blocks known as sequencing, branching, and looping.

Sequential instructions simply tell the computer what to do one instruction at a time. Branching instructions tell the computer to choose between two or more different sets of instructions. Looping instructions tell the computer to repeat one or more instructions multiple times.

Every program uses sequencing, branching, and looping instructions. When you understand how these three basic buildings blocks can create any type of a program, you'll know how to build your own programs on any type of computer in any programming language you decide to use.

Chapter 5
Getting Started

In This Chapter

- Learning BASIC
- Learning C++
- Learning Revolution

The best way to learn anything is to start practicing, make mistakes, feel foolish, and then try again. If you want to learn computer programming, you should start writing programs on your computer as soon as possible.

Most books teach programming by using a specific programming language, which can give you the false impression that the way a specific programming language works is the way all computer programming works. This book is different because it first shows you general programming principles that anyone can understand. After you grasp these basic programming concepts, then this book provides examples in three different programming languages: BASIC, C++, and Revolution. By studying all three programming examples, you can see how different languages look and solve the same types of problems.

The programming language you learn and use is less important than the ideas you have and the programs you create. You can create the same program in any programming language, so just focus on the language you like best, get really good at using it, and you'll get further ahead in your programming career than someone who's worried about the superiority of one programming language over another.

In this chapter, you see how different languages can display the words `It works!` on-screen.

Learning BASIC

If you're interested in learning to program, you may wonder, "Why not jump right in and start learning C++?" There's nothing wrong with learning C++ right away, but the cryptic nature of C++ can be as confusing to a novice programmer as reading and writing Chinese or Arabic can be to a native English speaker. If you try to learn C++ right away, the technical details of learning the language can often interfere with understanding the general principles of programming.

That's why this book introduces programming concepts, using BASIC for a couple of reasons:

- **BASIC was specially designed to teach beginners how to program,** so it's one of the easiest languages for anyone to learn. Most BASIC commands are similar to English words, which makes learning easier in much the same way that native English speakers find that learning to read and write French or Spanish is easier than learning to read and write Arabic and Chinese.
- **BASIC is powerful,** so after you learn BASIC, you can apply your BASIC programming skills right away to create commercial-quality programs.

To help you learn BASIC, this book's CD comes with two BASIC compilers called Liberty BASIC and REALbasic. Liberty BASIC uses a simple BASIC dialect so you can start learning programming right away. After you understand how programming in the BASIC language works, you can graduate to REALbasic, which offers a more advanced BASIC dialect that includes object-oriented programming features, commonly found in more powerful programming languages like C++.

Appendix B gives instructions for installing and using Liberty BASIC on Windows and REALbasic on Windows and Macintosh computers. Liberty BASIC is a shareware program, so if you find it useful, consider paying for it. REALbasic is a trial version that you can use for a limited time. When this trial period is over, you have to buy a copy of REALbasic if you want to continue using it.

Getting to know Liberty BASIC

Liberty BASIC closely follows the goals of the original BASIC programming language, which emphasizes simplicity. The entire Liberty BASIC program to display `It works!` on-screen consists of a single line:

```
PRINT "It works!"
```

The philosophy of BASIC

In the early days of computers, programming was slow. First you had to write your commands and store them in a file. Then you had to compile them into a program. Finally, you had to run your program to test whether it worked. If it didn't work, you had to edit your commands, compile them again, and run the new program once more.

The problem was that most compilers were slow. For a large program, it was customary to compile a program overnight and then return the next morning to see whether it worked. Obviously, such a slow process made programming tedious and frustrating. So the whole idea behind BASIC was to make programming fun by giving you instant feedback on whether your program would work.

Instead of using a compiler, the first BASIC language used an interpreter so programmers could type a BASIC command into the computer and immediately see whether it would work. Not only did BASIC give instant feedback so people could program faster, but it also used more English-like words for its commands to make programming easier, especially for beginners. In fact, BASIC is actually an acronym that stands for Beginner's All-purpose Symbolic Instruction Code.

Although BASIC compilers are now just as fast as BASIC interpreters, the central goal of BASIC remains the same: Make programming easy for beginners while still being powerful enough to create commercial-quality programs.

In BASIC, you can type commands in all uppercase (`PRINT`), lowercase (`print`), or a combination of the two (`Print`).

Almost anyone can figure out how the previous Liberty BASIC program works without knowing anything about programming. Novices often start learning to program in BASIC because it makes programming easy and simple. When you understand the fundamental principles of programming, you can always graduate to a more powerful (and complicated) language like C++, or you can just continue using BASIC.

Getting to know REALbasic

REALbasic is an object-oriented version of BASIC that includes rapid application development (RAD) features that let you design a user interface by drawing buttons, menus, and other types of controls on a window.

To write a REALbasic program, you typically design the user interface and then write BASIC code to make user interface actually respond to the user and do something useful. REALbasic programs consist of two parts: a user interface and the BASIC code that makes the user interface work. So to display `It works!` on-screen, you could create a user interface with a single button on it, as shown in Figure 5-1.

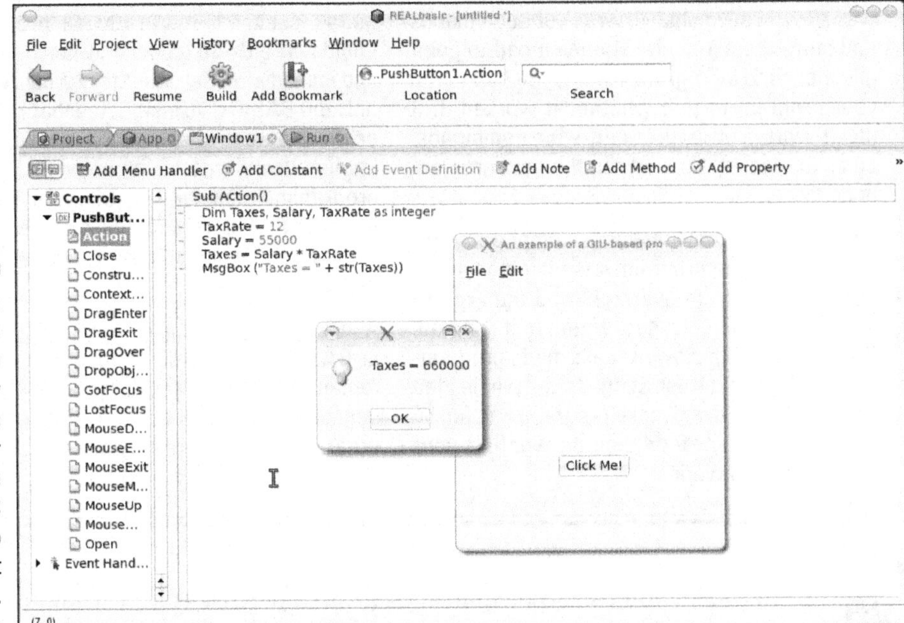

Figure 5-1: A REALbasic program typically consists of a user interface with BASIC code to make it work.

When you run this program, it displays the user interface and waits until the user clicks the button. The moment the user clicks the button, the following BASIC code runs:

```
Sub Action()                                   →1
  MsgBox "It works!"                           →2
End Sub                                        →3
```

This REALbasic program is stored in the REALbasic Sample Programs folder as `Chapter 5 - It Works.bas.`

Although still fairly easy to understand, the REALbasic program consists of three lines that work as follows:

→1 The `Sub` keyword is short for *subprogram* and identifies the BASIC code as a self-contained chunk of code that's part of a larger program (hence the prefix *sub-* in subprogram). The `Action` keyword tells the computer to run the commands in this subprogram when the user clicks the button displayed on the user interface in Figure 5-1.

→2 The `MsgBox` command tells the computer to display a small window, called a message box, on-screen with the words `It works!` shown inside.

→3 The `End Sub` keywords define the end of the subprogram.

Learning C++

C++ is currently one of the most widely used languages in the world today, so gaining some familiarity with C++ and related programming languages (such as C, C#, and Java) is important.

Although this book won't cover everything about C++, it shows you enough to understand how C++ programs work. After you understand C++, you can apply your knowledge to learning more about C++ or similar languages such as C# or Java.

If you have Windows, you can install the gcc compiler, and an accompanying editor and debugger called Dev-C++, off this book's CD. If you have Mac OS X, you can install a free C++ compiler on your Macintosh that runs under a collection of tools called Xcode. (You can copy and install Xcode from the original discs that came with your Macintosh, or you can download and install the latest version of Xcode from Apple's Web site at `http://developer.apple.com/tools/xcode`.)

The gcc compiler is free. Xcode also uses the gcc compiler but includes an editor to help you write C++ programs on a Macintosh. The gcc compiler (`http://gcc.gnu.org`) is open source. If you find the gcc compiler useful, consider donating either your time or money to helping make the gcc compiler even better than before.

A C++ program to display `It works!` on-screen might look like this:

```
#include <iostream>
#include <stdio.h>
int main()
{
 cout << "It works!\n";
 cout << "\nPress ENTER to continue..." << endl;
 getchar();
 return 0;
}
```

The design of the C++ language

Most programming languages, like BASIC, provide a large collection of keywords, or commands, that you can combine in different ways to tell a computer what to do. The more keywords or commands a language provides, the more powerful the programs you can create.

Unfortunately, when a language offers a huge library of keywords, the language compiler must be able to recognize all these keywords, whether or not programmers ever use the keywords. As a result, creating compilers for such languages can be difficult.

The C++ language takes a different approach. Rather than bog down the compiler with a huge library of keywords, the C++ language contains a much smaller library of keywords. This makes it easy to write C++ compilers for different computers, which in turn means more computers can run a C++ program.

Of course, having a small library of keywords means you have only a handful of keywords to give the computer instructions. So C++ solves this problem by including a library of commands, created from this handful of C++ keywords, and stored in separate files. To use a command stored in a C++ library, you just have to tell the C++ compiler which library file you want to use. Two of the most common library files that C++ programs use are the `iostream.h` and the `stdio.h` files, which give you commands for accepting data and printing data to the screen.

Because C++ is designed for efficiency (from the computer's point of view), it tends to be cryptic (from a human point of view).

This C++ program is stored in the C++ Sample Programs folder as `Chapter 5 - It Works.cpp`.

If this C++ program looks a bit weird, it is. Here's how each line in the C++ program works:

→1 The `#include` command tells C++ to include the library file called `iostream.h`.

Some C++ compilers let you abbreviate the filename by dropping the `.h` file extension, so you'd use `#include <iostream>` rather than `#include <iostream.h>` in this example.

→2 The second `#include` command tells C++ to include the library file called `stdio.h`.

→3 The `int main()` defines the start of your program. Every C++ program is called a *main* program. The `int` keyword identifies your main program to represent an integer value, which in this sample program means absolutely nothing and serves only to confuse beginners. (Now you know why learning C++ is much harder than learning BASIC.) The empty parentheses `()` tells the computer that the program doesn't need any additional data to run.

→4 The left curly bracket `{` defines the start of your program.

→5 The `cout` command tells the computer to print the phrase `It works!` on-screen. The `\n` symbols tell the computer to move the cursor to a new line after it prints `It works!` on the screen. The semicolon `;` defines the end of the command.

→6 The `cout` command prints `Press ENTER to continue` on-screen. The `\n` symbols tell the computer to move the cursor to a new line after it prints `It works!` on the screen. The semicolon `;` defines the end of the command.

→7 The `getchar()` waits for the user to press a key.

→8 The `return 0` command assigns the number 0 to the main program. Some C++ compilers require this, others don't.

→9 The right curly bracket `}` defines the end of your program.

C++ programs almost always look more cryptic than similar BASIC programs (especially the simple one-line Liberty BASIC program). As a general rule, C++ makes easy things hard and hard things easy. As you can see from the previous C++ program, you have to write a lot of commands just to print `It works!` on-screen.

C++ is a powerful but unforgiving language. Make a single mistake, and your C++ program could crash a computer. Despite this problem, C++ still remains the most popular language to use, which explains why programs like Microsoft Windows, Photoshop, and Quicken are all written in C++ (or a combination of C and C++ code). (This also explains why programs like Microsoft Windows tend to crash a lot and constantly need patching to make sure they work properly.)

Learning Revolution

Revolution is a unique scripting language that uses English-like commands to program a computer. As a result, it's easy to understand while also demonstrating that not all programming languages need to work like BAISC or look as cryptic as C++.

Perhaps the biggest drawback of traditional programming languages like BASIC and C++ is that you must tell the computer what to do and then how to do it, step by step. Scripting languages like Revolution allow you just to tell the computer what you want it to do without getting bogged down in the details for how to do it. Revolution offers three advantages over traditional programming languages:

- Revolution programs are often shorter than equivalent programs written in other languages such as BASIC or C++.

The design of the Revolution language

In 1987, Apple developed a unique program called HyperCard, which it gave away for free with every Macintosh computer. HyperCard combined the features of a paint program with a database program and included its own programming language called HyperTalk. HyperTalk was designed to be easy to write and understand by using plain English commands. For many people, HyperCard and HyperTalk made programming fun and accessible for the first time.

Unfortunately, Apple couldn't make money by giving HyperCard away for free, so it eventually stopped improving the program. Around this time, an independent programmer decided to develop an equivalent HyperCard clone, called MetaCard, which would run on Windows, Macintosh, and UNIX (including Linux) computers.

Eventually, a company in Scotland bought the rights to MetaCard and made it even easier to use. This new program was dubbed Revolution and its programming language, based on the original HyperTalk language, was dubbed Transcript. (The AppleScript language, used on current Macintosh computers, bears a striking similarity to the original HyperTalk language, so if you understand AppleScript, you already know much of the Revolution language, too.)

So the basic design philosophy of Revolution is to make programming easy by hiding the details of programming and letting you focus on writing descriptive English-like commands to tell the computer what to do.

- Revolution uses English-like commands to make programs much easier to understand and modify.
- Because you don't have to worry about how the computer does something, you can concentrate more on the design of your program.

Programmers familiar with traditional languages like BASIC or C++ might find Revolution initially confusing, but the fundamental programming principles apply to Revolution, as well. By browsing through Revolution program examples, you can see that there is more than one way to write a program.

Appendix B gives instructions for installing Revolution on a Windows or Macintosh computer. Revolution is a trial version that you can use for a limited time. After this trial period is over, you have to buy a copy of Revolution if you want to continue using it.

To create a program to display `It works!` on-screen, a Revolution program might look like this:

```
on mouseUp                              →1
    put "It works!" into message        →2
end mouseUp                             →3
```

This Revolution program is stored in the Revolution Sample Programs folder as `Chapter 5 - It Works.rev`.

Like REALbasic, Revolution programs often rely on a user interface and then provide Revolution commands to make the user interface work. The previous code runs only when the user clicks a button in a Revolution program, as shown in Figure 5-2.

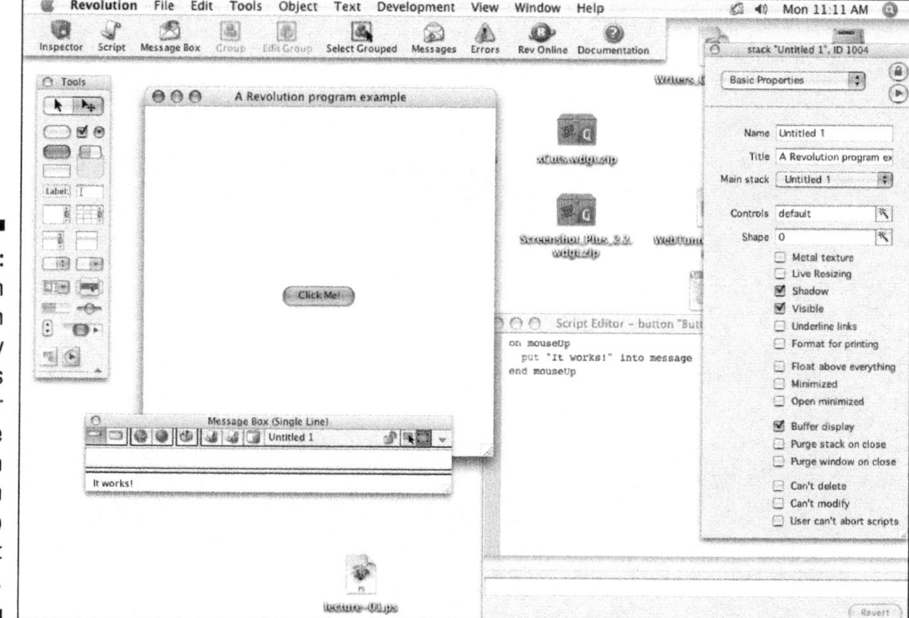

Figure 5-2: A Revolution program typically consists of a user interface with Revolution code to make it work.

Here's how each line in the Revolution program works:

→1 The `on mouseUp` command tells the computer that this is the start of a program that runs whenever the user releases the mouse button in the process of clicking.

→2 The `put` command tells Revolution to display or "put" the phrase `It works!` on-screen.

→3 The `end mouseUp` command defines the end of your program.

Chapter 6

The Structure of a Computer Program

In This Chapter

- Putting together a program
- Discovering the three parts of programming
- Using subprograms
- Looking at the real purpose of programming

A computer program is nothing more than a list of instructions that tell the computer what to do. Because programmers don't like to tell people, "I'm writing a list of instructions," they use euphemisms and say things like, "I'm writing code," where the magic word *code* is just another word that means "a list of instructions."

The simplest program can consist of a single instruction, as in the following Liberty BASIC program:

```
PRINT "I am a useless program"
```

As you can guess, this program does no more than print `I am a useless program` on-screen.

Programmers often refer to each instruction in a program as a *line of code.* When you save a program to a file, programmers refer to this file as the *source code* of the program. The source code of every program contains the secret step-by-step instructions that make the program work.

Each line of code acts like a single building block. The more lines of code you put together, the bigger the programs you can create, as shown in Figure 6-1. If you want to create a program that prints `I am a useless program` and `Because this is all I can do`, you write two lines of code, such as

```
PRINT "I am a useless program"
PRINT "Because this is all I can do"
```

```
PRINT "I am a useless program"
```

```
PRINT "Because this is all I can do"
```

Figure 6-1: Each line of code acts like a building block to create bigger and more powerful programs.

In general, the more lines of code you add to a program, the more things your program can do. However, you can write the same program literally in a million different ways. One person might write a two-line program whereas another might write a five-line program, yet both programs do the exact same thing, as this snippet shows:

```
PRINT "I am a ";
PRINT "useless ";
PRINT "program"
PRINT "Because this ";
PRINT "is all I can do"
```

In this example, written in Liberty BASIC, the semicolon tells the computer to keep printing text on the same line. However, in another programming language, the semicolon may mean something else entirely.

Try to keep your programs as small and straightforward as possible. Not only are small programs easier to write, but they're also easier to understand and modify later.

Designing a Program

Designing a program involves two crucial steps:

1. **Identify what you want the program to do.**

   The first step is fairly easy (because it's always easy to tell someone else what to do). You might want a program that balances your budget, plays Chinese checkers, or removes the sound of static from a poorly recorded audio file.

2. **Tell the computer, step by step, how to do what you want it to do.**

   The second (and much harder) step is to figure out how to achieve your desired result. This process of telling the computer what to do, step by step, is what programming is really all about regardless of the programming language you ultimately use.

When you have a clear idea about what you want your program to do and you know how you want to make the computer work, the next task is writing the instructions, in a particular programming language, that tells the computer what to do.

Spaghetti programming

In the early days of computers, many programs were small and simple, so programmers could often start writing their programs without any planning whatsoever. They'd write part of a program, test it, and add more instructions over and over again until the program finally worked (if it ever did).

Unfortunately, this haphazard approach to programming often lead to something called *spaghetti programming,* which gets its name from the idea of untangling strands of spaghetti.

In a well-organized program, you can easily see where a program starts, where it ends, and how it proceeds step by step. In a spaghetti program, the programmer just starts typing commands without any thought of organization whatsoever, which can be like dumping your laundry on the floor and then wondering why you can never find a matching pair of socks in a hurry.

In a small program, dumping commands haphazardly may be troublesome but still manageable. In a large program, such haphazard spaghetti programming can make a program completely incomprehensible so no one (including the original programmer) can figure out how it works ever again (if it ever works). Figure 6-2 shows how confusing a spaghetti program can look.

The code used in the program for Figure 6-2 is the following:

```
GOTO [LabelOne]
[LabelFour]
 PROMPT "How much money do you have"; MyCash
 GOTO [LabelThree]
[LabelTwo]
 END
[LabelOne]
GOTO [LabelFour]
[LabelThree]
 PRINT "You owe me = "; MyCash * .95
 GOTO [LabelTwo]
```

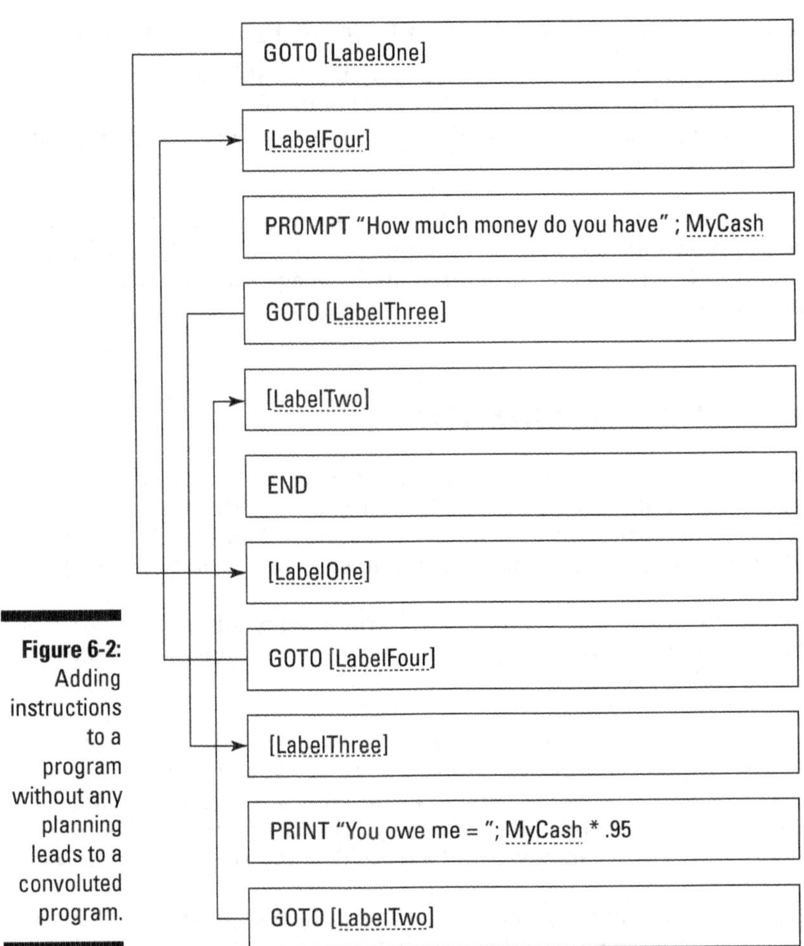

Figure 6-2: Adding instructions to a program without any planning leads to a convoluted program.

Believe it or not, this program actually works, but trying to follow the logic is nearly impossible. Reorganizing the program can create the much simpler equivalent program:

```
PROMPT "How much money do you have:"; MyCash
PRINT "You owe me ="; MyCash * .95
END
```

Which version of the program do you think is easier to read, understand, and modify?

The three parts of every program

A program like Microsoft Windows may appear to have nothing in common with a video game like World of Warcraft. However, no matter how diverse their purposes may be, every program consists of nothing more than instructions (lines of code) that tell the computer what to do, step by step.

The specific instructions stored in each program determine what that program does, but every program works the same no matter what type of program you write or what programming language you use.

In every program, you can find instructions organized in one of three ways: sequential, branching, or looping. By combining sequential, branching, and looping instructions, you can write any type of program.

Sequential instructions

Sequential simply means that the program follows instructions, one after another, from the first instruction at the top to the last instruction at the bottom, as shown in Figure 6-3.

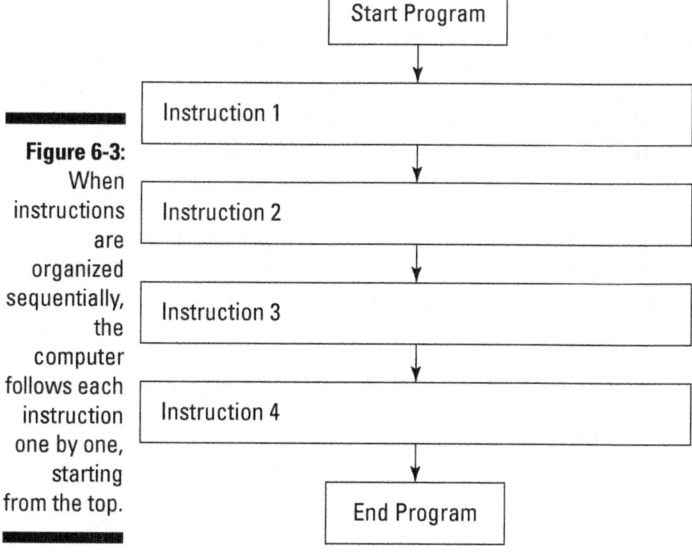

Figure 6-3: When instructions are organized sequentially, the computer follows each instruction one by one, starting from the top.

Every program organizes most of its instructions sequentially, but few programs organize all of their instructions sequentially. The reason is that if a program organizes all of its instructions sequentially, the program can run through its instructions exactly once before it stops.

Such a program might be handy for creating simple programs that print `I am a useless program` on-screen, but such programs ignore any data they might receive from the user. No matter how many times you press a key or click the mouse, running the following two-line Liberty BASIC program always displays `I am a useless program` on-screen followed by `Because this is all I can do.`

```
PRINT "I am a useless program"
PRINT "Because this is all I can do"
```

Branching instructions

To make programs more useful and responsive, they need to accept and react to outside data. When you play a video game and a monster appears on-screen, the game needs to react differently if you shoot and kill the monster or if the monster eats and kills you. If you shoot and kill the monster, the game lets you keep playing. If the monster kills and eats you, the game displays the words `GAME OVER` on-screen.

Branching instructions simply tell the computer to run different instructions depending on the value of certain data. When you delete a file, many programs ask, `Do you really want to delete the file?`. If you click the Yes button, the program follows the instructions to delete the file. If you click the No button, the program follows a different set of instructions, as shown in Figure 6-4.

The following Liberty BASIC program shows how a simple branching instruction can work. If the user types the letter Y, the program displays the message `Deleting file`. If the user types any other letter, the program displays the message `File NOT deleted`.

```
PROMPT "Do you want to delete the file? (Y or N)"; answer$

IF answer$ = "Y" THEN

  NOTICE "Deleting file"

ELSE

  NOTICE "File NOT deleted"

END IF

END
```

Branching instructions let a program respond to data. Branching instructions typically contain two or more alternative instructions, but the computer can follow only one of these sets of instructions at a time.

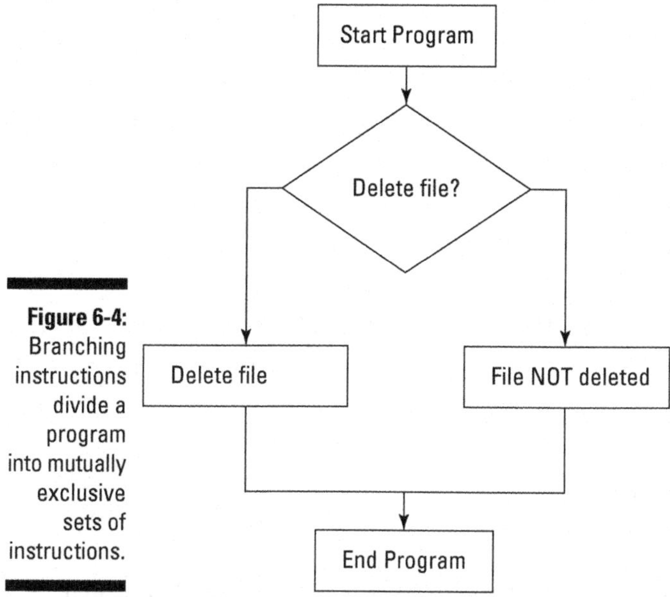

Figure 6-4: Branching instructions divide a program into mutually exclusive sets of instructions.

Looping instructions

No matter how many sequential or branching instructions a program has, it runs only once before stopping. To keep a program running until you want it to stop, you need to use looping instructions.

Looping instructions make the computer repeat one or more instructions. In a video game, a loop might keep running all the instructions in the program until the game character dies. Then the loop stops and the program (and game) ends, as shown in Figure 6-5.

Besides keeping a program running until the user wants to quit, looping instructions save you from having to type nearly identical instructions over and over again.

Suppose you wanted to print the numbers 1 through 5 on-screen. You could use the following Liberty BASIC program:

```
PRINT 1
PRINT 2
PRINT 3
PRINT 4
PRINT 5
```

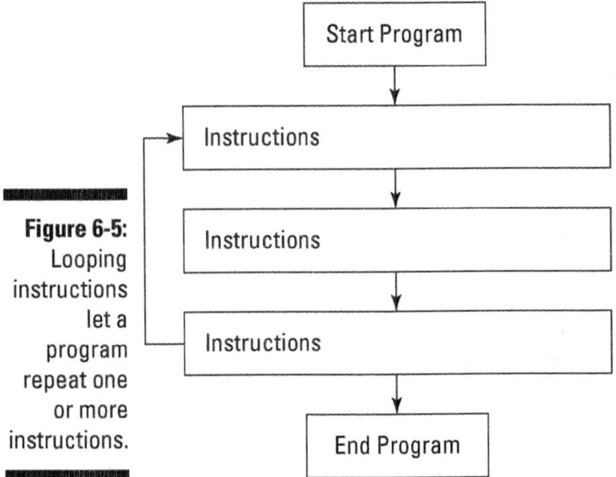

Figure 6-5: Looping instructions let a program repeat one or more instructions.

Typing multiple instructions may be tedious, but still tolerable for a small number of instructions. However, if you want a program that prints the numbers 1 through 1000 on-screen, you would have to type nearly a thousand identical instructions.

Obviously, typing that many instructions over and over again is a waste of time, so that's where looping instructions come in handy. Looping instructions tell the computer to repeat one or more lines of code, eliminating the need for you to type them yourself. A Liberty BASIC looping program that prints the numbers 1 through 5 on-screen might look like this:

```
FOR X = 1 TO 5
   PRINT X
NEXT X
```

Although this looping instruction looks more cryptic than the straightforward list of five instructions that printed the numbers 1 through 5 on-screen, the looping instruction requires much less typing. Even better, if you want to print the numbers 1 though 1000 on-screen, you just have to rewrite the looping instruction like this:

```
FOR X = 1 TO 1000
   PRINT X
NEXT X
```

The building blocks of programming

Every program in the world has been built by using the three basic building blocks (sequential, branching, and looping instructions). Figure 6-6 shows how these three building blocks can create the Liberty BASIC program in Listing 6-1, which asks for a password.

Listing 6-1: Enter Your Password

```
password$ = ""
WHILE password$ <> "open"
  PROMPT "Enter your password"; password$
  IF password$ = "open" THEN
    NOTICE "Welcome to the FBI's secret computer network"
  ELSE
    NOTICE "Try again"
  END IF
WEND
END
```

Although you find out more about branching (Chapter 9) and looping (Chapter 10) instructions later in this book, you can break this program in the following parts:

Sequential instructions

```
password$ = ""
WHILE password$ <> "open"
  PROMPT "Enter your password"; password$
  IF password$ = "open" THEN
    NOTICE "Welcome to the FBI's secret computer
        network"
  ELSE
    NOTICE "Try again"
  END IF
WEND
END
```

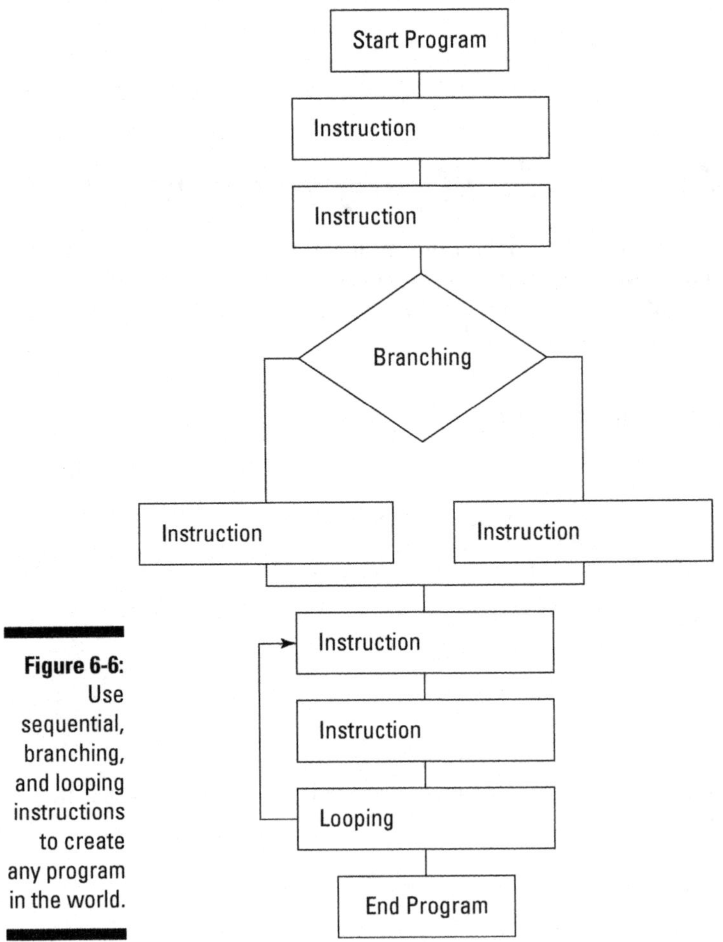

Figure 6-6: Use sequential, branching, and looping instructions to create any program in the world.

Branching instruction

```
password$ = ""
WHILE password$ <> "open"
  PROMPT "Enter your password"; password$
  IF password$ = "open" THEN
    NOTICE "Welcome to the FBI's secret computer
        network"
  ELSE
    NOTICE "Try again"
  END IF
WEND
END
```

Looping instruction

```
password$ = ""
WHILE password$ <> "open"
  PROMPT "Enter your password"; password$
  IF password$ = "open" THEN
    NOTICE "Welcome to the FBI's secret computer
        network"
  ELSE
    NOTICE "Try again"
  END IF
WEND
END
```

Dividing and Conquering with Subprograms

In general, the more complicated the task, the larger your program needs to be. The larger your program gets, the harder it can be to read and understand. Reading a large program can be like trying to read a long novel printed on a scroll rather than on separate pages.

Just as books divide large text into separate pages for easy reading, so do programmers divide large programs into separate parts. When you divide a large program into smaller parts, those smaller parts are called *subprograms.*

Rather than clutter your main program with a long list of instructions, subprograms let you group related instructions in one place, making your main program smaller and easier to read and understand.

In the Liberty BASIC program shown earlier in Listing 6-1, you can store most of the instructions in a subprogram, so your main program looks like this:

```
' This is the main program
GOSUB [password]
END
```

This Liberty BASIC program tells the computer to run all the instructions in the `[password]` subprogram, which looks like this:

```
' This is the subprogram
[password]
password$ = ""
WHILE password$ <> "open"
  PROMPT "Enter your password"; password$
  IF password$ = "open" THEN
    NOTICE "Welcome to the FBI's secret computer network"
  ELSE
    NOTICE "TRY AGAIN"
  END IF
WEND
RETURN
```

Figure 6-7 shows how you can divide a large program into multiple subprograms, where subprograms act like super building blocks that you can use to create a large program.

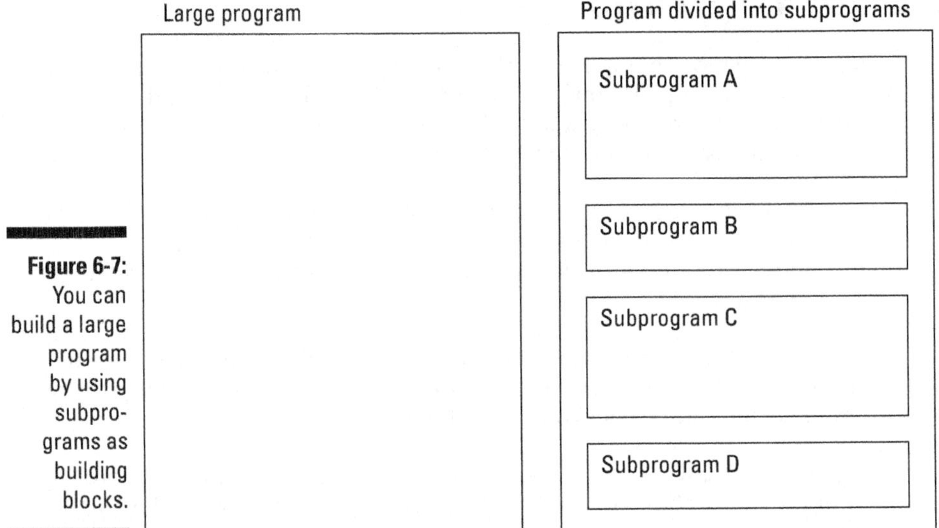

Figure 6-7: You can build a large program by using subprograms as building blocks.

By dividing a single program into subprograms, you gain the following advantages:

- Subprograms divide a large program into smaller parts to make reading and writing large programs easier.
- Subprograms isolate related program instructions. So if you need to modify a program later, you just need to modify a subprogram, much like removing a defective brick from a wall and putting in a better one.

Creating libraries of subprograms

When you divide a large program into a bunch of smaller programs, you're doing nothing more than rearranging and organizing your instructions. Unfortunately, a large program written as one long list of instructions is barely any smaller than the same large program divided into multiple subprograms. Because the larger a program gets, the harder it can be to understand, programmers found a way to take subprograms out of the main program file and store them in separate files.

Now instead of a program consisting of a single, massive file, it can consist of two, three, or even several thousand separate files, as shown in Figure 6-8.

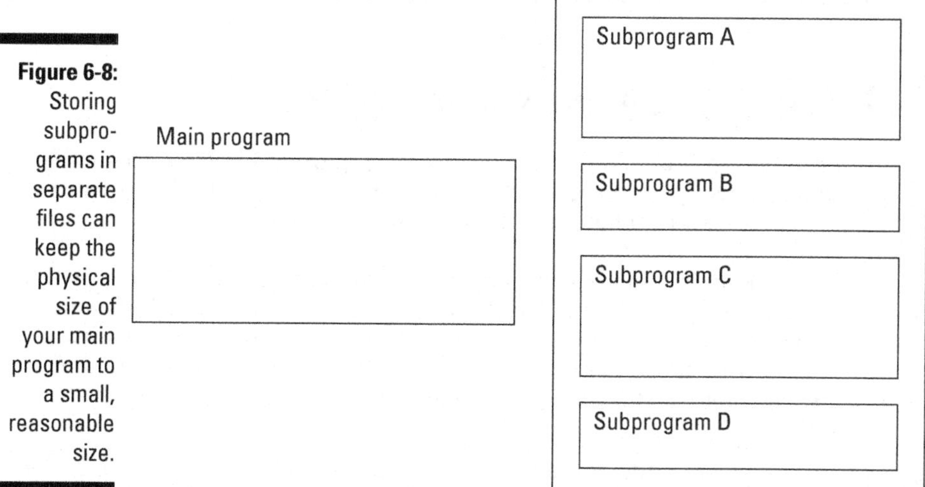

Figure 6-8: Storing subprograms in separate files can keep the physical size of your main program to a small, reasonable size.

By storing subprograms in separate files, reading and understanding your program is much simpler. Instead of scrolling through one massive file that contains your main program and all of its subprograms, you can just open the file that contains the subprogram you want.

A second advantage is that storing subprograms in separate files also lets you reuse subprograms. By storing commonly used subprograms in files, you can create libraries of useful subprograms, copy them to another computer, and reuse them in other programs.

One file might contain subprograms that calculate different mathematical equations, and a second file might contain subprograms that display graphics on-screen. By creating and reusing libraries of subprograms, you can keep your main program size to a minimum.

If you ever look at the structure of a typical C++ program, you might see code that looks like this:

```
#include <stdio.h>
#include <iostream.h>
int main()
{
    return 0;
}
```

The two `#include` commands simply tell the computer to use (or include) the subprograms stored in the separate files named `iostream.h` and `stdio.h`.

Dividing programs into objects

Storing subprograms in separate files helps keep programs to a reasonable size while allowing programmers to share libraries of useful subprograms. Unfortunately, two problems arose with subprogram libraries:

- If programmers found a subprogram library useful, they often copied it for their own programs. Unfortunately, this meant that you had multiple copies of the same subprogram library. If you found a mistake in your subprogram library and fixed it, guess what? Now you'd have to find and fix that same mistake in every single copy of that same subprogram library.
- Programmers often copied a useful subprogram library and then added their own subprograms to that library file, which meant that you not only had multiple copies of a subprogram library, but you could also have slightly different versions of that same subprogram library scattered among multiple programmers.

To solve these twin problems, computer scientists invented something called object-oriented programming (often abbreviated as OOP, as in "Oops, you spent four years studying the wrong programming language in college").

The basic idea behind objects is that instead of making physical (duplicate) copies of subprograms, you maintain a single, physical copy of subprograms but allow others to make "virtual" copies of those subprograms, as shown in Figure 6-9.

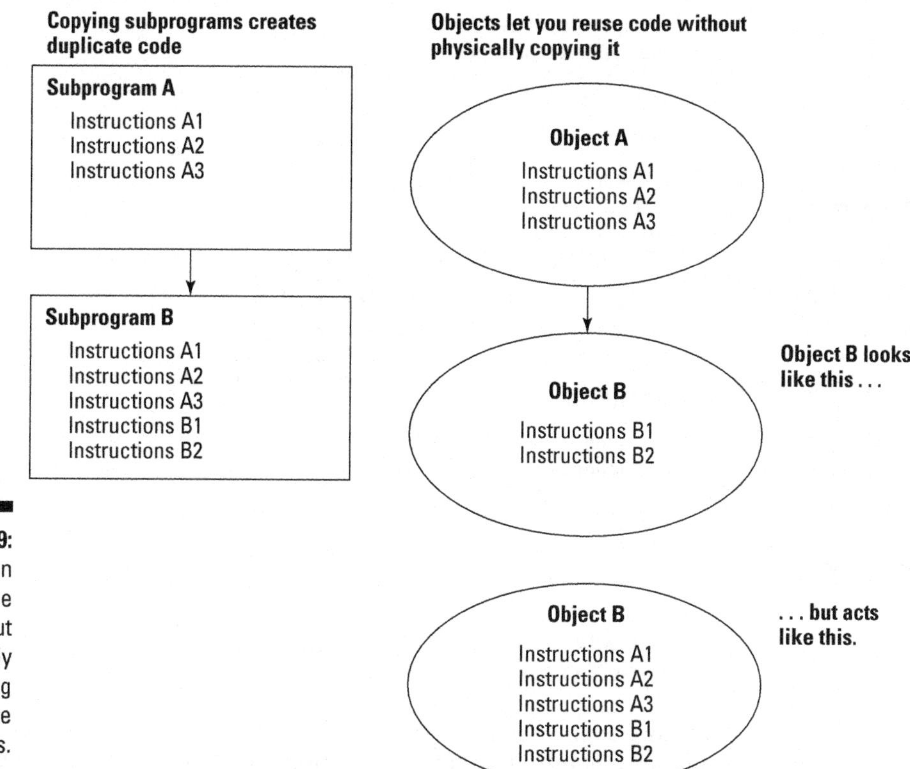

Figure 6-9: Objects can share code without physically making duplicate copies.

The virtual copies of subprograms work exactly the same as any physical copies. The main advantage is that you can't modify a virtual copy of a subprogram. This prevents five different programmers from copying a subprogram and making five different versions.

If programmers need a subprogram to fix a problem, they need to modify only the original subprogram stored in an object. This automatically updates any virtual copies of the subprogram anywhere else in the program.

If programmers want to create slightly different versions of a subprogram, they just need to create a copy of the virtual subprogram and then make any modifications, which is known as *polymorphism.* They can either add new instructions or overwrite any existing instructions stored in the original subprogram object, as shown in Figure 6-10.

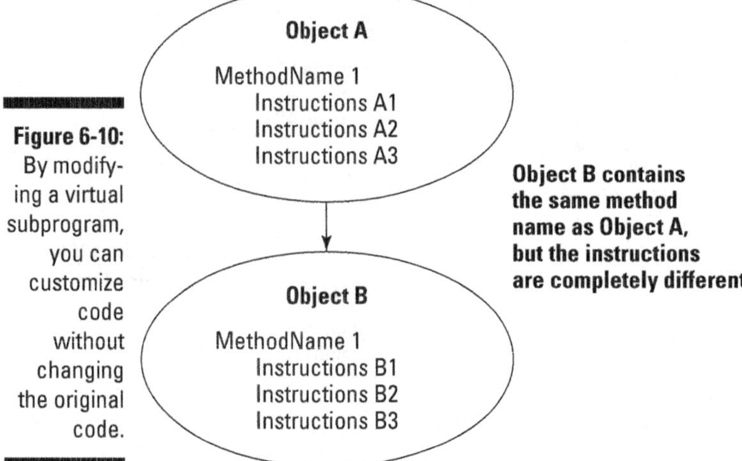

Figure 6-10: By modifying a virtual subprogram, you can customize code without changing the original code.

Any changes made to a virtual subprogram won't affect or modify the original subprogram. By sharing subprograms as objects, you gain two advantages:

- You store a single copy of subprograms that others can freely share. Updating a subprogram in one location automatically updates any virtual copies of that subprogram throughout an entire program.
- Others can modify any virtual subprograms without physically copying or altering the original subprogram.

Object-oriented programming offers other features as well, which you can find more about in Chapter 13. For now, remember that object-oriented programming is just another way to help you create, organize, and maintain large programs without losing your mind.

Ultimately, the real purpose of any programming technique, whether it's dividing a large program into multiple subprograms or using object-oriented programming techniques, is to make programming easier for you.

Chapter 7

Variables, Constants, and Comments

In This Chapter

- Using variables
- Creating and using constants
- Adding comments to your code

Every program works with data. The simplest programs just use the same data to do something over and over again, such as printing "It works!" on-screen. Programs that do only one thing may be useful in certain situations, like controlling a traffic signal, but most programs work by accepting data from the outside world, manipulating that data somehow, and then spitting it back out in some useful form.

When a program accepts data (called *input*), it stores that data in its memory. Of course, it can't just dump data anywhere in its memory like tossing a pair of socks in a closet. Instead, a program stores data in a specific location (called an *address*) in memory. To retrieve that data again, the program retrieves it from that same memory address.

Unfortunately, storing and retrieving data by specific memory addresses can get cumbersome. If you forget the memory address where you stored data, you might never find that data again. If you give the computer the wrong memory address to retrieve data from, it retrieves the wrong data. If you try to store data in a memory address that already contains data, you could wipe out the existing chunk of data.

Storing data in memory addresses can be as cumbersome as trying to talk to someone based on his or her physical location. If you want to talk to someone in front of you, you don't say, "To the guy standing 2.64 meters at a 37.2 degree angle to me, I want to talk to you." Instead, it's much easier to call the person by name (ignoring their physical location altogether) and just say,

"Hey, Joe, I want to talk to you." Likewise, forcing programmers to refer to data based on memory addresses isn't as easy as letting programmers refer to data by name. When programming languages let you store data in something you can name, that something is called a *variable.*

Variable names make programming easier for you (but harder for the computer because if you don't take care of worrying about memory addresses, the computer has to do it). The general rule with computers is that the more you force the computer to do, the slower your program is, but the easier the program is for you to write. The trade-off with computer programming is almost always computer speed versus programmer convenience.

Many programming languages, like assembly language and C++, still let you store and manipulate data by using memory addresses, which can be as powerful and dangerous as probing your brain with a scalpel to remove a tumor. If you know what you're doing, you can create fast, efficient programs, but if you don't know what you're doing or you make a mistake, manipulating memory addresses is a sure recipe for disaster in the form of a program that can crash your entire computer.

Creating Variables

A variable simply acts like a box that can hold data. Each variable can have a descriptive name so you can identify which variable to use when storing and retrieving data. Variables have the following two uses:

- Storing inputted data
- Storing calculations that use inputted data or previous calculations

When you store data in a variable, the computer handles the specific memory address to store your data; all you have to worry about is the name of the variable where you stored your data. When you want to retrieve the data again, you just refer to the data by its variable name, and the computer knows the exact memory address it needs to find your data.

In general, you create a variable in three steps:

1. Give each variable a unique, descriptive name.
2. Define what type of data each variable can hold.
3. Assign data (numbers or letters) to each variable.

Variables can hold any type of data, such as numbers or text. However, a variable can store only one chunk of data at a time. The moment you stuff another chunk of data in a variable, the variable dumps the old data and cheerfully stores the new data. The contents of a variable may vary at any given time, hence the name *variable.*

Naming variables

You can give variables any name you want, such as the name of your dog or variations of four-letter words. However, it's a good idea to use descriptive names that help identify the type of data that the variable holds, such as `FirstName` or `CustomerIDNumber`.

Each variable must have a unique name to keep your computer from getting confused. In some languages, the variable names `LastName`, `lastname`, and `Lastname` are considered identical. Other languages, such as C++, are *case-sensitive.* A case-sensitive language considers a variable called `LastName` to be completely different from another variable called `lastName`. Unless every letter in a variable name is identical (including upper- and lowercase letters), a case-sensitive language considers variables to be two completely different items.

When naming variables in a case-sensitive language like C++, a common error is to name a variable something like `CustomerAge` but try to store data in that variable as `customerAge`. (Note that the first letter is lowercase rather than uppercase.) When naming variables, be consistent. Some programmers always capitalize the first letter of a variable name (`Customer`), but others always type the first letter as lowercase (`customer`). Some programmers always capitalize the first letter of each word (`MyStudentNumber`), but others don't (`Mystudentnumber`). Whatever you do, do it consistently to save yourself a lot of headaches trying to identify your variables later on.

In some programming languages, you can name your variables and stuff data in them at the same time, as in the following Liberty BASIC program that creates variables. One variable (`Salary`) stores data that represents a user's salary, and the second variable (`TaxOwed`) stores a calculation.

```
Salary = 25000
TaxOwed = Salary * 0.95
PRINT "This is how much tax you owe = $"; TaxOwed
END
```

This is how the Liberty BASIC program works:

→1 Tells the computer, "Create a variable named `Salary` and store the number `25000` in that variable."

→2 Tells the computer, "Create a variable called `TaxOwed`. Then multiply the number stored in the `Salary` variable by the number `0.95` and store the result of this calculation in `TaxOwed` variable."

→3 Prints `This is how much tax you owe = $` followed by the number that the variable `TaxOwed` represents.

→4 Tells the computer that the program has ended.

In most programming languages, you use the equal sign (=) to assign a value to a variable. However, in Revolution, you use the magic `into` command instead, as follows:

```
put 25000 into Salary                                        →1
put Salary * 0.95 into TaxOwed                               →2
put "This is how much tax you owe = $" && TaxOwed
         into message                                        →3
```

This is how the Revolution program works:

→1 Tells the computer, "Put the number `25000` into a variable named `Salary`."

→2 Tells the computer, "Multiply the number stored in the `Salary` variable by the number `0.95` and put the result of this calculation in a variable named `TaxOwed`."

→3 Tells the computer, "Take the text, `This is how much tax you owe = $` and include the number stored inside the `TaxOwed` variable and put all of this text in the message box that appears onscreen." (The `&&` symbol tells the computer to "add" the number stored in the `TaxOwed` variable to the end of the `This is how much tax you owe = $` line.)

Defining the data type of a variable

Programming languages like Liberty BASIC and Revolution let you create a variable and stuff it with data right away. This makes programming easy because you can create variables whenever you need them. Unfortunately, it also encourages sloppy programming for two reasons:

- You have to search your code, line by line, to find all the different variables your program creates and what type of data it stores in them.
- You can easily store the wrong type of data in a variable by mistake.

Consider the following Liberty BASIC code. The code works but doesn't make any logical sense because nobody can have 1.48 numbers of children.

```
Children = 1.48
MonthlyPayment = 350
PRINT "You owe = "; Children * MonthlyPayment
END
```

In this example, the `Children` variable should hold only whole numbers and not decimal numbers.

To avoid storing inappropriate data in a variable, many programming languages do something called *type-checking.* Type-checking forces you to define the type of data a variable can hold, and then it checks to make sure you don't try to store the wrong type of data in that variable. In this way, type-checking acts like a filter that allows only valid data into the variable.

Programming languages that force you to define the type of data a variable can hold are also known as *type-safe* languages.

If you don't define what type of data a variable can hold, it's possible to store the wrong type of data in a variable. If your program tries to work with the wrong type of data, it could crash or just mess up very badly.

In type-safe languages such as REALbasic and C++, you must define both the name of a variable and the type of data it can hold. Only after you have defined (or *declared*) both the variable name and its data type can you stuff data in that variable.

The three most common types of data that variables can hold are

- **Whole numbers (such as 3, 45, or 102):** Often referred to as *integers.*
- **Decimal numbers (such as 34.04679, 3.1415, or 26.943):** Often referred to as *single* or *double* to represent single-precision or double-precision numbers. Single- or double-precision refers to how many decimal places the computer uses to store a number. Double-precision numbers can store more decimal places than single-precision numbers.
- **Text (such as "a", "my cat", "fat", or "I like frogs"):** Often referred to as *strings.*

Understanding data types

The three most common data types are integers, decimal numbers, and strings. However, some programming languages offer other data types such as Boolean (which can only hold a `True` or `False` value), byte (which is a subset of an integer but can hold only values ranging from 0 to 255), and long (which can hold extremely large or small integer values).

The main reason for these other data types is to give programmers the freedom to choose the data type that most closely fits the acceptable range of values a program needs to store in a variable. For example, an integer variable type can hold both positive and negative numbers, but a byte data type can hold only values ranging from 0 to 255. So if you need to create a variable to hold someone's age, you should declare your variable as a byte because a person's age can never be negative nor higher than 255. Additional data types simply help you further restrict what types of values a variable can hold.

The following REALbasic code example shows how to declare a variable named `Children` and define it to hold only whole numbers (also called integers).

```
Dim Children As Integer
```

Dissecting this REALbasic code reveals the following:

1. The `Dim` command is short for *dimension,* which is just a fancy way of saying "I declare a variable. . . ."
2. Immediately following the `Dim` command is the name of the variable, which is `Children`. So the first two words in the REALbasic code tell the computer, "I declare a variable named Children. . . ."
3. The last two words, `As Integer`, define the data type as an integer. So the entire REALbasic code tells the computer, "I declare a variable named `Children` as an `Integer` data type." At this point, the `Children` variable can hold only integers.

Declaring a variable named `Children` and defining it to hold only integer data in C++ might look like this:

```
int Children;
```

Dissecting the preceding C++ code reveals the following:

1. The `int` command is short for integer and tells the computer, "I want to create a variable that can hold only integer values. . . ."

2. `Children` is the actual variable name, so the first two lines tell the computer, "I want to create a variable that can hold only integer values, and the name of the variable is `Children`."
3. The semicolon tells the computer, "That's the end of my variable declaration."

C++ commands tend to be much shorter (and harder to read) than equivalent BASIC commands. C++ resembles shorthand whereas BASIC resembles actual words.

If you declare a variable to hold only integers, you can never accidentally store decimal numbers (3.1415) or text (twenty-five thousand) in the variable by mistake.

Assigning a value to a variable

Variables are useless until you store data in them. When you store data in a variable, it's called *assigning* a value to a variable.

As soon as you create a variable, it's a good idea to assign an initial value to that variable, such as `0` or an empty string like `""`. In some programming languages, declaring a variable automatically fills that variable with random data. If you forget to clear out a variable by storing an initial value and you then try to use that variable in a calculation, the random data automatically stored in a variable could crash your program.

The simplest way to assign a value to a variable is to use the equal sign. This method enables you to assign a number or string to a variable, as in the following Liberty BASIC example:

```
CEOSalary = 9000000
Message2Workers$ = "So I make more than I'm worth."
```

In the first line, you assign the number `9000000` to a variable by the name of `CEOSalary`. In the second line, you assign the string `So I make more than I'm worth.` to the variable `Message2Workers$`.

If you assign a string to a variable in Liberty BASIC, the variable name must include the dollar sign (`$`) at the end. If you assign a number to a variable, don't include a dollar sign in the variable name. In other dialects of BASIC, such as REALbasic, you don't have to use the dollar sign at the end of a variable that contains strings. Like spoken languages, programming languages consist of minor variations (dialects) that force you to do something that another version of that same language may ignore completely.

To use the preceding Liberty BASIC code in REALbasic, you first have to declare your two variables before assigning a value to them, as shown here:

```
Dim CEOSalary As Integer
Dim Message2Workers As String
CEOSalary = 9000000
Message2Workers = "So I make more than I'm worth."
```

Similarly, you must declare your variables first in C++, as in this example:

```
#include <iostream.h>
#include <stdio.h>
using namespace std;
int main()
{
    int CEOSalary;
    string Message2Workers;
    CEOSalary = 9000000;
    Message2Workers = "So I make more than I'm worth.";
    cout << "\nPress ENTER to continue..." << endl;
    getchar();
    return 0;
}
```

The C++ language doesn't include a string data type, so you have to add the `using namespace std;` command near the top of your program. This provides commands that define a string data type that you can use in your C++ program.

Using variables in C++ is usually a two-step process. First, you must declare a variable name and its data type. Second, you have to assign a value to the variable. To save time, C++ lets you declare a variable and assign a value to it all in a single line such as

```
int CEOSalary = 9000000;
```

This C++ code tells the computer, "Create a variable that can only hold integer values (`int`), name the variable `CEOSalary`, and store the number `9000000` in it."

In most programming languages, you assign a value to a variable by using the equal sign (=). However, in Revolution, you assign a value to a variable by using the `into` command, as shown here:

```
put 9000000 into CEOSalary
put "So I make more than I'm worth." into Message2Workers
```

Using Constants

Variables can change values while the program's running; that's why they're called *variables* (because their values can vary). Sometimes, you may want to use a fixed value throughout your program. Look at the following program. Can you figure out what the number `0.1975` stands for?

```
Balance = 43090
OurProfit = Balance * 0.1975
Balance = Balance + OurProfit
PRINT "Pay this amount, or we'll get you = "; Balance
PRINT "Today's current loan sharking interest rate = ";
    .1975
END
```

A quick glance at the preceding program shows that the meaning of the number `0.1975` isn't obvious. Because the meaning of numbers isn't always clear without additional explanation, programmers use *constants*. A constant is nothing more than a descriptive name that represents a fixed value.

Older versions of the BASIC programming language, such as Liberty BASIC, don't support constants. Newer versions of BASIC (such as REALbasic) do support constants.

To see how constants can be helpful, look over the following REALbasic program:

```
Dim Balance, OurProfit As Single
Const InterestRate = 0.1975
Balance = 43090
OurProfit = Balance * InterestRate
Balance = Balance + OurProfit
MsgBox "Pay this amount = $" + str(Balance)
```

By reading this program, you can clearly see that the number `0.1975` represents an interest rate, which then makes the fourth line much easier to understand:

```
OurProfit = Balance * InterestRate
```

In this line, the value of the `OurProfit` variable is calculated by multiplying the variable `Balance` by the constant value of `InterestRate`.

By replacing a descriptive name (constant) to represent a fixed value, you can make the meaning of numbers easier to understand. Although the preceding REALbasic program is fairly small, imagine a program that consists of a million lines of code and uses the value of `0.1975` (as the interest rate) 20 times. What happens if you want to change the interest rate from `0.1975` to `0.2455`? You have to change it all 20 times where it appears, which means you have to take the time to find it and change it all 20 times (while hoping that the value of `0.1975` isn't also used somewhere else that you don't know about).

Rather than go through this hassle, constants let you assign a fixed value to a descriptive name and then use that descriptive name throughout your program. If you need to change the value of that constant, you just need to change it once and its value automatically changes throughout the rest of your program.

- Constants offer two key advantages:
- Descriptive constant names make fixed values easier to understand.
- Storing a value as a constant lets you update that value just once no matter how large your program is.

To define a constant in the C++ programming language, you need to use the `const` keyword followed by the data type, the constant name, and the value to define the constant, as shown here:

```
const double interestrate = 0.1975;
```

This C++ code tells the computer, "Create a constant that can represent a double-precision number (decimal number), name the constant `interestrate`, and set the value of the constant to `0.1975`."

To define a constant in Revolution, you just have to use the `constant` keyword followed by the constant name and its value:

```
constant InterestRate = 0.1975
```

Commenting Your Code

If you write a small program, anyone can readily understand how it works by following it line by line. But if you write a large program, understanding what the program does can prove difficult for others (and even for you) without spending a long time studying each line.

To make understanding (and ultimately maintaining) a program easier (because programmers are notoriously lazy), every programming language allows you to insert comments into your source code. Comments are often used to explain the following:

- Who wrote the program (so you know who to blame)
- The creation and last modification dates of the program

- What the program does
- How the program works
- Where the program gets, saves, and outputs data
- Any known problems with the program

Every programming language provides different ways to create comments.

In Liberty BASIC, you can add comments in one of the following two ways:

- By using the `REM` (short for *remark*) statement
- By using an apostrophe (`'`)

The following program shows how to use both the `REM` statement and the apostrophe to insert comments into a program. Although you can use both types of comments in a single program, you might want to use only one or the other for consistency's sake.

```
 ' Created on March 29, 2007
' Written by John Doe
' This program displays a not-so-subtle
' message to potential copycats to
' come up with their own ideas rather
' than steal mine.
REM This program does nothing more than
REM print a message on-screen to
REM insult any potential authors browsing
REM through this book in hopes of stealing
REM ideas to use in a competing book.
NOTICE "Don't steal ideas from this book!"
END ' This last line ends the program
```

Because comments are for the benefit of humans only, the computer looks at the preceding Liberty BASIC program and sees only this:

```
NOTICE "Don't steal ideas from this book!"
END
```

Comments exist solely for your benefit. The computer completely ignores any comments that you insert in a program. So make your comments useful but not too wordy; otherwise, they become more of a nuisance than an aid.

In C++, you can use two slash characters to create comments such as

```
// This is a C++ comment
```

In REALbasic, you can use the `REM` keyword, an apostrophe (`'`), or double slashes (`//`) to create a comment.

In Revolution, you can use the hash symbol (#) or two dashes (--) to create a comment such as

```
-- This is a comment in Revolution
# This is a comment in Revolution too
```

Comments typically take up a single line, but if you want to create a comment that appears on several lines, you can type the comment character in front of every line. However, many programming languages such as C++ and Revolution (but not Liberty BASIC or REALbasic) offer the /* and */ symbols to identify the beginning and ending of your comments, as in this example:

```
/* Created on March 29, 2007
Written by John Doe
This program displays a not-so-subtle
message to potential copycats to
come up with their own ideas rather
than steal mine.
This program does nothing more than
print a message on-screen to
insult any potential authors browsing
through this book in hopes of stealing
ideas to use in a competing book. */
```

Besides adding explanations to the source code of a program, programmers often use comments to temporarily ignore one or more lines of code to test certain parts of the code. Rather than delete an entire line, test to see whether the program works, and retype the deleted line, you can just comment out the line, as follows:

```
NOMAINWIN
' A = SQR((B * B) + (C + C))
END
```

If you run this program, Liberty BASIC sees only the following:

```
NOMAINWIN
END
```

To restore the commented line, just remove the apostrophe so that Liberty BASIC sees the program like this:

```
NOMAINWIN
A = SQR((B * B) + (C + C))
END
```

Chapter 8

Crunching Numbers and Playing with Strings

In This Chapter

- Performing mathematical operations
- Using built-in math functions
- Manipulating strings
- Converting strings and numbers

The most useful programs accept data (*input*), manipulate that data somehow, and then spit out a useful answer (*output*). The two types of data that your programs manipulate are *numbers* and *words* (known as *strings*).

Some common number-manipulating programs include spreadsheets, accounting programs, and even video games (because they need to calculate the correct way to display jet fighters or dragons popping on-screen to enable you to mow them down with a machine gun). Common string-manipulating programs include databases (which store, sort, and rearrange such data as names), word processors, and foreign-language translation programs.

Adding, Subtracting, Dividing, and Multiplying

The four basic ways to manipulate numbers are adding, subtracting, dividing, and multiplying. By using these four mathematical operations, you can create any type of complicated mathematical formula.

To add, subtract, divide, or multiply two numbers (or two variables that represent numbers), you use the symbols shown in Table 8-1.

Table 8-1 Mathematical Operators

Mathematical Operation	*Symbol to Use*	*Example*	*Result*
Addition	+	2 + 5	7
Subtraction	–	77 – 43	34
Division	/ (forward slash)	20 / 4	5
Multiplication	*	4 * 7	28
Integer Division	\ (backward slash)	23 / 4	5
Modulo	mod	23 mod 4	3
Exponentiation	^	2 ^ 3	8

The division symbol (/) usually appears in two places on your keyboard: on the same key as the question mark (?) and on the numeric keypad. The exponentiation symbol (^) appears on the 6 key. You can also use the subtraction symbol (–) to indicate negative numbers, such as –34.5 or –90.

Although you already understand how addition, subtraction, division, and multiplication work, you may be less familiar with integer division, modulo, and exponentiation.

Integer division divides two numbers and returns only the integer portion of the result. So dividing 25 by 6 would normally give you 4.167, but with integer division, the decimal portion of the number gets chopped off, and the result is simply 4.

Modulo is a form of division that divides two numbers and returns only an integer remainder. So dividing 25 mod 6 would return 1 (because 6 goes into 25 four times, leaving a remainder of 1).

Exponentiation simply multiplies one number by itself several times. The formula 4 ^ 3 tells the computer to take the number 4 and multiply it by itself three times. So 4 ^ 3 really means 4 * 4 * 4, or 64.

C++ unary operators

Mathematical operators, such as addition (+) and multiplication (*), are known as binary operators because they operate on two different values. In C++, you can also use something called unary operators, which operate on a single value. The most common C++ unary operators are ++ (which increments a value by one) and –, (which decrements a value by one).

You can place a unary operator before or after a variable (for example, `++i` or `i++`). The placement of the unary operator defines when to alter the variable. Consider the following C++ code:

```
int x;
int y;
int z;
x = 5;
y = x++   // y = 5 but x = 6
z = ++y   // z = 6 and y = 6
```

In the line `y = x++`, the value of `x` is `5` and is first assigned to `y`, which now holds the number `5`. Then the ++ unary operator increments the value of `x` by one so `x` now stores the number `6`. In the line `z = ++y`, the unary operator first increments the value of `y`. Because `y` holds the number `5`, the ++ unary operator increments it to `6`, and this value gets stored in the `z` variable.

Unary operators are often used to count in a `FOR-NEXT` loop (see Chapter 10) although you can use them anywhere.

Working with precedence

Consider the following formula, which multiples two variables and stores the result in a third variable called `TaxYouOwe`:

```
TaxYouOwe = NetIncome * TaxRate
```

Such a simple formula is easy to understand; you just multiply the values that both variables represent. Of course, you can create more powerful mathematical formulas by combining addition, subtraction, division, or multiplication, as in the following example:

```
TaxYouOwe = PastTaxes + NetIncome * TaxRate
```

If the value of `PastTaxes` is `2500`, the value of `NetIncome` is `50000`, and the value of `TaxRate` is `1.01`, the computer looks at the formula as follows:

```
TaxYouOwe = 2500 + 50000 * 1.01
```

So now the question is what does the computer do first? Does it add 2,500 to 50,000 and then multiply the whole thing by 1.01 (in which case the answer is 53,025) or multiply 50,000 by 1.01 first and then add 2,500 (in which case the answer is 53,000)?

Because the result of combining addition, subtraction, division, and multiplication in a single formula can be so confusing, programming languages use something known as *precedence,* which tells the computer which mathematical operations to calculate first. Most programming languages calculate mathematical operators in the following order, from top (first) to bottom (last):

- Exponentiation (^)
- Multiplication (*) and division (/)
- Integer division (\)
- Modula arithmetic (mod)
- Addition (+) and subtraction (–)

The computer always calculates operators from left to right if operators are equal in precedence, such as multiplication and division or addition and subtraction.

Before running the following Liberty BASIC program, try to figure out how the computer calculates a result:

```
MyMoney = 3 + 4 ^ 5 - 8 / 5 * 7
PRINT MyMoney
END
```

This is how Liberty BASIC calculates the value of `MyMoney`:

1. Because the computer calculates exponential values first, Liberty BASIC calculates the value of `4 ^ 5`, which is `1024`. The formula now looks like this:

   ```
   MyMoney = 3 + 1024 - 8 / 5 * 7
   ```

2. Next, the computer calculates all multiplication and division. Because multiplication and division have equal precedence, the computer starts calculating with the first multiplication or division operator that it finds,

moving from left to right. The computer calculates the value of `8 / 5` first (`1.6`) and then multiplies it by `7`. So the formula now looks like this:

```
MyMoney = 3 + 1024 - 11.2
```

3. Finally, the computer calculates all addition and subtraction, moving from left to right. First it calculates the value of `3 + 1,024` (which is `1027`), and then it subtracts `11.2` from `1027`. Thus the final answer looks like this:

```
MyMoney = 1015.8
```

Using parentheses

Trying to remember the precedence of different mathematical operators can prove confusing. Even worse is that the ordinary precedence of mathematical operators can mess up the way that you want the computer to calculate a result. Suppose that you typed the following Liberty BASIC program:

```
BigValue = 3 + 4 ^ 5
PRINT BigValue
END
```

With this program, the computer first calculates the exponential value of `4 ^ 5` (which is `1024`), and then it adds `3` to it, for a total of `1027`.

But what if you really want the computer to add `3` to `4` and then perform the exponential? In this case, you must use parentheses to tell the computer, "Hey, add `3` to `4` first and then calculate the exponential," as in the following example:

```
BigValue = (3 + 4) ^ 5
PRINT BigValue
END
```

This program adds `3` and `4` to get `7`, so the formula becomes `BigValue = 7 ^ 5`, or `16807`.

Anytime that the computer sees something trapped within parentheses, it calculates those values first. Then it uses its normal rules of precedence to figure out how to calculate the rest of the formula.

Use parentheses to enclose only one mathematical operator at a time, such as `(3 + 4)`. Although you can use parentheses to enclose multiple mathematical operators, such as `(3 + 4 ^ 5)`, doing so essentially defeats the purpose of using parentheses to make clear what the computer is to calculate first. You can, of course, use multiple parentheses to create fairly complex formulas, as in the following formula:

```
EasyTaxCode = ((3 + 4) ^ 5 / 3 - 8) / 5 * -7
```

Without the parentheses in the preceding formula, the computer would calculate an entirely different result.

Using Built-In Math Functions

By combining mathematical operators, you can create practically any type of mathematical formula. But creating some mathematical formulas may prove too cumbersome, so as a shortcut, many programming languages provide built-in mathematical functions that you can use. Table 8-2 lists the names of common mathematical functions.

Table 8-2 Common Built-in Mathematical Functions

Function	*What It Does*
`ABS (x)`	Returns the absolute value of `x`
`ACS (x)` or `ACOS (x)`	Returns the arccosine of `x`
`ASN (x)` or `ASIN (x)`	Returns the arcsine of `x`
`ATN (x)` or `ATAN (x)`	Returns the arctangent of `x`
`COS (x)`	Returns the cosine of `x`
`EXP (x)`	Returns a number raised to a specified power `x`
`LOG (x)`	Returns the natural logarithm of `x` (Note: The value of `x` must be a positive, nonzero number.)
`SIN (x)`	Returns the sine of `x`
`SQR (x)` or `SQRT (x)`	Returns the square root of `x`
`TAN (x)`	Returns the tangent of `x`

If you don't understand terms like arcsine or logarithm, you probably don't need to use them anyway. The important point to remember is that all programming languages include built-in mathematical functions that you can use if you need them.

To see how the Liberty BASIC mathematical functions work, run the following program and type different numbers (negative, positive, decimal, and so on) between 0 and 1.0 to see how the program works:

```
PROMPT "Type in a number"; AnyNumber
PRINT "The ABS value = "; ABS(AnyNumber)
PRINT "The ACS value = "; ACS(AnyNumber)
PRINT "The ASN value = "; ASN(AnyNumber)
PRINT "The ATN value = "; ATN(AnyNumber)
PRINT "The COS value = "; COS(AnyNumber)
PRINT "The EXP value = "; EXP(AnyNumber)
PRINT "The LOG value = "; LOG(ABS(AnyNumber))
PRINT "The SIN value = "; SIN(AnyNumber)
PRINT "The SQR value = "; SQR(AnyNumber)
PRINT "The TAN value = "; TAN(AnyNumber)
PRINT
END
```

You can use only positive numbers with the `LOG` function or in calculating a square root.

This Liberty BASIC program is stored in the Liberty BASIC Sample Programs folder as `Chapter 8 - Math Functions.bas`.

Unlike many programming languages, C++ doesn't have built-in math functions. Instead, C++ compilers come with a library of math functions written in C++. You don't have to worry about how these math functions work; you can just use them by adding the #include <math.h> command at the top of your program, as shown here:

```
#include <iostream.h>
#include <stdio.h>
#include <math.h>
int main()
{
  double anyNumber;
  cout << "Enter a number: ";
  cin >> anyNumber;
  cout << "The ABS value = "; cout << abs(anyNumber);
  cout << "\nThe ACOS value = "; cout << acos(anyNumber);
  cout << "\nThe ASIN value = "; cout << asin(anyNumber);
  cout << "\nThe ATAN value = "; cout << atan(anyNumber);
  cout << "\nThe COS value = "; cout << cos(anyNumber);
  cout << "\nThe EXP value = "; cout << exp(anyNumber);
  cout << "\nThe LOG value = "; cout << log(anyNumber);
  cout << "\nThe SIN value = "; cout << sin(anyNumber);
  cout << "\nThe SQRT value = "; cout << sqrt(anyNumber);
  cout << "\nThe TAN value = "; cout << tan(anyNumber);
  cout << "\nThe ACOS value = "; cout << acos(anyNumber);
  cout << "\nPress ENTER to continue..." << endl;
  getchar();
  return 0;
}
```

This C++ program is stored in the C++ Sample Programs folder as `Chapter 8 - Math Functions.cpp`.

A mathematical function accepts a value and uses that value to calculate a result. So you can assign a mathematical function to a variable, as the following REALbasic program demonstrates:

```
Dim x, y as Single                                    →1
x = 0.52                                              →2
y = cos(x)                                            →3
MsgBox str(y)                                         →4
```

This REALbasic program tells the computer to do the following:

- →1 Declares two variables `x` and `y` that can hold only a single-precision (decimal) number.
- →2 Stores the value `0.52` into the `x` variable.
- →3 Gives the value `0.52` to the cosine (`cos`) mathematical function. The cosine mathematical function calculates the cosine of `0.52`, which is `0.8678191`. This value gets stored in the `y` variable.
- →4 The `str` command converts the number `0.8678191` into the string `"0.8678191"`, which it then displays in a message box created by the `MsgBox` command.

This REALbasic program is stored in the REALbasic Sample Programs folder as `Chapter 8 - Math Functions.rb`.

Mathematical functions work the same way in Revolution, as the following program shows:

```
put 0.52 into x                                       →1
put cos(x) into y                                     →2
put y into message                                    →3
```

This Revolution program tells the computer to do the following:

- →1 Stores the value `0.52` into a variable called `x`.
- →2 Gives the value of `x` (`0.52`) to the cosine mathematical function, which returns the value `0.876819` and stores this value in a variable named `y`.
- →3 Displays the value of the `y` variable on-screen in a message box defined by the `message` command.

This Revolution program is stored in the Revolution Sample Programs folder as `Chapter 8 - Math Functions.rev`.

Manipulating Strings

Besides manipulating numbers, computers can also manipulate strings. A string is anything that you can type from the keyboard, including letters, symbols (such as #, &, and +), and even numbers used to identify something such as a mailing address (3095 Main Street) or a person (student number 80895).

Most programming languages identify a string as anything that appears inside quotation marks, as in the following Liberty BASIC example:

```
PRINT "Everything enclosed in quotation marks"
PRINT "is a string, including the numbers below:"
PRINT "72 = 9 * 8"
PRINT "You can even mix letters and numbers like this:"
PRINT "I made $4,500 last month and still feel broke."
END
```

In the preceding program, the formula `"72 = 9 * 8"` is actually a string, even though it consists of numbers. That's because anything inside quotation marks is a string, including any numbers.

Declaring variables as strings

As with numbers, you can use strings directly in your program, as follows:

```
PRINT "Print me."
PRINT 54
END
```

Just as with numbers, you may want to store strings in variables so you can reuse that particular string over and over again by typing just the variable rather than the entire string.

Unfortunately, every programming language tends to use different ways to declare a variable to hold a string data type. In Liberty BASIC, you never declare variables until you actually assign data to them. When assigning a string to a variable, the variable name must include the dollar sign (`$`) at the end of the variable name, as follows:

```
MyName$ = "Bo the Cat"
```

In Revolution, you can assign a string to a variable (just like you can assign a number to a variable) by using the `into` command like so:

```
put "Bo the Cat" into MyName
```

In REALbasic, you can declare a variable to hold string data types, as follows:

```
Dim MyName As String
```

The C++ language won't recognize string data types, so you must use a library file called `std`, which you can include in your program by adding the following:

```
using namespace std;
```

This command tells your C++ program to use a library file called `std`, which defines a string data type. After you include the `std` library file, you can declare a string variable such as:

```
string myName;
```

So an entire C++ program that declares a string variable might look like this:

```
#include <iostream.h>
#include <stdio.h>
using namespace std;
int main()
{
    string myName;
    myName = "Bo the Cat";
    cout << myName;
    cout << "\nPress ENTER to continue..." << endl;
    getchar();
    return 0;
}
```

Smashing strings together

Unlike with numbers, you can't subtract, divide, or multiply strings. But you can add strings (which is technically known as *concatenating strings*). To concatenate two strings, you use the plus sign (+) to essentially smash two strings into a single string, as the following Liberty BASIC example shows:

```
MyName$ = "Joe Smith"                    →1
PRINT "Hello, " + MyName$                →2
END                                      →3
```

This Liberty BASIC program tells the computer to do the following:

→1 Creates a string variable called `MyName$` and stuffs it with the string `"Joe Smith"`.

→2 Prints the string `"Hello, "` followed by the string stored in the `MyName$` variable, so the entire line prints out `Hello, Joe Smith`.

→3 Tells the computer that the program is at an end.

If you concatenate strings, make sure that you leave a space between the two strings so that they don't appear smashed together (`likethis`). In the previous example, notice the space in the second line following the word `Hello` and the comma.

Both REALbasic and C++ also let you use the plus sign (+) to concatenate strings. However, Revolution uses the dual ampersand symbols (`&&`) to concatenate strings like so:

```
put "Joe Smith" into MyName
put "Hello, " && MyName into message
```

Converting Strings into Numbers (And Vice Versa)

A string can consist of letters, symbols, and numbers. The most common use for storing numbers as a string is when the numbers represent something special, such as a telephone number or address. If you want the computer to print a telephone number, you must store that number as a string, as shown here:

```
PRINT "555-1212"
```

This command prints the string `555-1212` on-screen. The quotation marks tell the computer, "Anything inside the quotation marks is a string." What happens if you try the following command?

```
PRINT 555-1212
```

Liberty BASIC interprets this command to mean, "Subtract the number 1,212 from the number 555 and print the result (which is –657) on-screen."

Although the number `53` and the string `"53"` may look identical to a human, computers treat numbers as entirely different from strings. To a computer, the number `53` is as completely different from the string `"53"` as a painting of a cat is different from a real cat.

Converting strings into numbers

The problem with strings is that when users enter numbers, the computer may treat those numbers as strings, but your program may need to use those numbers as data. If a program stores a number as a string but needs to use that number as data, the program needs to convert that number (as a string) into data.

To convert a string into data, most programming languages come with special string-to-data and data-to-string conversion commands. In Liberty BASIC, you can convert a string into a number by using the `VAL` function, which works like this:

```
VAL("String")
```

The `VAL` function tells Liberty BASIC, "Take a string (such as `"45"`) and turn it into a number." If you have a string `"45"` and use the `VAL` function, Liberty BASIC converts that string `"45"` into the number `45`.

If you use the `VAL` function on a string that doesn't represent a number, such as the string `"Hello!"`, the `VAL` function returns a zero value.

To see how the `VAL` function works, run the following Liberty BASIC program:

```
YearBorn$ = "1964"                                  →1
PRINT "You were born in " + YearBorn$               →2
Age = 2007 - VAL(YearBorn$)                         →3
PRINT "In 2007, you were this old = "; Age          →4
END                                                 →5
```

This Liberty BASIC program tells the computer to do the following:

→1 Creates a string variable called `YearBorn$` and stuffs it with the string `"1964"`.

→2 Prints the string `"You were born in "` followed by the string stored in the `YearBorn$` variable, so the entire line prints `You` were born in 1964. In this line, the computer treats "1964" as a string.

→3 The VAL function converts the string "1964" to the number 1964. Then it subtracts 1964 from 2007 and stores the calculated result in the Age variable.

→4 Prints the string In 2007, you were this old = and then prints the number stored in the Age variable, which is 2007 – 1964 (43).

→5 This line marks the end of the program.

REALbasic uses the same Val function to convert a string into data, as shown here:

```
Dim YearBorn as string                              →1
Dim Age as integer                                  →2
YearBorn = "1964"                                   →3
MsgBox "You were born in " + YearBorn               →4
Age = 2007 - Val(YearBorn)                          →5
MsgBox "In 2007, you were this old = " + Str(Age)   →6
```

This REALbasic program tells the computer to do the following:

→1 Creates a string variable called YearBorn.

→2 Creates an integer variable called Age.

→3 Stores the string "1964" into the YearBorn string variable.

→4 Uses the MsgBox command to display a box on-screen that shows the string "You were born in " followed by the string stored in the YearBorn variable, so the entire line prints You were born in 1964. In this line, the computer treats "1964" as a string.

→5 The Val function converts the string "1964" to the number 1964. Then it subtracts 1964 from 2007 and stores the calculated result (43) in the Age variable.

→6 Uses the MsgBox command to display a box on-screen that shows the string In 2007, you were this old = and then uses the Str function to convert the Age variable (43) to the string "43". So the entire line prints out In 2007, you were this old = 43.

One problem with type-safe languages like REALbasic is that they restrict what type of data can go into variables (to prevent errors in your program), but they can also make programming more cumbersome when you want to treat a number as both a string and data.

The following Revolution program automatically detects when a number should be treated as a string and when it should be treated as data. Although this has the potential for causing errors, it also gives you the freedom to concentrate on the logic of your program and not worry about trivial details like converting strings into data (and vice versa).

```
put "1964" into YearBorn                                         →1
put "You were born in " && YearBorn into message                 →2
wait for 5 seconds                                               →3
put 2007 - YearBorn into Age                                     →4
put "In 2007, you were this old = " && Age into message          →5
```

This Revolution program tells the computer to do the following:

→1 Stores the string "1964" in a variable called YearBorn.

→2 The two ampersand symbols (&&) tack the string "1964" onto the other string "You were born in ". Then this line display You were born in 1964 in a message box on-screen.

→3 Tells the computer to wait for five seconds. Without this command, Revolution would rush into the rest of the program and the message box displayed in line 2 would appear and disappear in the blink of an eye.

→4 Automatically converts the string "1964" into the number 1964. Then subtracts the number 1964 from 2007 and stores the result (43) in a variable called Age.

→5 Converts the Age variable number (43) into the string "43" and then the two ampersand symbols (&&) tack the "43" string onto the end of the "In 2007, you were this old = " string. Then this line displays In 2007, you were this old = 43 in a message box that appears on-screen.

The main difference between Revolution and the previous two BASIC examples is that Revolution is smart enough to figure out when to treat a number as data and when to treat a number as a string without having to define any data conversion yourself.

The C++ language doesn't recognize strings as valid data types, although you can define a string data type by using the using namespace std; command at the top of your programs. However, C++ doesn't provide any built-in commands for converting strings into numbers (and vice versa), so many programmers simply write their own conversion programs and store them in library files that they can reuse later.

Converting a number into a string

Rather than convert a string into a number, you might want to go the other way and convert a number into a string.

In Liberty BASIC, you can convert a number into a string by using the `STR$` function, which works like this:

```
STR$(Number)
```

The following Liberty BASIC program shows how to use the `STR$` function to convert the `BossIQ` variable into a string:

```
BossIQ = 34                                                    →1
NewString$ = "This is the IQ of your boss = " +
          STR$(BossIQ)                                         →2
PRINT NewString$                                               →3
END                                                            →4
```

This Liberty BASIC program tells the computer to do the following:

→1 Stores the number `34` in a variable called `BossIQ`.

→2 Uses the `STR$` function to convert the number stored in the `BossIQ` variable (`34`) into a string (`"34"`). Then it pastes the two strings together to store `This is the IQ of your boss = 34` in a string variable called `NewString$`.

→3 Prints the string `This is the IQ of your boss = 34` on-screen.

→4 Defines the end of the program.

In this example, Liberty BASIC lets you declare a number variable and convert that number into a string. Here's the equivalent REALbasic program that converts a number into a string by using the `Str` function:

```
Dim BossIQ as Integer
Dim NewString as String
BossIQ = 34
NewString = "This is the IQ of your boss = " + Str(BossIQ)
MsgBox NewString
```

In Revolution, you don't need to give an explicit command to convert a number into a string; the computer does this conversion for you automatically, as the following program demonstrates:

```
put 34 into BossIQ
put "This is the IQ of your boss = " && BossIQ into
          message
```

Chapter 9

Making Decisions with Branching Statements

In This Chapter

- Understanding Boolean expressions
- Using `IF-THEN` statements
- Using `SELECT CASE` statements

The whole purpose of a program is to make the computer behave in a certain way. The most primitive programs act exactly the same way each time that you run them, such as displaying `Hello, world!` or the name of your cat on-screen.

Such primitive programs may work fine for learning to program, but they're relatively useless otherwise because most programs need to accept data and modify their behavior based on any data that they receive.

Each time that you feed the program different data, the program may spit out a different answer. To find out how to give your program the capability to make decisions, you must use something called *branching* or *control statements.*

A branching or control statement simply provides the computer with two or more alternative instructions to follow based on certain data. Based on how much money you have stored in your bank account, an automated teller machine may either let you withdraw $100 or display a message on-screen telling you `Insufficient funds available`, but it can never do both.

Using Boolean Expressions

To make any decision, you first need to ask a question such as, "Do I feel like eating a hamburger?" If the answer is yes, you go to a restaurant that serves hamburgers. If the answer is no, you eat something else.

Computers work in a similar way. Although people can ask questions, computers check something called a *Boolean expression.* A Boolean expression is a computer's way of asking a Yes or No question.

Boolean expressions are part of Boolean algebra, which was named after a man by the name of George Boole. (If you study hard and create your own branch of mathematics, someone may name it after you, too.)

Boolean expressions compare two values. An expression can be either true or false, as shown in Table 9-1.

Table 9-1 Evaluating Boolean Expressions

Boolean Expression	*What It Means*	*Boolean Value*
`4 < 54`	4 is less than 54	True
`4 > 54`	4 is greater than 54	False
`4 = 54`	4 is equal to 54	False
`4 <= 54`	4 is less than or equal to 54	True
`4 >= 54`	4 is greater than or equal to 54	False
`4 <> 54`	4 is not equal to 54	True

Symbols such as <, >, =, <=, >=, and <> are known as *relational operators.*

In most programming languages, you can use the equal sign to test a Boolean expression such as `(MyIQ = 120)`. However in C++ (and other C-derivative languages like Perl), you must use the double equal sign symbol (==) to test for equality such as `(MyIQ == 120)`. If you use a single equal sign, your C++ program won't work right.

A Boolean expression isn't very useful by itself, so programmers often use it in branching statements to determine which set (or branch) of instructions the computers should follow at any given time.

The simplest type of a branching statement is called an `IF-THEN` statement, which offers one alternative set of instructions to follow if a certain Boolean expression is true. An `IF-THEN` statement typically looks like this:

```
IF (Boolean expression is True) THEN
   One or more instructions
END IF
```

In C++, an `IF-THEN` statement looks slightly different:

```
if (Boolean expression is True)
   {
          One or more instructions
   }
```

In C++, the two big differences are that the word `THEN` is not used and that you must enclose any instructions to follow within curly brackets.

To see how `IF-THEN` statements work, look at the following Liberty BASIC program:

```
IF (4 < 54) THEN                                    →1
 PRINT "This prints on-screen."                     →2
END IF                                              →3
END                                                 →4
```

This Liberty BASIC program tells the computer to do the following:

- →1 Tells the computer to evaluate the Boolean expression `(4 < 54)`. Because this is true (`4` is less than `54`), the computer can proceed to the second line.
- →2 Tells the computer to print the message `This prints on-screen.`
- →3 Identifies the end of the `IF-THEN` statement.
- →4 Tells the computer that the program is at an end.

To see how `IF-THEN` statements work in C++, look over the following equivalent program:

```
if (4 < 54)
   {
   cout << "This prints out on-screen.";
   }
```

Storing Boolean expressions in variables

Many programming languages let you define a variable as a Boolean data type.

In REALbasic, you can define a variable as a Boolean data type like this:

```
Dim Guilty As Boolean
```

In C++, you can define a variable as a Boolean data type like this:

```
bool Guilty;
```

You can just stuff a Boolean expression into a variable in Liberty BASIC and Revolution because neither of these languages forces you to declare your variables ahead of time like C++ or REALbasic.

You can then assign a Boolean expression to a variable in the following way:

```
Guilty = (4 < 54)
```

This example assigns the value of `True` to the variable `Guilty`. The preceding statement tells the computer, "The Boolean expression of `(4 < 54)` is true. Thus the value of the `Guilty` variable is `True`."

To see how a variable can hold a Boolean value, try the following Liberty BASIC program:

```
Guilty = (4 < 54)
IF Guilty THEN
 PRINT "Slap him on the wrist and let him go."
END IF
END
```

Each time that you run the preceding program, it prints the message `Slap him on the wrist and let him go.`

Here's what the equivalent program looks like in Revolution:

```
put 4 < 54 into Guilty
if Guilty then
  put "Slap him on the wrist and let him go." into message
end if
```

Using variables in Boolean expressions

The sample program in the preceding section uses a Boolean expression `(4 < 54)` that's fairly useless because it's always true. Every time that you run the program, it just prints the message `Slap him on the wrist and let him go.`

For greater flexibility, Boolean expressions usually compare two variables or one variable to a fixed value, as in the following examples:

```
(MyIQ >= AnotherIQ)
(Taxes < 100000)
```

The value of the first Boolean expression `(MyIQ < AnotherIQ)` depends on the value of the two variables `MyIQ` and `AnotherIQ`. Run the following Liberty BASIC program to see how it follows a different set of instructions, depending on the value of the `MyIQ` and `AnotherIQ` variables:

```
PROMPT "What is your IQ"; MyIQ
PROMPT "What is the IQ of another person"; AnotherIQ
IF (MyIQ >= AnotherIQ) THEN
 PRINT "I'm smarter than you are."
END IF
IF (MyIQ < AnotherIQ) THEN
 PRINT "You have a higher IQ to make up for your lack of
         common sense."
END IF
END
```

This Liberty BASIC program is stored in the Liberty BASIC Sample Programs folder as `Chapter 9 - Boolean Example.bas`.

If you run this program and type different values for `MyIQ` and `AnotherIQ`, the program behaves in two possible ways: printing on-screen either `I'm smarter than you are.` or `You have a higher IQ to make up for your lack of common sense.`

By using variables in Boolean expressions, you give your program the flexibility it needs to handle different data.

Using Boolean operators

Rather than examine a single Boolean expression, your program may need to examine two or more Boolean expressions. For example, the following program checks the Boolean expression `(Salary > 500)` and `(Bribes > 700)`. Only if both Boolean expressions are true does the program print `You don't need to pay any taxes.`, as the following Liberty BASIC program shows:

```
PROMPT "How much money did you make"; Salary
PROMPT "How much money did you donate to political
         candidates"; Bribes
IF (Salary > 500) THEN
 IF (Bribes > 700) THEN
   PRINT "You don't need to pay any taxes."
 END IF
END IF
END
```

Rather than force the computer to evaluate Boolean expressions one at a time, you can get the computer to evaluate multiple Boolean expressions by using *Boolean operators.* A Boolean operator does nothing more than connect two or more Boolean expressions to represent a `True` or a `False` value.

The two most common Boolean operators are

- AND
- OR

The AND operator

The AND operator links two Boolean expressions. By rewriting the previous program using the AND operator, you can simplify the program as follows:

```
PROMPT "How much money did you make?"; Salary
PROMPT "How much did you donate to politicians?"; Bribes
IF (Salary > 500) AND (Bribes > 700) THEN
 PRINT "You don't need to pay any taxes."
END IF
END
```

In this case, the program prints the message `You don't need to pay any taxes` only if both `(Salary > 500)` and `(Bribes > 700)` are true. If either Boolean expression is false, this program doesn't print anything.

Run the preceding program and use the values in Table 9-2 to see what happens.

Table 9-2 Different Values Determine How the AND Operator Works

Value of Salary	*Value of Bribes*	*What the Program Does*
100	100	Nothing
900	100	Nothing
100	900	Nothing
900	900	Prints the message

The AND operator can represent a `True` value only if both Boolean expressions that it connects also are true.

To show how the AND operator works, programmers like to draw something known as a *truth table,* which tells you whether two Boolean expressions that the AND operator connects represent a `True` or a `False` value. Table 9-3 is a truth table listing the values for the following two Boolean expressions:

```
(Boolean expression 1) AND (Boolean expression 2)
```

Table 9-3 The Truth Table for the AND Operator

Value of (Boolean Expression 1)	*Value of (Boolean Expression 2)*	*Value of the Entire (Boolean Expression 1) AND (Boolean Expression 2)*
False	False	False
True	False	False
False	True	False
True	True	True

The equivalent Revolution program looks similar to the Liberty BASIC version. The only main differences are the commands used to ask the user to type data. In the following Revolution program, the `ask` command asks the user to type an answer, which gets stored temporarily in the `it` variable, which you must then store in a more descriptive variable:

```
ask "How much money did you make?"
put it into Salary
ask "How much did you donate to politicians?"
put it into Bribes
if (Salary > 500) and (Bribes > 700) then
  put "You don't need to pay any taxes." into message
end if
```

In C++, the AND operator consists of a double ampersand symbol (`&&`), as in this example:

```
(Boolean expression 1) && (Boolean expression 2)
```

Notice that C++ uses the double ampersand to represent the Boolean AND operator, but Revolution uses the double ampersand to concatenate strings. When using different programming languages, watch out for ways that different languages use identical symbols or commands that mean entirely different things.

The following code shows the equivalent C++ program:

```
#include <iostream.h>
#include <stdio.h>
int main()
{
   int Salary;
   int Bribes;
   cout << "How much money did you make? ";
   cin >> Salary;
   cout << "How much did you donate to politicians? ";
   cin >> Bribes;
   if ((Salary > 500) && (Bribes > 700))
   {
   cout << "You don't need to pay any taxes.";
   }
   cout << "\nPress ENTER to continue..." << endl;
   getchar();
   return 0;
}
```

This C++ program is stored in the C++ Sample Programs folder as `Chapter 9 - And Operator.cpp`.

The OR operator

The `OR` operator links two Boolean expressions but produces a `True` value if either Boolean expression represents a `True` value. For an example of how this operator works, run the following program:

```
PROMPT "How far can you throw a football"; Football
PROMPT "What is your IQ"; IQ
IF (Football > 50) OR (IQ <= 45) THEN
 PRINT "You have what it takes to become a professional!"
END IF
END
```

In this case, the program prints the message `You have what it takes to become a professional!` if either `(Football > 50)` is true or `(IQ <= 45)` is true. Only if both Boolean expressions are false does the program refuse to print anything.

Run the preceding program and use the values in Table 9-4 to see what happens.

Table 9-4 Different Values Determine How the OR Operator Works

Value of Football	*Value of IQ*	*What the Program Does*
5	70	Nothing
70	70	Prints the message
5	5	Prints the message
70	5	Prints the message

The `OR` operator can represent a `False` value only if both Boolean expressions that it connects are false.

Table 9-5 is a truth table to show how the `OR` operator works for Boolean expressions in the following example:

```
(Boolean expression 1) OR (Boolean expression 2)
```

Table 9-5 The Truth Table for the OR Operator

Value of (Boolean Expression 1)	*Value of (Boolean Expression 2)*	*Value of the Entire (Boolean Expression 1) OR (Boolean Expression 2)*
False	False	False
True	False	True
False	True	True
True	True	True

In C++, the `OR` operator consists of a double vertical line symbol (| |), as shown here:

```
(Boolean expression 1) || (Boolean expression 2)
```

Here's the equivalent C++ program:

```
#include <iostream.h>
#include <stdio.h>
int main()
{
   int Football;
   int IQ;
   cout << "How far can you throw a football? ";
   cin >> Football;
   cout << "What is your IQ? ";
   cin >> IQ;
   if ((Football > 50) || (IQ <= 45))
   {
   cout << "You have what it takes to become a
          professional!";
   }
   cout << "\nPress ENTER to continue..." << endl;
   getchar();
   return 0;
}
```

This C++ program is stored in the C++ Sample Programs folder as `Chapter 9 - Or Operator.cpp`.

Exploring IF-THEN Statements

The most common branching instruction is the `IF-THEN` statement. This statement checks whether a certain condition is true. If the condition is true, it tells the computer to follow one or more instructions.

The `IF-THEN` statement looks as follows:

```
IF (Boolean expression) THEN
 ' Follow one or more instructions listed here
END IF
```

For an example of how this statement works, type and run the following program:

```
PROMPT "Do you eat cow lips? (Type Y for Yes or N for
         No)"; Answer$
IF (Answer$ = "Y") THEN
 PRINT "I have a nice hot dog you might like then."
END IF
END
```

Only if the user types Y (using uppercase) does the program print the message `I have a nice hot dog you might like then.` If the user types anything else (such as *y* or *c*), the program skips over the `PRINT` command and does nothing.

An `IF-THEN` statement can run multiple instructions, as this example shows:

```
PROMPT "How many cats do you own"; Answer
IF (Answer >= 1) THEN
 PRINT "You have my sympathies."
 PRINT "Have you ever thought of getting"
 PRINT "your head examined real soon?"
END IF
END
```

Using IF-THEN-ELSE Statements

The `IF-THEN` statement tells the computer to follow one or more instructions only if a certain condition is true. If that condition is false, the computer ignores all the instructions trapped inside the `IF-THEN` statement.

The `IF-THEN-ELSE` statement is slightly different because it tells the computer to follow one set of instructions in case a condition is true and a different set of instructions if that same condition is false. Here's an example of the `IF-THEN-ELSE` statement:

```
IF (Boolean expression) THEN
  ' Follow one or more instructions
  ' listed here
ELSE
  ' If the condition is false, then follow these
  ' instructions instead
END IF
```

In C++, the `IF-THEN-ELSE` statement looks like this:

```
if (Boolean expression)
   {
   // Follow one or more instructions
   // listed here
   }
else
   {
   // If the condition is false, then follow these
   // instructions instead
   }
```

For an example of how the IF-THEN-ELSE statement works, run the following Liberty BASIC program and see what happens:

```
PROMPT "How long were you in medical school"; Answer
IF (Answer > 4) THEN
 PRINT "Congratulations! You should be able to"
 PRINT "play a good game of golf in no time."
ELSE
 PRINT "You may not have been in medical school for"
 PRINT "very long, but at least you should know"
 PRINT "how to put on a white lab coat."
END IF
END
```

The Liberty BASIC programs waits for the user to type a number, which gets stored in the `Answer` variable. If the user typed in a number greater than 4 (such as 5 or 109298), the program prints `Congratulations! You should be able to play a good game of golf in no time.`

However, if the user typed in a number equal or less than 4 (such as 4 or 1), the program prints `You may not have been in medical school for very long, but at least you should know how to put on a white lab coat.`

This Liberty BASIC program is stored in the Liberty BASIC Sample Programs folder as `Chapter 9 - If Then Else.bas`.

Here's the equivalent C++ program:

```
#include <iostream.h>
#include <stdio.h>
int main()
{
   int Answer;
   cout << "How long were you in medical school? ";
   cin >> Answer;
   if (Answer > 4)
      {
      cout << "Congratulations! You should be able to\n";
      cout << "play a good game of golf in no time.";
      }
   else
      {
      cout << "You may not have been in medical school
           for\n";
      cout << "very long, but at least you should know\n";
      cout << "how to put on a white lab coat.";
      }
   cout << "\nPress ENTER to continue..." << endl;
   getchar();
   return 0;
}
```

This C++ program is stored in the C++ Sample Programs folder as `Chapter 9 - If Then Else.cpp`.

Unlike the `IF-THEN` statement, the `IF-THEN-ELSE` statement always forces the computer to follow one set of instructions no matter what. In this program, if the answer is greater than `4`, the computer prints `Congratulations! You should be able to play a good game of golf in no time.`

If the answer isn't greater than `4`, the computer prints `You may not have been in medical school for very long, but at least you should know how to put on a white lab coat.`

The `IF-THEN-ELSE` statement always makes the computer follow one set of instructions. If you use the ordinary `IF-THEN` statement, the computer may or may not do anything.

Here's an equivalent Revolution program. The `wait for 3 seconds` command keeps each string displayed in the message box before displaying the next one. Notice that the `IF-THEN` statement in Revolution works identically to Liberty BASIC:

```
ask "How long were you in medical school?"
put it into Answer
if (Answer > 4) then
  put "Congratulations! You should be able to" into
         message
  wait for 3 seconds
  put "play a good game of golf in no time." into message
else
  put "You may not have been in medical school for" into
         message
  wait for 3 seconds
  put "very long, but at least you should know" into
         message
  wait for 3 seconds
  put "how to put on a white lab coat." into message
end if
```

This Revolution program is stored in the Revolution Sample Programs folder as `Chapter 9 - If Then Else.rev`.

Many programming languages also include an `IF-THEN-ELSEIF` statement, which lets you combine multiple `IF-THEN` statements into a single statement such as

```
IF (Boolean expression 1) THEN
  ' Follow one or more instructions
  ' listed here
ELSEIF (Boolean expression 2)
  ' Follow one or more instructions
  ' listed here
END IF
```

An IF-THEN-ELSEIF statement runs only if one of its Boolean expressions is true. Otherwise it's possible that none of its instructions run. In C++, an IF-THEN-ELSEIF statement looks like this:

```
if (Boolean expression 1)
  {
  // Follow one or more instructions here
  }
else if (Boolean expression 2)
  {
  // Follow one or more instructions here
  }
```

Working with SELECT CASE Statements

One problem with the IF-THEN statement is if you need to test multiple conditions, you need to write multiple IF-THEN statements as the following Liberty BASIC program shows:

```
PROMPT "How old are you"; Answer
IF (Answer = 21) THEN
 PRINT "Congratulations! You may be able to rent a"
 PRINT "car in some states."
END IF

IF (Answer = 20) THEN
 PRINT "You can't rent a car, but you're pre-approved"
 PRINT "for 20 different credit cards."
END IF

IF (Answer = 19) THEN
 PRINT "You're still officially a teenager."
END IF

IF (Answer = 18) THEN
 PRINT "You're old enough to join the military and"
 PRINT "fire an automatic rifle, but you still can't"
```

```
 PRINT "buy beer legally. Figure that one out."
END IF

IF (Answer = 17) THEN
 PRINT "You can see R-rated movies on"
 PRINT "your own (but you've probably done that for
         years)."
END IF
END
```

As an alternative to multiple `IF-THEN-ELSE` statements, many programming languages offer a `SELECT CASE` statement, which looks like this:

```
SELECT CASE Variable
CASE Value1
  ' Follow these instructions if the Variable = Value1
CASE Value2
  ' Follow these instructions if the Variable = Value2
END SELECT
```

The `SELECT CASE` statement provides different instructions depending on the value of a particular variable. If you rewrite the preceding program that uses multiple `IF-THEN-ELSE` statements to use `SELECT CASE` statements, the program looks like this:

```
PROMPT "How old are you"; Answer
SELECT CASE Answer
CASE 21                                                    →3
 PRINT "Congratulations! You may be able to rent a"
 PRINT "car in some states."
CASE 20                                                    →6
 PRINT "You can't rent a car, but you're pre-approved
 PRINT "for 20 different credit cards."
CASE 19                                                    →9
 PRINT "You're still officially a teenager."
CASE 18                                                   →11
 PRINT "You're old enough to join the military and"
 PRINT "fire an automatic rifle, but you still can't"
 PRINT "buy beer legally. Figure that one out."
CASE 17                                                   →15
 PRINT "You can see R-rated movies on"
 PRINT "your own (but you've probably done that for
         years)."
END SELECT
END
```

This Liberty BASIC program is stored in the Liberty BASIC Sample Programs folder as `Chapter 9 - Select Case 1.bas`.

Here's how this program works

- **→3-5** If the user types 21, the program prints `Congratulations! You may be able to rent a car in some states.`
- **→6-8** If the user types 20, the program prints `You can't rent a car, but you're pre-approved for 20 different credit cards.`
- **→9-10** If the user types 19, the program prints `"You're still officially a teenager."`
- **→10-14** If the user types 18, the program prints `You're old enough to join the military and fire an automatic rifle, but you still can't buy beer legally. Figure that one out.`
- **→15-17** If the user types 17, the program prints `You can see R-rated movies on your own (but you've probably done that for years).`

Of course, if the user types any value that the `SELECT CASE` statement doesn't list, such as 22 or 16, the `SELECT CASE` statement doesn't run any instructions.

To make sure that the computer follows at least one set of instructions in a `SELECT CASE` statement, just add a `CASE ELSE` command at the very end, as shown in this Liberty BASIC program:

```
PROMPT "How old are you"; Answer
SELECT CASE Answer
CASE 21                                                      →3
 PRINT "Congratulations! You may be able to rent a"
 PRINT "car in some states."
CASE 20                                                      →6
 PRINT "You can't rent a car, but you're pre-approved
 PRINT "for 20 different credit cards."
CASE 19                                                      →9
 PRINT "You're still officially a teenager."
CASE 18                                                      →11
 PRINT "You're old enough to join the military and"
 PRINT "fire an automatic rifle, but you still can't"
 PRINT "buy beer legally. Figure that one out."
CASE 17                                                      →15
 PRINT "You can see R-rated movies on"
 PRINT "your own (but you've probably done that for
        years)."
CASE ELSE                                                    →18
 PRINT "This sentence prints out if the user does NOT"
 PRINT "type numbers 17, 18, 19, 20, or 21."
END SELECT
END
```

This Liberty BASIC program is stored in the Liberty BASIC Sample Programs folder as `Chapter 9 - Select Case 2.bas.`

The program works like this:

- **→3-5** If the user runs this program and types 21, the program prints `Congratulations! You may be able to rent a car in some states.`
- **→6-8** If the user types 20, the program prints `You can't rent a car, but you're pre-approved for 20 different credit cards.`
- **→9-10** If the user types 19, the program prints `You're still officially a teenager.`
- **→11-14** If the user types 18, the program prints `You're old enough to join the military and fire an automatic rifle, but you still can't buy beer legally. Figure that one out.`
- **→15-17** If the user types 17, the program prints `You can see R-rated movies on your own (but you've probably done that for years).`
- **→18-20** If the user types any other number (such as 54 or 97, the program prints `This sentence prints out if the user does NOT type numbers 17, 18, 19, 20, or 21.`

Rather than a `SELECT CASE` statement, C++ and Revolution offer an equivalent `switch` statement. In C++, the `switch` statement looks like this:

```
switch (variable)
{
   case value1:
      // One or more instructions
      break;
   case value2:
      // One or more instructions
      break;
}
```

Within a `switch` statement, you must type a `break;` command after each statement. If you omit the `break;` command, C++ runs all the instructions stored in the `switch` statement along with any instructions stored in any following case blocks.

Listing 9-1 shows what the equivalent C++ program looks like.

Listing 9-1: Using the switch-break Commands in C++

```
#include <iostream.h>
#include <stdio.h>
int main()
{
   int Answer;
   cout << "How old are you? ";
   cin >> Answer;
   switch (Answer)
      {
      case 21:
         cout << "Congratulations! You may be able to rent
           a\n";
         cout << "car in some states.";
         break;
      case 20:
         cout << "You can't rent a car, but you're pre-
           approved\n";
         cout << "for 20 different credit cards.";
         break;
      case 19:
         cout << "You're still officially a teenager.";
         break;
      case 18:
         cout << "You're old enough to join the military
           and\n";
         cout << "fire an automatic rifle, but you still
           can't\n";
         cout << "buy beer legally. Figure that one out.";
         break;
      case 17:
         cout << "You can see R-rated movies on\n";
         cout << "your own (but you've probably done that
           for years).";
         break;
      default:
         cout << "This sentence prints out if the user
           does NOT\n";
         cout << "type numbers 17, 18, 19, 20, or 21.";
      }
   cout << "\nPress ENTER to continue..." << endl;
   getchar();
   return 0;
}
```

Instead of using `CASE-ELSE`, the C++ `switch` statement uses the keyword `default` to provide a list of instructions that run if none of the previous case statements ran.

This C++ program is stored in the C++ Sample Programs folder as `Chapter 9 - Switch.cpp`.

The Revolution program in Listing 9-2 uses a `switch` statement much like C++ does.

Listing 9-2: Using the switch-break Commands in Revolution

```
ask "How old are you?"
   put it into Answer
   switch Answer
     case 21
        put "Congratulations! You may be able to rent a"
               into message
        wait for 3 seconds
        put "car in some states." into message
        break
     case 20
        put "You can't rent a car, but you're pre-approved"
               into message
        wait for 3 seconds
        put "for 20 different credit cards." into message
        break
     case 19
        put "You're still officially a teenager." into
               message
        break
     case 18
        put "You're old enough to join the military and "
               into message
        wait for 3 seconds
        put "fire an automatic rifle, but you still can't"
               into message
        wait for 3 seconds
        put "buy beer legally. Figure that one out." into
               message
        break
     case 17
        put "You can see R-rated movies on" into message
        wait for 3 seconds
        put "your own (but you've probably done that for
               years)." into message
        break
     default
           put "This sentence prints out if the user does
               NOT" into message
           wait for 3 seconds
           put "type numbers 17, 18, 19, 20, or 21." into
               message
  end switch
```

This Revolution program is stored in the Revolution Sample Programs folder as `Chapter 9 - Switch.rev`.

Checking a range of values

The `SELECT CASE` statement can check whether a variable exactly matches a specific value, such as the number `21` or the string `"yes"`. But sometimes you may want to run a set of instructions if a variable falls within a range of values, such as any number between `1` and `4`. In that case, you must list all the possible values on a single `CASE` statement, as in the following example:

```
CASE 1, 2, 3, 4
```

This Liberty BASIC program checks whether a variable represents a number between `1` and `10`:

```
PROMPT "How many water balloons do you have? "; Answer
SELECT CASE Answer
CASE 1, 2, 3, 4                                          →3
 PRINT "You need more water balloons."
CASE 5, 6, 7, 8                                          →5
 PRINT "Now you need a target."
CASE ELSE                                                →7
 PRINT "What are you? A peace-loving hippie freak?"
END SELECT
END
```

This Liberty BASIC program is stored in the Liberty BASIC Sample Programs folder as `Chapter 9 - Select Case Range.bas`.

The program works like this:

- **→3-4** If the user types a number from 1 to 4, the program prints `You need more water balloons.`
- **→5-6** If the user types a number from 5 to 8, the program prints `Now you need a target.`
- **→7-8** If the user types any number less than 1 or greater than 8, the program prints `What are you? A peace-loving hippie freak?`

Make sure that you don't use the same value on two separate `CASE` statements, as happens in the following example:

```
PROMPT Type a number. "; Answer
SELECT CASE Answer
CASE 1, 2
 PRINT "This always prints if you type a 2."
CASE 2, 3
 PRINT "This never prints if you type a 2."
END SELECT
```

In the preceding `SELECT CASE` statement, the program prints `This always prints if you type a 2` if the user types 2, but the program never prints the instructions under the second `CASE` statement (`CASE 2, 3`). That's because the first `CASE` statement runs first, preventing the second `CASE` statement from getting a chance to run at all.

In C++ and Revolution, you must stack multiple case statements that define different values. Listing 9-3 shows the C++ program.

Listing 9-3: Checking for a Range of Values in a C++ switch Statement

```
#include <iostream.h>
#include <stdio.h>
int main()
{
   int Answer;
   cout << "How many water balloons do you have?";
   cin >> Answer;
   switch (Answer)                                        →8
      {
      case 1:
      case 2:
      case 3:
      case 4:
         cout << "You need more water balloons.";
         break;                                           →15
      case 5:
      case 6:
      case 7:
      case 8:
         cout << "Now you need a target.";
         break;                                           →21
      default:
         cout << "What are you? A peace-loving hippie
           freak?";
      }
      cout << "\nPress ENTER to continue..." << endl;
      getchar();
      return 0;
}
```

This C++ program is stored in the C++ Sample Programs folder as `Chapter 9 - Switch Range.cpp`.

Here's how Listing 9-3 works:

- →**8-14** If the user types a value of 1 through 4, the C++ program prints `You need more water balloons.`
- →**15-20** If the user types a value of 5 through 8, the program prints `Now you need a target.`
- →**21-27** If the user types any other value, the program prints `What are you? A peace-loving hippie freak?`

Checking a relational operator

Sometimes, checking for an exact value or a range of values may still prove too limiting. For greater flexibility, you may compare a variable to another value by using one of those friendly symbols known as *relational operators.* A relational operator enables the `SELECT CASE` statement to determine whether a variable is greater than (>); less than (<); greater than or equal to (>=); less than or equal to (<=); or not equal to (<>) a specific value.

To use a relational operator, you must use a slightly different version of the `CASE` statement, as shown in the following example:

```
PROMPT "How many cats do you own"; Answer
SELECT CASE
CASE (Answer <= 5)
 PRINT "You need more cats."
CASE (Answer > 5)
 PRINT "Are you out of your mind?"
END SELECT
END
```

This Liberty BASIC program is stored in the Liberty BASIC Sample Programs folder as `Chapter 9 - Select Case Relational.bas`.

If the user types any number equal to or less than 5, the program prints `You need more cats`. If the user types any number greater than 5, the program prints `Are you out of your mind?`

The two crucial differences when using relational operators in a `SELECT CASE` statement are

- The SELECT CASE variable (which is Answer in the preceding example) doesn't appear directly after the SELECT CASE command.
- The relational expression (such as Answer <= 5) appears directly after each CASE statement.

Make sure that your relational operators don't overlap another part of the SELECT CASE statement, as happens in the following example:

```
SELECT CASE
CASE (Answer < 10)
 PRINT "This always prints."
CASE (Answer < 12)
 PRINT "This prints only if the user types 11."
END SELECT
```

In this SELECT CASE statement, the program prints This always prints if the user types any number less than 10, but the program prints the instructions under the second CASE statement (Answer < 12) only if the user types 11.

In REALbasic, the SELECT CASE statement looks like this when using relational operators:

```
Dim Answer as integer
Answer = val(EditField1.text)
Select Case Answer
Case is <= 5
  MsgBox "You need more cats."
Case is  > 5
  MsgBox "Are you out of your mind?"
End Select
```

Notice that the REALbasic code differs from the Liberty BASIC code in two ways.

- The beginning of the Select Case statement contains the name of the variable to check (Select Case Answer).
- Each Case statement uses the Case is command followed by a relational operator and a value such as <= 5.

This REALbasic program is stored in the REALbasic Sample Programs folder as Chapter 9 - Select Case Relational.bas.

Although C++ doesn't let you use relational operators in a `switch` statement, Revolution does, as shown here:

```
ask "How many cats do you own?"
put it into Answer
switch
  case (Answer <= 5)
    put "You need more cats." into message
    break
  case (Answer > 5)
    put "Are you out of your mind?" into message
    break
end switch
```

This Revolution program is stored in the Revolution Sample Programs folder as `Chapter 9 - Switch Range.rev`.

Chapter 10

Repeating Yourself with Loops

In This Chapter

- Looping a fixed number of times with the `FOR-NEXT` loop
- Looping with the `WHILE` and `WEND` commands

Ideally, programming would mean doing as little work as possible while making the computer do as much work as possible. The less code you need to write, the smaller your programs will be, making them easier to create, fix, and modify.

One way that programmers write as little code as possible is by reusing existing code, and one of the simplest ways to do that is to make the computer repeat one or more instructions over and over again, using a loop.

Creating Loops

When you make a computer repeat one or more instructions, that's called a *loop.* Consider the following program, which prints the numbers 1 through 5 on-screen:

```
PRINT 1
PRINT 2
PRINT 3
PRINT 4
PRINT 5
END
```

If you want to expand this program to print five million numbers, guess what? You must type five million instructions. Because you really don't want to type that many instructions, you can use loops to make the computer repeat the same instructions multiple times. The computer does the hard work.

Consider the following, which in programming lingo is called a FOR-NEXT loop (see the next section to find out more about FOR-NEXT loops):

```
FOR I = 1 TO 5
  PRINT I
NEXT I
END
```

As you can see, loops allow you to write shorter programs. This program prints the following:

```
1
2
3
4
5
```

If you run this program, it does exactly the same thing as the first BASIC program. The loop version, however, can print five million numbers as easily as it can print five numbers. (Just change the number 5 in the program to 5000000.)

Although loops can help create shorter programs, the trade-off is that loops are also harder to read and understand than a straightforward list of instructions. If you create a loop, make sure that you write a comment in the program to explain exactly what you expect the loop to do. (See Chapter 7 for more information about comments.)

A loop forces the computer to run the same instructions over and over, but eventually the computer needs to know when to stop. To tell the computer when to stop looping, you need to use a *condition* that represents a True or False value.

In the world of mathematics and programming, anything that represents a True or False value is known as a *Boolean expression;* see Chapter 9. An example of a Boolean expressions is 4 > 9.48 (which has a False value).

Looping a Fixed Number of Times

The simplest loop repeats a group of instructions a fixed number of times, as in the previous example, which repeats the PRINT command five times. To loop a fixed number of times, programming languages use something called a FOR-NEXT loop.

A `FOR-NEXT` loop typically consists of three items:

- A variable used to count how many times the loop has repeated
- An initial start value such as 1
- An ending value

The following shows the structure of a typical `FOR-NEXT` loop in Liberty BASIC:

```
FOR counter = start TO end
  ' One or more instructions
NEXT counter
```

This loop tells the computer to repeat a fixed number of times the instructions between the `FOR` and `NEXT` commands. The *`start`* and *`end`* values determine the number of repeats, and the *`counter`* value is a variable that keeps track of how many times the loop has run. A typical Liberty BASIC `FOR-NEXT` loop looks like this:

```
FOR I = 1 TO 10                                    →1
 PRINT "The square of "; I; " is "; I * I          →2
NEXT I                                             →3
END                                                →4
```

This Liberty BASIC program is stored in the Liberty BASIC Sample Programs folder as `Chapter 10 - For Next.bas`.

If you run this Liberty BASIC program, here's what happens:

→1 Creates the variable `I` and tells the computer to start counting from number `1` and stop counting at `10`.

→2 Tells the computer to print `The square of 1 is 1`. Each time this line runs, the value of `I` is different, so the final output from the program looks like this:

```
The square of 1 is 1
The square of 2 is 4
The square of 3 is 9
The square of 4 is 16
The square of 5 is 25
The square of 6 is 36
The square of 7 is 49
The square of 8 is 64
The square of 9 is 81
The square of 10 is 100
```

→3 Tells the computer to increment the value of `I` by the next value.

→4 Tells the computer that the program is at an end.

If the start value is less than the end value, the `FOR-NEXT` loop doesn't run at all, as in the following example:

```
FOR I = 8 TO 2
  ' This doesn't work at all
NEXT I
```

In C++, the `FOR-NEXT` loop looks like this:

```
for (initialization; conditional; increment)
  {
  // One or more instructions
  }
```

The *initialization* part declares a variable for counting and assigns it an initial value. The *conditional* part defines the condition that causes the loop to stop repeating itself. The *increment* part defines how the loop counts (such as by 1). The following C++ program is equivalent to the preceding `FOR-NEXT` loop program in Liberty BASIC:

```
#include <iostream.h>
#include <stdio.h>
int main()
{
   for (int i = 1; i <= 10; i++)
     {
     cout << "The square of " << i << " is " << i * i <<
          "\n";
     }
   return 0;
}
```

This C++ program is stored in the C++ Sample Programs folder as `Chapter 10 - For Next.cpp`.

The initialization part of the `FOR-NEXT` loop declares an integer variable called `i` and sets its initial value to `1`.

The letters *i*, *j*, and *x* are often used as a counting variable in `FOR-NEXT` loops, but you're free to make up your own variable name if you want.

The conditional part of the `FOR-NEXT` loop tells the computer to keep looping as long as the value of the `i` variable is less than or equal to `10`.

The increment part, `i++`, tells the computer to add `1` to the `i` variable each time to loop runs.

In Revolution, you can create a repeating loop by using the `repeat with` command, which is similar to a `FOR-NEXT` loop, as shown here:

```
repeat with i = 1 to 10
    put "The square of " && i && " is " && i * i
    wait for 3 seconds
end repeat
```

This Revolution program is stored in the Revolution Sample Programs folder as `Chapter 10 - Repeat With.rev`.

Counting with different numbers

Most `FOR-NEXT` loops count from `1` to another fixed value, such as `10`. The `FOR-NEXT` loop, however, can count from any number to any other number, as in the following example:

```
FOR I = 8 TO 14
 PRINT "The value of I ="; I
NEXT I
END
```

This loop repeats seven times and prints the following:

```
The value of I = 8
The value of I = 9
The value of I = 10
The value of I = 11
The value of I = 12
The value of I = 13
The value of I = 14
```

You can also use negative numbers for the start and end values, as follows:

```
FOR counter = -5 TO 3
  ' One or more instructions
NEXT counter
```

Unless you have a good reason for choosing different numbers to start and end, always start at number 1. Starting at 1 makes determining how many times the `FOR-NEXT` loop repeats easier for you or anyone else running the program.

Counting in increments

A `FOR-NEXT` loop counts by one, but if you like, you can use the `STEP` command in the following way to make the `FOR-NEXT` loop count in increments other than one:

```
FOR counter = 1 TO 4 STEP increment
  ' One or more instructions
NEXT counter
```

If, for example, you want to count by twos, you can use the following FOR-NEXT loop:

```
FOR I = 1 TO 8 STEP 2
  PRINT "The value of I = "; I
NEXT I
```

If you run this Liberty BASIC program, the FOR-NEXT loop doesn't repeat eight times, but rather four times and prints this:

```
The value of I = 1
The value of I = 3
The value of I = 5
The value of I = 7
```

To increment by other values besides 1, REALbasic also lets you use the STEP command, as shown here:

```
Dim I as Integer
For I = 4 to 10 Step 2
    MsgBox "The value of I is = " + Str(I)
Next
```

In C++, you can change the increments that the FOR-NEXT loop counts just by changing the increment value. So if you want to increment by 2, you can type **i = i + 2** as follows:

```
#include <iostream.h>
#include <stdio.h>
int main()
{
   for (int i = 1; i <= 10; i = i + 2)
      {
      cout << "The current value is " << i << "\n";
      }
   cout << "\nPress ENTER to continue..." << endl;
   getchar();
   return 0;
}
```

This C++ program is stored in the C++ Sample Programs folder as Chapter 10 - For Next Increment.cpp.

The C++ program prints the following:

```
The current value is 1
The current value is 3
The current value is 5
```

```
The current value is 7
The current value is 9
```

Revolution also allows you to count in increments by using the `step` command as in this example:

```
repeat with i = 1 to 10 step 2
    put "The value of i is " && i
    wait for 3 seconds
end repeat
```

Counting backward

In Liberty BASIC, you can make a `FOR-NEXT` loop count backward by using a negative number for the increment value, which is the only time that you can have the start value greater than the end value, as shown in the following example:

```
FOR I = 6 TO -8 STEP -3
  PRINT "The value of I = "; I
NEXT I
```

If you run this program, the `FOR-NEXT` loop repeats five times, printing the following results:

```
The value of I = 6
The value of I = 3
The value of I = 0
The value of I = -3
The value of I = -6
```

In many programming languages, such as REALbasic, you can count backward by one by using the `DOWNTO` command as follows:

```
Dim I as Integer
For I = 4 Downto -2
    MsgBox "The value of I is = " + Str(I)
Next
```

If you use the `DOWNTO` command by itself, REALbasic counts backward. However, if you use the `DOWNTO` command with a negative number for the `STEP` command, REALbasic actually counts forward, as in the following:

```
Dim I as Integer
For I = 4 Downto -2 Step -2
    MsgBox "The value of I is = " + Str(I)
Next
```

In REALbasic, the `FOR-NEXT` loop doesn't need to mention the counting variable in the `NEXT` command that defines the end of the loop.

Instead of counting 4, 2, 0, and –2, the `DOWNTO` and the `STEP -2` commands count forward from 4, 6, 8, and so on. Because the `FOR-NEXT` loop ends only when the value of `I` equals `-2`, this creates an endless loop that causes your program to count forever.

To count backward in C++, you just have to decrement the counting variable (for example, `i = i - 2`). Here's what that looks like:

```
#include <iostream.h>
#include <stdio.h>
int main()
{
   for (int i = 10; i >= 1; i = i - 2)
     {
     cout << "The current value is " << i << "\n";
     }
   cout << "\nPress ENTER to continue..." << endl;
   getchar();
   return 0;
}
```

This C++ program is stored in the C++ Sample Programs folder as `Chapter 10 - For Next Backward.cpp`.

In Revolution, you can count backward by using the `down to` command (note the space between `down` and `to`) as follows:

```
repeat with i = 7 down to 4
    put "The value of i is " && i
    wait for 3 seconds
end repeat
```

If you want to count backward by increments other than `1`, you need to use the `down to` command along with the `step` command that displays a negative number, as shown here:

```
repeat with i = 10 down to 4 step -2
    put "The value of i is " && i
    wait for 3 seconds
end repeat
```

Using a WHILE Loop

The `FOR-NEXT` loop is handy for repeating one or more instructions a fixed number of times. Of course, sometimes you won't know exactly how many times to repeat a group of instructions. In this case, you need to create a loop that repeats while a certain condition remains true, which is often called a `WHILE` loop.

In Liberty BASIC, the `WHILE` loop looks like this:

```
WHILE (Boolean expression is true)
  ' One or more instructions
WEND
```

To repeat one or more instructions, you just sandwich them between the `WHILE` and `WEND` commands, as shown in the following Liberty BASIC example:

```
I = 0                                        →1
WHILE I < 5                                  →2
  PRINT "This is the value of I = "; I       →3
  I = I + 1                                  →4
WEND                                         →5
END                                          →6
```

This program does the following:

→1 Creates the variable `I` and sets its value to `0`.

→2 Tells the computer to start a loop running the two instructions sandwiched between the `WHILE` and `WEND` commands while the Boolean expression `I < 5` is true.

→3 Tells the computer to print `This is the value of I = 0` the first time that the `WHILE-WEND` loops runs and `This is the value of I = 1` the second time that the `WHILE-WEND` loop runs, and so on.

→4 Tells the computer to add one to the value of the variable `I`.

→5 Tells the computer to check whether the Boolean expression `I < 5` is still true. If false, the program skips to the sixth line. If `I` represents the number `0`, `1`, `2`, `3`, or `4`, the program returns to the top of the loop on the second line. The computer repeats the loop four times to print the following:

```
This is the value of I = 0
This is the value of I = 1
This is the value of I = 2
This is the value of I = 3
This is the value of I = 4
```

→6 Tells the computer that this is the end of the program.

In C++, the `WHILE` loop looks like this:

```
while (Boolean condition)
  {
  // One or more instructions
  }
```

The equivalent C++ program that counts from 0 to 4 looks like this:

```
#include <iostream.h>
#include <stdio.h>
int main()
{
   int i;
   i = 0;
   while (i < 5)
     {
     cout << "This is the value of i = " << i << "\n";
     i = i + 1;
     }
   cout << "\nPress ENTER to continue..." << endl;
   getchar();
   return 0;
}
```

This C++ program is stored in the C++ Sample Programs folder as `Chapter 10 - While.cpp`.

In Revolution, the equivalent `WHILE` loop looks like this:

```
put 0 into i
repeat while i < 5
  put "The value of i is " && i
  put i + 1 into i
  wait for 3 seconds
end repeat
```

This Revolution program is stored in the Revolution Sample Programs folder as `Chapter 10 - Repeat While.rev`.

A `WHILE` loop stops only when a certain condition changes. If this condition never changes, the `WHILE` loop could get stuck in something known as an *endless loop*, which means that the computer follows a set of instructions but never stops. If a program gets caught in an endless loop, the program may appear to freeze on-screen. Usually, the only way to get out of an endless loop is to kill the running program (or turn the computer off and then on again).

The UNTIL Loop Variation

Besides the `WHILE` loop, many programming languages offer a variation known as the `UNTIL` loop. Whereas the `WHILE` loop keeps repeating while a certain condition remains true, an `UNTIL` loop keeps repeating until a certain condition becomes true.

In REALbasic, you can use a DO-LOOP in place of a WHILE loop such as the following:

```
Dim I as integer
I = 0
DO
  MsgBox "This is the value of I = " + Str(I)
  I = I + 1
LOOP UNTIL I >= 5
```

The preceding DO-LOOP always runs at least once before checking its Boolean condition (I >= 5). You can also rewrite the DO-LOOP to check a Boolean condition before running the loop like so:

```
Dim I as integer
I = 0
DO UNTIL I  >= 5
  MsgBox "This is the value of I = " + Str(I)
  I = I + 1
LOOP
```

This REALbasic program is stored in the REALbasic Sample Programs folder as Chapter 10 - Do Loop.rb.

If you check a Boolean condition before running a loop, it's possible that the loop won't run at all. If you check a Boolean condition at the end of a loop, the loop always runs at least once.

In C++, you can check a Boolean condition at the end of a WHILE loop by using a variation called the DO-WHILE loop, as in this example:

```
#include <iostream.h>
#include <stdio.h>
int main()
{
   int i;
   i = 0;
   do                                                    →3
     {
     cout << "This is the value of i = " << i << "\n";
     i = i + 1;                                          →6
     }
   while (i < 5);                                        →8
   cout << "\nPress ENTER to continue..." << endl;
   getchar();
   return 0;
}
```

This C++ program is stored in the C++ Sample Programs folder as Chapter 10 - Do While.cpp.

→3-8 Defines the DO-WHILE loop that repeats as long as the Boolean expression (I M 5) is true.

→6 Adds 1 to the value of i. Without this line changing the value of i, this loop would repeat endlessly.

In Revolution, you can create a REPEAT UNTIL loop like the following:

```
put 0 into i
repeat until i >= 5
  put "The value of i is " && i
  put i + 1 into i
  wait for 3 seconds
end repeat
```

This Revolution program is stored in the Revolution Sample Programs folder as Chapter 10 - Repeat Until.rev.

Watching Out for Endless Loops

One of the trickiest parts of using a loop is avoiding a condition known as an endless loop. Unlike FOR-NEXT loops, which run a fixed number of times and then stop, most types of loops rely on a Boolean expression to become true or false in order to stop the loop.

That means it's possible for a loop to repeat itself zero, one, three, nine, or a million times, depending on the Boolean expression. When you create a loop, always make sure that the loop will stop running eventually. If you don't, your program will get stuck in an endless loop, which means your program will appear to freeze and do nothing while the user angrily bangs on the keyboard and smacks the mouse around.

Endless loops #1: Failing to modify the Boolean expression inside the loop

One common cause of an endless loop occurs whenever the Boolean expression of a loop never changes to tell the computer to stop running the instructions inside the loop, as in the following program:

```
I = 1
WHILE I < 5
 PRINT "This loop never ends."
WEND
END
```

This loop never stops because the value of I never changes. Thus the Boolean expression I < 5 always remains true, so the WHILE loop keeps running the instructions between the WHILE and WEND commands. In this case, the program just keeps printing This loop never ends.

To fix this problem, you need to insert a command inside the WHILE loop to change the variable in the Boolean expression. One option is to insert the command I = I + 1, as shown in the following example:

```
I = 1
WHILE I < 5
 PRINT "This loop eventually ends."
 I = I + 1
WEND
END
```

Endless loops #2: Failing to initialize a Boolean expression outside the loop

Another variation of the endless loop occurs if you forget to define the value of a variable outside the WHILE loop, as in the following program:

```
WHILE I < 5
 I = 1
 PRINT "This loop never ends."
 I = I + 1
WEND
END
```

In this example, the value of variable I is always set to 1 at the beginning of the WHILE loop and then gets incremented to 2 at the end of the WHILE loop. But each time the WHILE loop runs, the value of I is reset to 1 so the Boolean expression I < 5 always remains true, and thus the loop never ends.

The correct way to use the preceding WHILE loop is to place the statement I = 1 right in front of the WHILE loop, as in the following example:

```
I = 1
WHILE I < 5
 PRINT "This loop will eventually end."
 I = I + 1
WEND
END
```

In this example, the value of the I variable is set to 1 before the computer runs the WHILE loop. When inside the WHILE loop, the value of I steadily increases until the value of `I` is equal to `5`, which makes the Boolean expression `I < 5` false; therefore, the `WHILE` loop ends.

The two key ways to preventing endless loops are to

- Make sure you initialize the Boolean variable outside of the loop.
- Make sure the Boolean expression will eventually change within the loop.

If possible, use `FOR-NEXT` loops that loop a fixed number of times so that you'll always be assured that the loop will terminate eventually.

Chapter 11

Dividing a Program into Subprograms

In This Chapter

- Understanding structured programming
- Dividing a program into modules
- Creating subroutines
- Creating functions

Writing a small program is easy. Writing a large program is difficult. So rather than struggle with writing a single large program, just write a bunch of small programs and paste them together like building blocks to create a much larger program.

That's the general theory behind programming. The most common way to divide a large program into a smaller one is to create a *subprogram.*

A subprogram is usually a small program designed to solve a single task, such as multiplying two numbers or verifying that the user types a correct password. For really complicated programs, you can break down a single subprogram into several smaller subprograms.

Suppose you want to write a program to break into another computer. The overall task is simple:

> Break into another computer.

Of course, you can't tell the computer just to break into another computer; the computer doesn't know how to do that. You must tell the computer, in specific detail, exactly how to do what you want it to do. So you must divide the overall task into smaller tasks, as follows:

1. Find the Internet Protocol (IP) address of the target computer.
2. Guess a password to access the system.
3. After gaining access, beep to notify the user.

Ideally, you can solve each task by using a separate subprogram that's completely independent of any other part of the program.

Programmers use subprograms for the following two reasons:

- **To make writing large programs easier:** By writing a bunch of small programs that perform specific tasks, you can paste together a bunch of subprograms to make a much larger program.
- **To store repetitive instructions in a single location:** Sometimes you need to run the same set of instructions over and over again. Rather than write these instructions each time that you need them, you can write them just once and store them in a subprogram that any other part of your program can run at any time.

Creating a Subprogram

When you create a subprogram, you can store the subprogram in one of two locations:

- **In the same file as your main program:** If you have a small number of subprograms, it's generally fine to store them in the same file as your main program, but the more subprograms you create, the larger your main file becomes.
- **In a separate file:** This technique keeps the main program file to a manageable size, but it also lets you create libraries of useful and tested subprograms that you can use in other projects.

Most C++ compilers include a collection of standard libraries that give C++ programs the ability to print messages on-screen or define a string data type. These C++ libraries are nothing more than separate files that contain tested C++ subprograms that you can reuse in every C++ program you create.

Although every programming language uses different syntax and commands for creating and running a subprogram, the general idea is the same no matter what computer or programming language you use: Define a subprogram by name and then run any commands stored in that subprogram by using that subprogram's name.

Creating a Liberty BASIC subprogram

To create a subprogram in Liberty BASIC, you need to perform the following tasks:

- Write any subprogram instructions after the `END` command in your main program.
- Identify the start of your subprogram with a unique name, enclosing it in square brackets `[like this]`.
- Identify the end of your subprogram by using the `RETURN` command, which tells the computer to return to the part of the program that was running before the subprogram ran.

You can choose any name for your subprogram, but you should choose a descriptive name. If your subprogram prints a warning message to the user, for example, you may want to name your subprogram `[warning]`.

The `RETURN` command identifies the end of your subprogram and tells the computer to return to the main program.

So a typical subprogram in Liberty BASIC looks as follows:

```
Main program instructions
Main program instructions
END

[subprogram]
Subprogram instructions
Subprogram instructions
RETURN
```

At this point, the computer totally ignores your subprogram because the computer starts at the top, beginning with the first instruction, and follows each succeeding instruction until it reaches the `END` command, which tells the computer to stop running the program before it can reach any of the instructions that your subprogram stores.

If you want your subprogram to run, you must insert a `GOSUB` command somewhere in your main program, as follows:

```
Main program instructions1
GOSUB [subprogram]
Main program instructions2
END

[subprogram]
Subprogram instructions
Subprogram instructions
RETURN
```

In the preceding example, the *`Main program instructions1`* line runs, and then the `GOSUB` command starts the subprogram running. After the subprogram instructions run, the `RETURN` command returns the computer to the line immediately following the GOSUB command. The computer then runs the *Main program instructions2* line until it stops at the END command.

To see a real program that you can try yourself, take a look at the following Liberty BASIC example:

```
PROMPT "What is your password?"; password$          →1
IF password$ = "open" THEN
  NOTICE "You typed a valid password."
ELSE
  NOTICE "Invalid password."
  GOSUB [hackeralert]
END IF
END                                                  →8

[hackeralert]                                        →10
PROMPT "Are you a hacker? (Y or N)?"; answer$
IF answer$ = "Y" THEN
  NOTICE "The police are on their way to pick you up now."
ELSE
  NOTICE "Then you must just be incompetent."
END IF
RETURN                                               →17
```

This Liberty BASIC program is stored in the Liberty BASIC Sample Programs folder as Chapter 11 - Subprogram.bas.

The program works like this:

- →1-8 These lines of code contain the main program instructions, starting with the PROMPT command and stopping with the END command.
- →10-17 The subprogram, [hackeralert], starts on line 10 ([hacker alert]) and stops on line 17 (RETURN). The only time that the [hackeralert] subprogram runs is when the user types an incorrect password in the first Prompt dialog box that asks What is your password?

Subprograms in Liberty BASIC divide a larger program into smaller parts, but everything still gets saved into a single file with a name such as PACMAN.BAS or BLACKJACK.BAS.

Creating a REALbasic subprogram

In REALbasic, subprograms are called *methods.* A method simply looks like this:

```
Sub MethodName()
  ' One or more instructions here
End Sub
```

MethodName is any descriptive name you want to use. You can save a method in the same file as your main program or in a separate file called a *module*.

To retrieve information from the user, REALbasic forces you to design a user interface so users can type data.

In REALbasic, a program consists of multiple methods that run when the user does something such as clicking a button. In Figure 11-1, clicking the Login button runs the following method:

```
Sub Action()
  Dim password as string
  password = EditField1.text
  If password = "open" Then
    MsgBox "You typed a valid password."
  Else
    MsgBox "Invalid password."
    HackerAlert()
  End If
End Sub
```

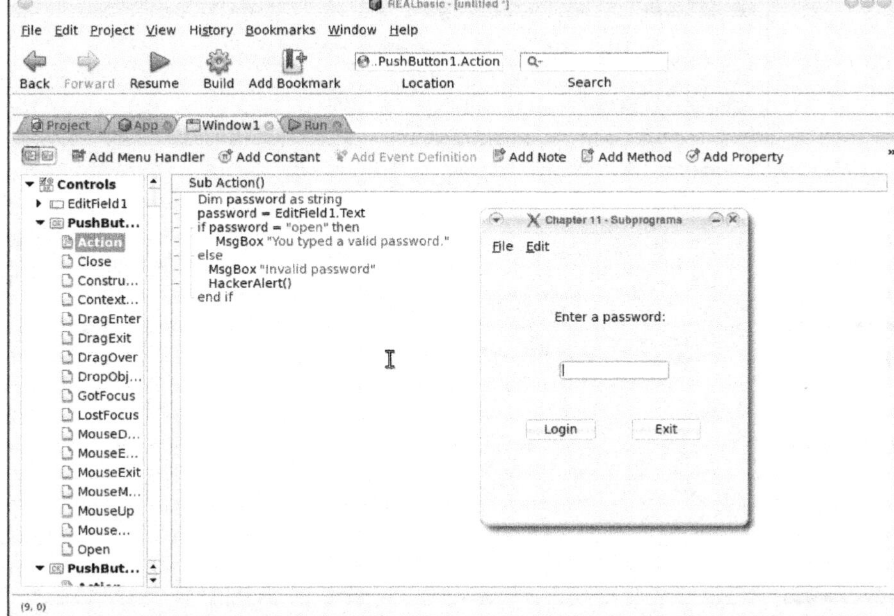

Figure 11-1: To retrieve data from the user in REALbasic, you must create a window and boxes as part of your program's user interface.

The preceding method retrieves the password from the text box named `EditField1`. If the user types an incorrect password, the program then runs the `HackerAlert()` method shown here:

```
Sub HackerAlert()
  Dim answer as integer
  answer = MsgBox ("Are you a hacker?", 4, "Hacker Alert")
  If answer = 6 Then ' Yes
    MsgBox "The police are on their way to pick you up
           now."
  Else 'No
    MsgBox "Then you must just be incompetent."
  End If
End Sub
```

This REALbasic program is stored in the REALbasic Sample Programs folder as `Chapter 11 - Subprogram.rb`.

This method uses the `MsgBox` command to open a dialog box that displays a Yes and No button along with the text `Are you a hacker?`, as shown in Figure 11-2.

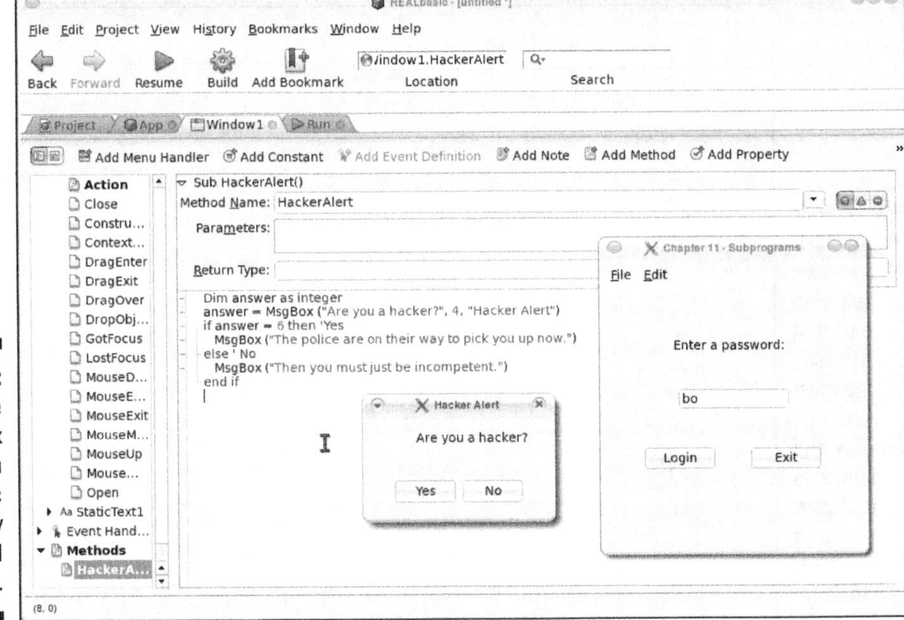

Figure 11-2: The MsgBox command in REALbasic can display a Yes and No button.

In the preceding method, the Yes button is identified by the number 6. (The No button is identified by the number 7, but the `IF-THEN` statement assumes if the user didn't click the Yes button, the user must have clicked the No button, so it doesn't explicitly check whether the user clicked the No button. You find out more about designing a user interface in Chapter 17.)

Creating a C++ subprogram

In C++, subprograms are called *functions.* Typically, you type your functions near the top of your program and then type the actual main program last, as follows:

```
#include <iostream.h>
#include <stdio.h>
using namespace std;

int hackerAlert ()
{
    string answer;
    cout << "Are you a hacker? (Y or N)?\n";
    cin >> answer;
    if (answer == "Y")
      {
      cout << "The police are on their way to pick you
            up.";
      }
    else
      {
      cout << "Then you must just be incompetent.";
      }
    return 0;
}
```

The `hackerAlert` function includes an empty pair of parentheses. The parentheses allow you to send data to the function, but the `hackerAlert` doesn't need any data to work so that's why its parentheses are empty.

The following C++ program shows how to run (or *call*) the `hackeralert` function. Notice that to run the `hackeralert` function, you just need to use the command `hackeralaert()`:

```
int main()
{
    string password;
    cout << "What is your password?";
    cin >> password;
    if (password == "open")
      {
      cout << "You typed a valid password.";
      }
```

```
    else
      {
      cout << "Invalid password.\n";
      hackerAlert();
      }
    cout << "\nPress ENTER to continue..." << endl;
    getchar();
    return 0;
}
```

These C++ programs are stored in the C++ Sample Programs folder as `Chapter 11 - Subprogram.cpp`.

The main program calls the `hackerAlert` function by its name, including its empty parentheses. If you're sending data to the `hackerAlert` function, you can type a specific value or variable inside those parentheses. By using functions, you essentially create your own programming commands.

Creating a Revolution subprogram

In Revolution, subprograms are called *handlers*. A handler typically runs when a certain event occurs or when specifically called to run. The following handler runs when the user clicks a button and releases the mouse button (`mouseUp`).

```
on mouseUp
  ask "What is your password?"
  put it into password
  if password = "open" then
    put "You typed a valid password." into message
  else
    put "Invalid password." into message
    HackerAlert
  end if
end mouseUp
```

The handler tells Revolution the name of the handler (subprogram) to run, which is `HackerAlert`. Inside the following `HackerAlert` handler, the `ask` command displays a dialog box and whatever the user types is stored in a special variable called `it`.

```
on HackerAlert
  ask "Are you a hacker? (Y or N)?"
  put it into answer
  if answer = "Y" then
    put "The police are on their way to pick you up." Into
         message
  else
    put "Then you must just be incompetent." Into message
  end if
end HackerAlert
```

This Revolution program is stored in the Revolution Sample Programs folder as `Chapter 11 - Subprogram.rev`.

When the user clicks the mouse, the on `mouseUp` handler runs and a dialog box appears asking, "What is your password?" If the user does not type the word *open*, the `HackerAlert` handler runs.

Running Subprograms

At the simplest level, a subprogram can do the exact same thing every time it runs. For example, it can display an error message on-screen whenever the program messes up. However, if a program can mess up in seventeen different ways, you'd have to write seventeen different subprograms just to display a different error message each time. To avoid writing multiple subprograms that do only one task, you can write a single subprogram that accepts data so it can perform different tasks.

When you create a subprogram that can accept data, you must define the following:

- How many chunks of data the subprogram can accept
- The type of data the subprogram expects

The list of variables that a subprogram can accept is called a *parameter list.* When you send data to a subprogram, that's called *passing a parameter.*

Programmers sometimes refer to parameters as *arguments.* Rather than "passing parameters," they say they're "passing arguments."

Passing parameters in Liberty BASIC

To create a subprogram that accepts data, you have to type the parameter list next to the subprogram name, as shown here:

```
SUB SubprogramName ParameterList
  ' One or more instructions here
END SUB
```

The parameter list needs to specify how many chunks of data to accept and what type of data to accept.

To specify how many chunks of data to accept, you need to create a variable for each chunk of data. If you want your subprogram to accept three chunks of data, your subprogram parameter list needs to define three variables, as shown here:

```
SUB SubprogramName Variable1, Variable2, Variable3
 ' One or more instructions here
END SUB
```

To specify what type of data the subprogram can accept, you need to define the variable to accept a number or a string. In Liberty BASIC, you can define a variable to hold numbers just by defining a variable name. To define a variable to hold strings, you must add the dollar sign ($) at the end of the variable name.

So if you want to create a subprogram that can accept a string and a number, your subprogram's parameter list might look like this:

```
SUB ErrorMessage Message$, ErrorNumber
 ' One or more instructions here
END SUB
```

When the preceding subprogram receives a string and a number, it stores the string in the `Message$` variable and the number in the `ErrorNumber` variable.

When you want to run the preceding subprogram, you have to use the `CALL` command followed by the subprogram name and the data you want to pass to the subprogram, as shown here:

```
CALL ErrorMessage "Fatal error!", 666
```

This instruction tells Liberty BASIC to run the `ErrorMessage` subprogram and pass it the string `"Fatal error!"` and the number `666`, as shown in Figure 11-3.

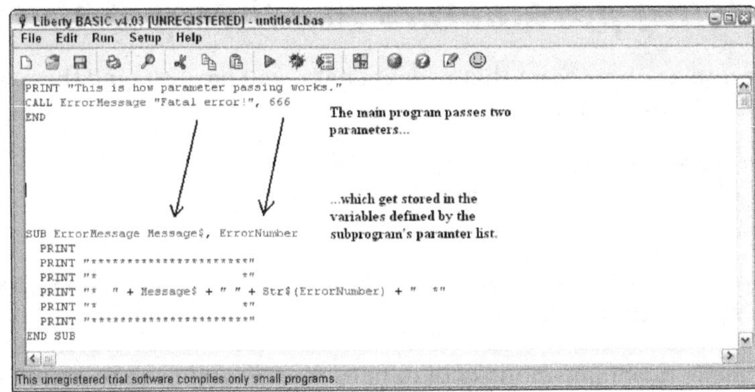

Figure 11-3: When you pass parameters to a subprogram, they get stored in that subprogram's variables defined by its parameter list.

To see how parameter passing works, run the following Liberty BASIC program:

```
PRINT "This is how parameter passing works."                →1
CALL ErrorMessage "Fatal error!", 666                       →2
END                                                         →3
```

The Liberty BASIC program works as follows:

→1 Prints the message "This is how parameter passing works."

→2 Uses the CALL command to tell the subprogram named ErrorMessage to run, and passes the string ("Fatal error!") and number (666) as a parameter to the ErrorMessage subprogram.

→3 Tells the computer this is the end of the program.

The ErrorMessage subprogram looks like this:

```
SUB ErrorMessage Message$, ErrorNumber
  PRINT
  PRINT "**********************"
  PRINT "*                    *"
  PRINT "*  " + Message$ + " " + Str$(ErrorNumber) + "  *"
  PRINT "*                    *"
  PRINT "**********************"
END SUB
```

This Liberty BASIC program is stored in the Liberty BASIC Sample Programs folder as Chapter 11 - Parameter.bas.

This subprogram accepts a string and stores it in the Message$ variable, and then it accepts a number and stores it in the ErrorNumber variable. Finally, it uses the Message$ and the ErrorNumber variables to print the following:

```
**********************
*                    *
*  Fatal error! 666  *
*                    *
**********************
```

When you call a subprogram, you must pass it the exact number of data chunks and the specific data types it's expecting. So the preceding ErrorMessage subprogram expects two data chunks: a string first and then a number. Check out these commands:

```
CALL ErrorMessage "Fatal error!"
CALL ErrorMessage 666, "Fatal error!"
CALL ErrorMessage "Fatal error!", "Hello"
```

None of these commands work, because they're either passing the subprogram the wrong number of data chunks or the wrong types of data chunks:

- The first line doesn't work because it passes only one parameter (the string `"Fatal error!"`), but the `ErrorMessage` subprogram is expecting a string and a number.
- The second line doesn't work because it passes two chunks of data but in the wrong order. The `ErrorMessage` subprogram expects a string first and then a number.
- The third line doesn't work because it passes two strings, but the `ErrorMessage` subprogram expects only one string (`Message$`) and one number (`ErrorNumber`).

If you pass the wrong number of parameters or the wrong type of parameters, your program won't work. So there.

Passing parameters in REALbasic

A REALbasic method (subprogram) with a parameter list looks like this:

```
Sub MethodName(Variable as DataType)
  // One or more instructions here
End Sub
```

If you want to define a method that accepts two parameters, a string and a number, you have to declare the first parameter as a string data type and the second parameter as a number data type, as in this example:

```
Sub ErrorMessage(Message as String, ErrorNumber as
      Integer)
  MsgBox Message + " " + Str(ErrorNumber)
End Sub
```

To run a REALbasic method, you just have to use the method's name. Look at the following method, which runs whenever the user clicks a button:

```
Sub Action()
  ErrorMessage("Fatal error!", 666)
End Sub
```

This REALbasic program is stored in the REALbasic Sample Programs folder as `Chapter 11 - Parameters.rb`.

Passing parameters in C++

A C++ subprogram is called a *function*. A typical function with a parameter list looks like this:

```
void FunctionName(DataType Variable)
  {
  // One or more instructions here
  }
```

In C++, every function can return a value, even the main function. Using the `void` data type tells C++ that this subprogram doesn't need to return a value.

Each C++ function must be assigned a data type, and then each variable in its parameter list must also be assigned a data type, as the following program demonstrates:

```
#include <iostream.h>
#include <stdio.h>
using namespace std;

void ErrorMessage (string Message, int ErrorNumber)     →1
{
   cout << "**********************\n";
   cout << "*                    *\n";
   cout << "*   " + Message + " " << ErrorNumber << "
          *\n";
   cout << "*                    *\n";
   cout << "**********************\n";
}                                                       →8
int main()
{
   cout << "This is how parameter passing works.\n";
   ErrorMessage("Fatal error!", 666);                   →12
   cout << "\nPress ENTER to continue..." << endl;
   getchar();
   return 0;
}
```

This C++ program is stored in the C++ Sample Programs folder as `Chapter 11 - Parameters.cpp`.

- **→1-8** These lines of code define the `ErrorMessage` function that can accept a string (`Message`) and an integer (`ErrorNumber`).
- **→12** This line of code calls the `ErrorMessage` function and passes it two parameters, `"Fatal error!"` and `666`.

To call a C++ function, you simply use the function name and pass it any parameters that it's expecting, such as a string and a number, as the preceding main program does in calling the `ErrorMessage` function.

Passing parameters in Revolution

A Revolution handler (subprogram) with a parameter list looks like this:

```
on HandlerName Variable
  -- One or more instructions here
end HandlerName
```

In Revolution, the parameter list is not enclosed in parentheses, as the following program demonstrates:

```
on mouseUp
  put "This is how parameter passing works." into message
  ErrorMessage "Fatal error!", 666
end mouseUp

on ErrorMessage Message, ErrorNumber
  put Message && " " && ErrorNumber into message
end ErrorMessage
```

This Revolution program is stored in the Revolution Sample Programs folder as `Chapter 11 - Parameters.rev.`

Revolution uses the two ampersand symbols (`&&`) to add strings together.

Using Functions

Subprograms typically perform a single, well-defined task such as moving a cartoon figure across the screen or verifying that the user entered a valid password. However, sometimes you might want a subprogram that simply calculates a single result, such as the result of a quadratic equation. In this situation, you need to create a specialized subprogram known as a *function.*

In C++ and many other languages derived from C, every subprogram is considered to be a function.

A function accepts data, performs some calculation with that data, and then returns a single result. Because functions represent a single value, you can assign a function to a variable or just use a function as part of a mathematical equation, as shown here:

```
Angle = cos(0.75)                 →1
Target = Range * sin(0.14)        →2
```

In the preceding two examples, this is how the computer behaves:

- →1 The `cos` function accepts the number `0.75`, calculates the cosine of `0.75`, and stores the result into a variable called `Angle`.
- →2 The `sin` function accepts the number `0.14`, calculates the sine of `0.14`, multiplies that value by the value stored in a variable called `Range`, and stuffs the entire multiplication result into a variable called `Target`.

Functions typically contain instructions that calculate some frequently used result, such as the tangent or logarithm of a number. That's why most programming languages include a library of built-in mathematical functions.

To create your own functions, you need to define

- The name of your function
- The type of data your function creates (such as an integer)
- A parameter list that defines the data the function needs
- One or more instructions that calculate a single value

Creating a Liberty BASIC function

A typical function in Liberty BASIC appears after the `END` statement in the main program and looks like this:

```
FUNCTION FunctionName(Data)
  ' One or more instructions
 FunctionName = value
END FUNCTION
```

Don't leave a space between the function name and the left parenthesis, or Liberty BASIC doesn't run your program.

If you want to create a function that calculates the cube of a number (multiplying the same number by itself three times), you use the following:

```
Answer = cube(3)                              →1
PRINT "The cube of 3 is = "; Answer           →2
END                                           →3

FUNCTION cube(x)                              →5
  cube = x * x * x                            →6
END FUNCTION                                  →7
```

This Liberty BASIC program is stored in the Liberty BASIC Sample Programs folder as `Chapter 11 - Function.bas.`

The preceding Liberty BASIC program appears on the first three lines, and the function appears on the last three lines. The program works like this:

- →1 Runs the function `cube` and passes it the number `3`. The result of the `cube` function gets stored in a variable called `Answer`.
- →2 Prints `The cube of 3 is =` followed by the value stored in the `Answer` variable.
- →3 Tells the computer that this is the end of the program.
- →5 Defines the function `cube`, which expects one number that it stores in the `x` variable.
- →6 Multiplies the variable `x` three times and stores the result in the `cube` function name.
- →7 Defines the end of the function.

The `cube` function represents a number value. If you want to create a function to represent a string value, you have to add the dollar sign (`$`) at the end of the function name such as:

```
FUNCTION FunctionName$(Data)
 ' One or more instructions
 FunctionName$ = value
END FUNCTION
```

Creating a REALbasic function

A REALbasic function looks like this:

```
Function FunctionName(Variable As DataType) As DataType
 ' One or more instructions here
 Return value
End Function
```

When defining a parameter list for a REALbasic function, you must create a variable name and define its data type just as you would declare a variable to use in the program. You must also define the function name as a data type. The last line in a REALbasic uses the `Return` command to assign a value to the function name.

To create a function that returns the cube of a number, you could use the following REALbasic program. This program consists of two methods. The first method (`Sub Action`) runs whenever the user clicks a button on the user interface. The second method (`Cube`) runs when called from the `Sub Action` method, as follows:

```
Sub Action()
  Dim Answer as integer
  Answer = Cube(3)
  MsgBox "The cube of 3 is = " + Str(Answer)
End Sub

Function Cube(x as Integer) As Integer
  Return x * x * x
End Function
```

This REALbasic program is stored in the REALbasic Sample Programs folder as `Chapter 11 - Function.rb`.

Creating a C++ function

A typical C++ function looks like this:

```
datatype functionname (datatype variable)
    {
      // One or more instructions here
      return value;
    }
```

A C++ function appears ahead of the main program. The following C++ program defines a `cube` function:

```
#include <iostream.h>
#include <stdio.h>
using namespace std;

int cube (int x)                                          →1
    {
     return x * x * x;
    }                                                     →4

int main()
    {
    int answer;
    answer = cube(3);                                     →9
    cout << "The cube of 3 is = " << answer;
    cout << "\nPress ENTER to continue..." << endl;
    getchar();
    return 0;
    }
```

This C++ program is stored in the C++ Sample Programs folder as `Chapter 11 - Function.cpp`.

- →1-4 Defines the `cube` function that accepts an integer parameter (stored in the `x` variable) and returns the value of that `x` variable multiplied three times.
- →9 This line "calls" the `cube` function and passes it the number `3`. Whatever value the `cube` function returns gets stored in the answer variable.

The main C++ program is actually just another function that happens to run first.

Creating a Revolution function

A Revolution function follows this format:

```
function functionName Variable
  -- One or more instructions here
  return value
end functionName
```

The following creates a Revolution function that calculates the cube of a number:

```
on mouseUp
  put cube(3) into answer
  put "The cube of 3 is = " && answer into message
end mouseUp

function cube x
  return x * x * x
end cube
```

This Revolution program is stored in the Revolution Sample Programs folder as `Chapter 11 - Function.rev`.

Chapter 12

Storing Stuff in Arrays

In This Chapter

- Creating an array
- Using an array to store data
- Creating dynamic arrays
- Making a multi-dimensional array

Variables are handy for storing data temporarily, but if you want to store a list of nearly identical data, you would have to create a series of nearly identically named variables. If you want to store the names of four people, you can use four different variables that are similarly named, such as

```
Name1$ = "Leo Fontaine"
Name2$ = "Jordan Preston"
Name3$ = "Rick Gene"
Name4$ = "Bo the Cat"
```

Naturally, this method is clumsy, and any time that programmers run into a problem that threatens to make programming harder than necessary, they come up with a solution to avoid the problem. In this case, the solution that programmers developed is known as an *array*, which can store a list of items.

Creating an Array

An ordinary variable can hold only one chunk of data at a time, such as a number or a name. The moment that you try to store another chunk of data in a variable, the variable erases the old data and saves the new data.

Unlike ordinary variables, an array is a single variable name that can hold a list of data. The only catch is that each chunk of data must represent the same data type, such as string or integer. To make an array, you must define the following three parts:

- The name of the array
- The number of items the array can hold (known as the *array index*)
- The type of data (integer, string, and so on) that the array can hold

Using arrays in Liberty BASIC

To create an array in Liberty BASIC, you use the `DIM` command, as follows:

```
DIM ArrayName(Number)
```

In this example, *`ArrayName`* is any valid variable name, and *`Number`* represents the total number of items that you want to store in the array.

As is true of other variables, an array can hold either numbers or strings. To define your array to hold strings, you need to add the dollar sign (`$`) to the end of the array name, as follows:

```
DIM ArrayName$(Number)
```

You define the size of an array with a single number, as follows:

```
DIM CatArray$(4)
```

This command actually creates an array that can hold five items because the array starts with the number 0 (zero), as shown in Figure 12-1.

When an array starts counting from zero, it's known as a *zero-based array*. In some programming languages, arrays start counting with the number one, so those arrays are known as a *one-based array*.

Figure 12-1: A zero-based array identifies the first item in an array with the number 0.

If you need to define several arrays, you can create them all on a single line, as shown here:

```
DIM CatArray$(45), DogArray(12), BirdArray$(87)
```

This line simply tells the computer to create three different arrays of size 46, 13, and 88. (Remember, the first item in an array is always numbered 0.) Both the `CatArray$` and `BirdArray$` arrays can hold only strings (because of the dollar sign at the end of their names), but the `DogArray` can hold only numbers. If you want, you can always define your arrays on separate lines, like this:

```
DIM CatArray$(45)
DIM DogArray(12)
DIM BirdArray$(87)
```

The first time you create an array in any programming language, it's usually a good idea to initialize that array by filling it with a fixed value (such as 0) or a space. If you don't initialize an array, the computer may cheerfully store random garbage in the array, which could mess up your program later.

To store data in an array, you must specify the array name and the index number of that array. So if you want to store the string `"Tasha"` in the number 4 index position of an array named `CatArray$`, use this line:

```
CatArray$(4) = "Tasha"
```

To retrieve data from an array, you need to specify the array name and the index number of that array, like this:

```
KoratName$ = CatArray$(4)
```

To store data in an array or retrieve data from it, use a loop such as a `FOR-NEXT` loop. The following program shows how a loop works with an array:

```
DIM NameArray$(3)
FOR I = 0 TO 3
 PROMPT "Type the name of someone you hate:"; Enemy$
 NameArray$(I) = Enemy$
NEXT I
FOR I = 0 TO 3
 PRINT NameArray$(I) + " sounds like the
         name of a moron."
NEXT I
END
```

This Liberty BASIC program is stored in the Liberty BASIC Sample Programs folder as `Chapter 12 - Array.bas`.

Here's how the computer runs the preceding program:

→1 Creates the array `NameArray`, which can hold three different strings.

→2 Starts a `FOR-NEXT` loop that runs three times.

→3 Displays a Prompt dialog box that tells the user, `"Type the name of someone you hate."` Whatever name the user types, the program stores it in the `Enemy$` string variable.

→4 Tells the computer, "Store the value of the `Enemy$` string variable in `NameArray$`. The first time that this `FOR-NEXT` loop runs, store the value of the `Enemy$` string variable in `NameArray$(1)`. The second time, store the `Enemy$` string variable in `NameArray$(2)`. The third time, store the `Enemy$` string variable in `NameArray$(3)`."

→5 Marks the end of the `FOR-NEXT` loop.

→6 Starts a second `FOR-NEXT` loop, which runs four times.

→7 Prints the value of `NameArray$` plus the string `" sounds like the name of a moron."` The first time the `FOR-NEXT` loop runs, this line prints the value stored in `NameArray$(0)`; the second time, it prints the value in `NameArray$(1)`, the third time, it prints the value in `NameArray$(2)`; and the fourth time, it prints the value in `NameArray$(3)`.

→8 Marks the end of the `FOR-NEXT` loop.

→9 Tells the computer that the program is at an end.

Using arrays in REALbasic

To create an array in REALbasic, you use the `DIM` command followed by a data type declaration, as shown here:

```
Dim ArrayName(Number) As DataType
```

In this example, *`ArrayName`* is any valid variable name, *`Number`* represents the total number of items that you want to store in the array, and *`DataType`* defines what type of information the array can hold, such as integer or string.

REALbasic arrays are zero-based. If you want to define an array that can hold six integers, write an array like this:

```
Dim IQArray(5) As Integer
```

This array can hold six items identified as `IQArray(0)`, `IQArray(1)`, `IQArray(2)`, `IQArray(3)`, `IQArray(4)`, and `IQArray(5)`.

The following REALbasic program demonstrates how to store and retrieve four strings in an array:

```
Dim NameArray(3) As String
Dim I As Integer
NameArray(0) = EditField1.text
NameArray(1) = EditField2.text
NameArray(2) = EditField3.text
NameArray(3) = EditField4.text
For I = 0 to 3
  MsgBox NameArray(I) + " sounds like the name of a
          moron."
Next
```

This REALbasic program is stored in the REALbasic Sample Programs folder as `Chapter 12 - Array.rb`.

Because REALbasic relies on retrieving data from a user interface, the preceding program displays four text boxes (named `EditField1`, `EditField2`, and so on) where the user can type four different names. Each name gets stored in a separate location in the array called `NameArray`. Then the `FOR-NEXT` loop opens a message box (using the `MsgBox` command) to display each name stored in the array called `NameArray` along with the message `sounds like the name of a moron.`

Using arrays in C++

To create an array in C++, you need to identify the data type of the array, the name of the array, and finally the number of items to store in the array. Here's what it looks like:

```
dataType ArrayName[Number];
```

In BASIC, you specify the number of array items with parentheses, but in C++, you use square brackets.

In this example, *`ArrayName`* is any valid variable name, *`Number`* represents the total number of items that you want to store in the array, and *`dataType`* defines what type of information the array can hold, such as integer or string.

In C++, arrays are zero-based. If you want to define an array that can hold five integers, write an array like this:

```
int IQArray[4];
```

This creates an array that can hold five items identified as `IQArray[0]`, `IQArray[1]`, `IQArray[2]`, `IQArray[3]`, and `IQArray[4]`.

The following C++ program demonstrates how to store and retrieve four strings in an array:

```
#include <iostream.h>
#include <stdio.h>
using namespace std;

int main()
{
   string namearray[3];                                    →1
   string enemy;                                           →2
   for (int i = 0; i <=3; i= i + 1)                        →3
     {
     cout << "Type the name of someone you hate\n";
     cin >> enemy;
     namearray[i] = enemy;
     }                                                     →8
   for (int i = 0; i <=3; i = i + 1)                       →9
     {                                                     →10
     cout << namearray[i] << " sounds like the
             name of a moron.\n";                          →11
     }                                                     →12
   cout << "\nPress ENTER to continue..." << endl;
   getchar();
   return 0;
}
```

This C++ program is stored in the C++ Sample Programs folder as `Chapter 12 - Array.cpp`.

Here's how it works:

- **→1-2** Creates an array called `namearray`, which can hold four (0–3) strings. Also creates a variable called enemy, which can hold a single string.
- **→3-8** Creates a `FOR` loop that runs four times and prints the message, `Type the name of someone you hate`. Each time the user types a name, the program stores the name in the enemy variable, which then gets copied into the string array called `namearray`.
- **→9-12** Creates a second `FOR` loop that runs four times and prints each person's name followed by `sounds like the name of a moron`.

In C++, you can initialize an array with data at the same time you create it. The number of initial data you store in the array defines its maximum size. So if you want to create an array of three integers that contain the numbers 34, 20, and 102, use the following line:

```
int arrayTest[] = {34, 20, 102};
```

Using arrays in Revolution

Unlike other programming languages, Revolution doesn't identify the items in an array by number. Instead, Revolution identifies array items by a *key* that can be any unique number or string.

Also unlike other programming languages, you don't need to declare an array name, its size, or the type of data it can hold ahead of time. In Revolution, you can create an array at the same time you store data in it for the first time.

The following example stores the number 75 in a newly created array called IQArray and associates it with a key named "Moron":

```
put 75 into IQArray["Moron"]
```

An array in Revolution is actually an *associative array.*

To retrieve data from a Revolution array, you need to identify both the array name and the key associated with the data you want to retrieve. This key can be a string or a number.

So if you previously stored the number 75 in an array named IQArray by using the key "Moron", you could retrieve this data by using the following:

```
put IQArray["Moron"] into message
```

The preceding command simply stores the value stored in the array named IQArray, identified by the "Moron" key. This value happens to be 75, so Revolution displays the number 75 in the message box.

The following Revolution program shows how to store and retrieve data in an array:

```
repeat with i = 0 to 3
  ask "Type the name of someone you hate."
  put it into NameArray[i]
end repeat
repeat with i = 0 to 3
  put NameArray[i] && "sounds like the name of a moron."
          into message
  wait for 3 seconds
end repeat
```

This Revolution program is stored in the Revolution Sample Programs folder as Chapter 12 - Array.rev.

The preceding program uses a repeat loop to display an ask dialog box four times that displays the message Type the name of someone you hate.

Each time the user types a name, the program stores that name in the array named `NameArray`.

The second repeat loop runs four times and displays the name, stored in `NameArray`, along with the message `sounds like the name of a moron`. After displaying each name in a message box, the program waits for three seconds before displaying the next name.

Creating Dynamic Arrays

One problem with defining a fixed size for an array is that you may allocate too much or too little space to hold all the data your program needs. If you make your array too small, it can't hold enough data. If you make the array too large, it holds mostly empty space, which wastes memory.

To solve these twin problems, many programming languages let you create *dynamic arrays*. As the name implies, a dynamic array can change in size while your program runs. It's possible to expand or shrink an array depending on the needs of the user at any given time.

The main advantage of a dynamic array is that you can resize it or completely erase it (thus freeing up memory) while the program is running. The disadvantage is that you must write specific commands to do so.

Resizing a dynamic array doesn't enable you to change the data type. If your original array held strings, your newly resized array must also hold strings.

Using dynamic arrays in Liberty BASIC

Liberty BASIC lets you resize any array by using the `REDIM` command, as in the following example:

```
REDIM VictimArray$(44)
```

This command tells the computer to take the existing array, `VictimArray$`, and change its size so that it can now hold 45 items.

If you change the size of an array, Liberty BASIC erases all the data stored in that array. If you want to preserve the contents of your array, you have to copy it into a second array, change the size of the first array, and then copy the data back in again. Otherwise, if you resize an array, you just lose any data already stored in it.

After you resize a dynamic array, you can stuff new data into it. To see how dynamic arrays work, try the following program:

```
DIM NameArray$(2)                                    →1
NameArray$(0) = "Ann Adams"                          →2
NameArray$(1) = "Bo Becker"                          →3
NameArray$(2) = "Calvin Coolidge"                    →4
FOR I = 0 TO 2                                       →5
  PRINT "NameArray$(" + Str$(I) + ") =
        " + NameArray$(I)                            →6
NEXT I                                               →7
REDIM NameArray$(4)                                  →8
NameArray$(4) = "Last name"                          →9
FOR I = 0 TO 4                                       →10
  PRINT "NameArray$(" + Str$(I) + ") =
        " + NameArray$(I)                            →11
NEXT I                                               →12
END                                                  →13
```

This Liberty BASIC program is stored in the Liberty BASIC Sample Programs folder as `Chapter 12 - Dynamic Array.bas`.

Here's how the computer runs the preceding program:

- →1 Creates the array `NameArray$`, which can hold three different strings (numbered 0, 1, and 2).
- →2 Stores the string `"Ann Adams"` in the index 0 of `NameArray$`.
- →3 Stores the string `"Bo Becker"` in the index 1 of `NameArray$`.
- →4 Stores the string `"Calvin Coolidge"` in the index 2 of `NameArray$`.
- →5 Starts a `FOR=NEXT` loop that runs three times, counting from 0 to 2.
- →6 Prints `"NameArray$("` followed by the current value of `I`, the string `") = "`, and the string stored in `NameArray$`. The first time it prints `Ann Adams`, the second time it prints `Bo Becker`, and the third time it prints `Calvin Coolidge`.
- →7 Marks the end of the `FOR-NEXT` loop.
- →8 The `REDIM` command erases everything currently stored in the `NameArray$` and then resizes it to hold five items numbered 0 to 4.
- →9 Stores the string `"Last name"` in index 4 of `NameArray$`.

→10 Starts a `FOR-NEXT` loop that repeats five times, counting from 0 to 4.

→11 Prints the contents of `NameArray$` starting from index 0 to index 4. Until the `PRINT` command prints the contents of index 4 of `NameArray$`, every index in the array will be empty.

→12 Marks the end of the `FOR-NEXT` loop.

→13 Tells the computer that the program is at an end.

Using dynamic arrays in REALbasic

REALbasic provides four different commands for resizing an existing array:

- `Append`: Adds one item to the end of an array. To use the `Append` command, you need to specify the array name along with the data you want to add or append to the end of the array, as in the following line:

```
ArrayName.Append NewData
```

- `Insert`: Inserts one item anywhere in an array. To use the `Insert` command, you need to specify the array name, the array index number where you want to insert new data, and the new data you want to insert into the array, like this:

```
ArrayName.Insert Index, NewData
```

- `Remove`: Deletes one item from an array. To use the `Remove` command, you need to specify the array name and the array index number that contains the data you want to delete (remove) from the array, as shown here:

```
ArrayName.Remove Index
```

- `Redim`: Changes the size of an entire array by any number you specify. To use the `Redim` command, you need to specify the array name along with a new size for that array. If you increase the size of an array, the new parts of the array are empty.

```
Redim ArrayName (Size)
```

If you decrease the size of an array, you may lose data currently stored in that array. If you have an array that consists of three items (`Dim NameArray(2) as String`) and you resize an array to hold only two items, your array cheerfully deletes any data previously stored in the deleted portion of the array, as shown in Figure 12-2.

Ann Adams	Bo Barker	Calvin Coolidge

The original array

Ann Adams	Bo Barker

Resizing an array can cut off existing data

Figure 12-2: When you decrease the size of an array, you can accidentally delete data stored in the cut-off portion of the array.

To see how REALbasic works with dynamic arrays, look at the following program:

```
Dim NameArray(2) as String                                    →1
Dim I as Integer
NameArray(0) = "Ann Adams"
NameArray(1) = "Bo Barker"
NameArray(2) = "Calvin Coolidge"                              →5
For I = 0 to 2
  MsgBox "NameArray(" + str(I) + ") = " + NameArray(I)
Next
NameArray.Append "David Duncan"                               →9
NameArray.Insert 1, "Ingrid Islander"                        →10
NameArray.Remove 2                                           →11
Redim NameArray(5)                                           →12
NameArray(5) = "Last name"                                   →13
For I = 0 to 5
  MsgBox "NameArray(" + str(I) + ") = " + NameArray(I)
Next
```

This REALbasic program is stored in the REALbasic Sample Programs folder as `Chapter 12 - Dynamic Array.rb`.

The REALbasic program works like this:

- →**1-5** Creates an array called `NameArray`, which can hold three strings, as shown in Figure 12-3.
- →**9** The `NameArray.Append` command adds the name `"David Duncan"` to the end of the array.

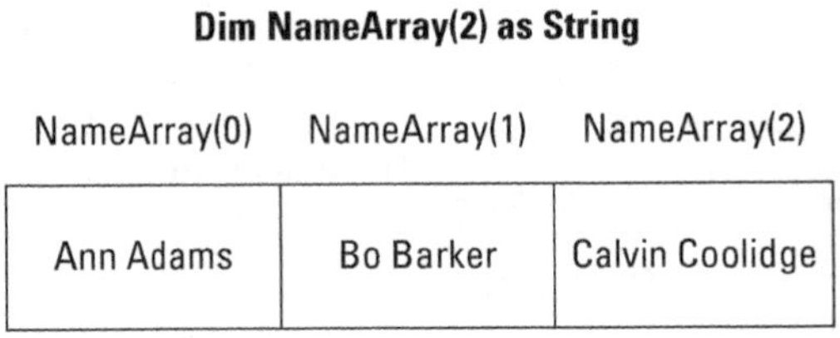

Dim NameArray(2) as String

NameArray(0)	NameArray(1)	NameArray(2)
Ann Adams	Bo Barker	Calvin Coolidge

Figure 12-3: The first three items in the NameArray.

→10 The `NameArray.Insert` command inserts the name `"Ingrid Islander"` in index 1, as shown in Figure 12-4.

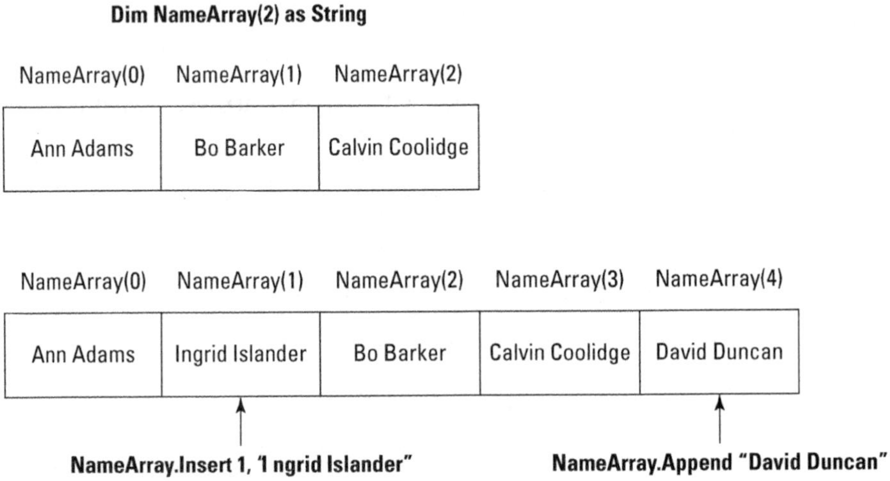

Dim NameArray(2) as String

NameArray(0)	NameArray(1)	NameArray(2)
Ann Adams	Bo Barker	Calvin Coolidge

NameArray(0)	NameArray(1)	NameArray(2)	NameArray(3)	NameArray(4)
Ann Adams	Ingrid Islander	Bo Barker	Calvin Coolidge	David Duncan

NameArray.Insert 1, 'I ngrid Islander" **NameArray.Append "David Duncan"**

Figure 12-4: The contents of the NameArray after the Append and Insert commands run.

→11 The `NameArray.Remove` command removes the string stored in index 2, which happens to be the `"Bo Barker"` string.

→12 The `Redim NameArray(5)` command expands the size of the array to hold six strings.

→13 Stores the string `"Last name"` in the last index of `NameArray` so the entire `NameArray` appears, as shown in Figure 12-5.

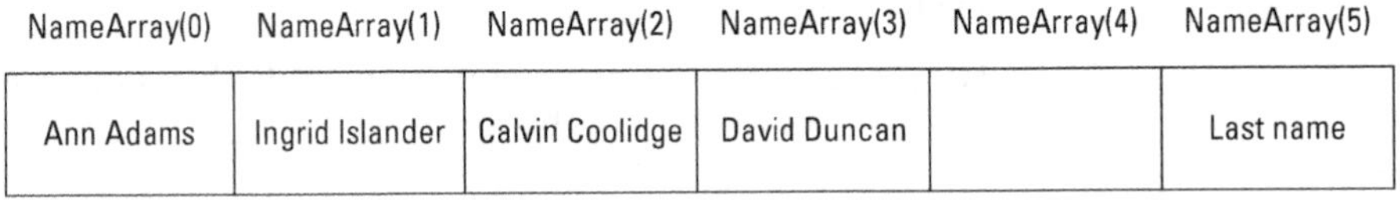

NameArray(0)	NameArray(1)	NameArray(2)	NameArray(3)	NameArray(4)	NameArray(5)
Ann Adams	Ingrid Islander	Calvin Coolidge	David Duncan		Last name

Figure 12-5: The final contents of the NameArray.

Dynamic arrays may be nice, but they can still hold only one type of data, such as numbers or strings. To avoid this limitation, REALbasic offers a *collection.* Essentially, a collection acts like an array that can hold any type of data. So one part of the collection may hold a number, another part of the collection may hold a string, and so on. Think of a collection as a super-flexible version of an array.

Using dynamic arrays in C++

In C++, you normally create a static array by identifying the data type, the array name, and its size. Here's what it looks like:

```
dataType ArrayName[Number];
```

You cannot resize a static array. If you want to create a dynamic array, you have to define it as follows:

```
dataType *ArrayName;
```

After you define a dynamic array by name and data type, you can then create the actual size of the array like this:

```
ArrayName = new dataType[Number];
```

To see how C++ creates dynamic arrays, check out the following program:

```
#include <iostream.h>
#include <stdio.h>
using namespace std;
int main()
{
   string *namearray;                                           →5
   namearray = new string[3];
   namearray[0] = "Ann Adams";
   namearray[1] = "Bo Barker";
   namearray[2] = "Calvin Coolidge";
   for (int i = 0; i <=2; i = i + 1)                           →10
     {
     cout << "NameArray[" << i << "] = " << namearray[i]
           << "\n";
     }
   namearray = new string[5];                                  →15
   namearray[4] = "Last name";
   for (int i = 0; i <=4; i = i + 1)                           →17
     {
     cout << "NameArray[" << i << "] = " << namearray[i]
           << "\n";
     }
   delete[] namearray;
   cout << "\nPress ENTER to continue..." << endl;
   getchar();
```

```
  return 0;
}
```

This C++ program is stored in the C++ Sample Programs folder as `Chapter 12 - Dynamic Array.cpp`.

This C++ program does the following:

→**5** Defines a dynamic array (`string *namearray;`) and then resizes it to hold three items (`namearray = new string[3]`).

→**10** The first `for` loop prints the following:

```
NameArray[0] = Ann Adams
NameArray[1] = Bo Barker
NameArray[2] = Calvin Coolidge
```

→**15** Resizes the array called `namearray` again to hold five strings (`namearray = new string[5]`).

When C++ resizes a dynamic array, it wipes out any data currently stored in that dynamic array.

→**17** The second `for` loop prints the following:

```
NameArray[0] =
NameArray[1] =
NameArray[2] =
NameArray[3] =
NameArray[4] = Last name
```

In C++, when you're done using the dynamic array, your program should use the `delete` command to free up memory used by the dynamic array, like this:

```
delete[] namearray;
```

Using dynamic arrays in Revolution

In Revolution, all arrays are dynamic arrays that you can resize by adding or removing data at any time. The following example shows how you can increase the size of an array just by adding new data to it:

```
put "Ann Adams" into NameArray[0]                    →1
put "Bo Becker" into NameArray[1]
put "Calvin Coolidge" into NameArray[2]              →3
repeat with i = 0 to 2                               →4
  put NameArray[i] into message
  wait for 3 seconds
end repeat                                           →7
put "Last name" into NameArray[4]                    →8
repeat with i = 0 to 4                               →9
```

```
   put NameArray[i] into message
   wait for 3 seconds
 end repeat                                                    →12
```

This Revolution program is stored in the Revolution Sample Programs folder as `Chapter 12 - Dynamic Array.rev.`

- →**1-3** Stores three names in the `NameArray`.
- →**4-7** Uses a `repeat` loop to yank out each name from `NameArray`, display it briefly in a message box, wait for three seconds, and then display another name from `NameArray` until all three names have appeared in the message box.
- →**8** Stores the string `"Last name"` in `NameArray`, which automatically resizes the array at the same time.
- →**9-12** Uses another `repeat` loop to yank out each name from `NameArray`, display it in a message box, wait three seconds, and then yank and display the next name from `NameArray`.

Creating a Multi-Dimensional Array

An ordinary array acts like a list. For greater flexibility (and complexity), you can also create multi-dimensional arrays. A two-dimensional array acts like a grid, as shown in Figure 12-6.

TwoD (1,2) as String

TwoD (0,0)	TwoD (1,0)
TwoD (0,1)	TwoD (1,1)
TwoD (0,2)	TwoD (1,2)

Figure 12-6: A two-dimensional array acts like a grid.

It's possible to create three-, four-, and even nine-dimensional arrays in some programming languages, but the more dimensions you create, the more confusing your array can become. For that reason, most programmers usually stick with one- or two-dimensional arrays.

Using two-dimensional arrays in Liberty BASIC

To create a two-dimensional array in Liberty BASIC, you just have to specify the array name and the two different sizes of the array, as shown here:

```
DIM ArrayName(X, Y)
```

ArrayName is any descriptive name for your array, and *X* and *Y* represent two integers that define the sizes of the two dimensions of the array. To see how Liberty BASIC can store data in a two-dimensional array, look at the following program:

```
DIM NameArray$(2,1)                                   →1
NameArray$(0,0) = "Ann Adams"                         →2
NameArray$(0,1) = "Bo Becker"
NameArray$(1,0) = "Calvin Coolidge"
NameArray$(1,1) = "David Duncan"
NameArray$(2,0) = "Ellen Eigel"
NameArray$(2,1) = "Frank Farley"                      →7
FOR I = 0 TO 2                                        →8
  FOR J = 0 TO 1
    PRINT "NameArray(" + Str$(I) + "," + Str$(J);
    PRINT ") = " + NameArray$(I, J)
  NEXT J
NEXT I                                                →13
END
```

This Liberty BASIC program is stored in the Liberty BASIC Sample Programs folder as `Chapter 12 - 2D Array.bas`.

- **→1** Creates a 3 x 2 two-dimensional array called `NameArray$`, which can hold strings.
- **→2-7** Stores six names in the two-dimensional `NameArray$`.
- **→8-13** Uses a nested loop to retrieve and print out each name from `NameArray$`, including its position in the array.

If you run this Liberty BASIC program, you see the following on-screen:

```
NameArray(0,0) = Ann Adams
NameArray(0,1) = Bo Becker
NameArray(1,0) = Calvin Coolidge
NameArray(1,1) = David Duncan
NameArray(2,0) = Ellen Eigel
NameArray(2,1) = Frank Farley
```

Using two-dimensional arrays in REALbasic

To create a two-dimensional array in REALbasic, you have to specify the array name, the two different sizes of the array, and the type of data to store in the array. Here's the basic structure:

```
Dim ArrayName(X,Y) As DataType
```

To see how REALbasic works with two-dimensional arrays, look over the following:

```
Dim NameString as string                                          →1
Dim NameArray(2,1) as string                                      →2
Dim I, J as integer                                               →3
NameArray(0,0) = "Ann Adams"                                      →4
NameArray(0,1) = "Bo Becker"
NameArray(1,0) = "Calvin Coolidge"
NameArray(1,1) = "David Duncan"
NameArray(2,0) = "Ellen Eigel"
NameArray(2,1) = "Frank Farley"                                   →9
For I = 0 to 2                                                    →10
  For J = 0 to 1
    NameString = "NameArray(" + Str(I) + "," + Str(J)
    NameString = NameString +  ") = " + NameArray(I, J)
    MsgBox NameString
  Next
Next                                                              →16
```

This REALbasic program is stored in the REALbasic Sample Programs folder as `Chapter 12 - 2D Array.rb`.

- **→1** Creates a string variable called `NameString`.
- **→2** Creates 3 x 2 two-dimensional array called `NameArray`, which can hold strings.
- **→3** Creates two integer variables called `I` and `J`.
- **→4-9** Stores six names into the `NameArray`.
- **→10-16** Uses two `FOR-NEXT` loops to retrieve a name from `NameArray` and display it in a message box, such as `"NameArray(2,1) = Frank Farley"`.

Using two-dimensional arrays in C++

To create a two-dimensional array in C++, you have to specify the data type of the array, the array name, and the two different sizes of the array in separate square brackets:

```
dataType ArrayName[X][Y]
```

To see how C++ works with two-dimensional arrays, look closely at the following program:

```
#include <iostream.h>
#include <stdio.h>
using namespace std;
int main()
{
   string namearray[3][2];                                  →1

   namearray[0][0] = "Ann Adams";                           →2
   namearray[0][1] = "Bo Barker";
   namearray[1][0] = "Calvin Coolidge";
   namearray[1][1] = "David Duncan";
   namearray[2][0] = "Ellen Eigel";
   namearray[2][1] = "Frank Farley";                        →7


   for (int i = 0; i <=2; i = i + 1)                        →8
     {
     for (int j = 0; j <=1; j = j + 1)
       {
       cout << "NameArray[" << i << "]" << "[" << j;
       cout << "] = " << namearray[i][j] << "\n";
       }
     }                                                      →15
   cout << "\nPress ENTER to continue..." << endl;
   getchar();
   return 0;
}
```

This C++ program is stored in the C++ Sample Programs folder as `Chapter 12 - 2D Array.cpp`.

- **→1** Creates a 3 x 2 two-dimensional array called `namearray`, which can hold strings.
- **→2-7** Stores six names in `namearray`.
- **→8-15** Uses two `for` loops to retrieve a name from `namearray` and display it in on screen in a string, such as `"NameArray[2][1] = Frank Farley"`.

Using two-dimensional arrays in Revolution

To create a two-dimensional array in Revolution, you just need to store data in an array name and specify the two dimensions, as the following program shows:

```
put "Ann Adams" into NameArray[0,0]                              →1
put "Bo Becker" into NameArray[0,1]
put "Calvin Coolidge" into NameArray[1,0]
put "David Duncan" into NameArray[1,1]
put "Ellen Eigel" into NameArray[2,0]
put "Frank Farley" into NameArray[2,1]                           →6
repeat with i = 0 to 2                                           →7
  repeat with j = 0 to 1
    put "NameArray[" & i & "," & j & "] = " &
          NameArray[i,j] into message
    wait for 3 seconds
  end repeat
end repeat                                                       →12
```

This Revolution program is stored in the Revolution Sample Programs folder as `Chapter 12 - 2D Array.rev`.

- **→1-6** Stores six names into a two-dimensional array called `NameArray`.
- **→7-12** Uses two `repeat` loops to yank a name out of `NameArray`, display it in a message box, wait three seconds, and then retrieve and display the next name in `NameArray`. The string in the message box looks like `"NameArray[2.1] = Frank Farley"`.

Chapter 13

Playing with Object-Oriented Programming

In This Chapter

- Isolating data with encapsulation
- Reusing code with inheritance
- Rewriting code with polymorphism

Object-oriented programming is the latest hope (or, to use correct programming lingo, the latest *methodology*) for pursuing the following Holy Trinity of software perfection:

- Simple and fast to create
- Easy to understand and modify
- Reliable and error-free

Creating a large program takes time. Often a large, complicated program can take so long to complete that by the time it's done it's already obsolete. The programmers have to start all over again, having wasted their time and money creating something that no one can use. (The FBI once spent $170 million dollars on a program called Virtual Case File to help fight terrorism. Because it never worked, the bureau decided to scrap the whole thing and buy commercially available software to help do the same thing for a fraction of the cost.)

Rather than create a new program from scratch, it's almost always easier to modify an existing program that already works. This is one reason why so many programmers are excited about open-source programs, which allow anyone to peek at and modify the source code to a program. By sharing open-source software, programmers can learn new tricks from existing programs that work, and they build on the successes of others.

Even if a program works, you still have no guarantee that it's reliable. *Reliability* means that the software works without crashing, freezing up, or acting erratically. Software reliability is especially critical with real-time systems, such as airplane navigation systems, computers that host corporate Web sites, and financial trading programs, where losing a single number can mean the loss of billions of dollars. Software reliability is so important because human lives and (more important, from a corporate point of view) millions of dollars depend on computers working.

Object-oriented programming attempts to solve these problems through three techniques known as

- Encapsulation
- Inheritance
- Polymorphism

Neither Liberty BASIC nor Revolution offer the true features of an object-oriented language. To use object-oriented programming, you have to use REALbasic or C++.

Encapsulation: Isolating Data

The reason for breaking a large program into smaller subprograms is to create independent building blocks. Unfortunately, although subprograms isolate groups of instructions together, they don't always isolate data.

The problem occurs when the instructions stored in one subprogram can still manipulate data used by another subprogram, as shown in Figure 13-1.

To solve this problem (and solving problems is something that programmers continually strive to do), programmers developed the idea of dividing and isolating large programs into *objects*.

An object isolates the following two items from the rest of a program:

- Data (also known as *properties*)
- Instructions (also known as *methods*) for manipulating that data

In a traditionally designed program, you often store data in one location and the instructions that manipulate that data in another location. Each subprogram can access the data it needs but can also access data used by another subprogram.

In comparison, an object-oriented program (depicted as ovals in Figure 13-2) lumps data and the instructions that manipulate that data in a single location (known by its official programming term as *encapsulation*). Encapsulation simply keeps one part of a program from messing with data that another part of the program uses.

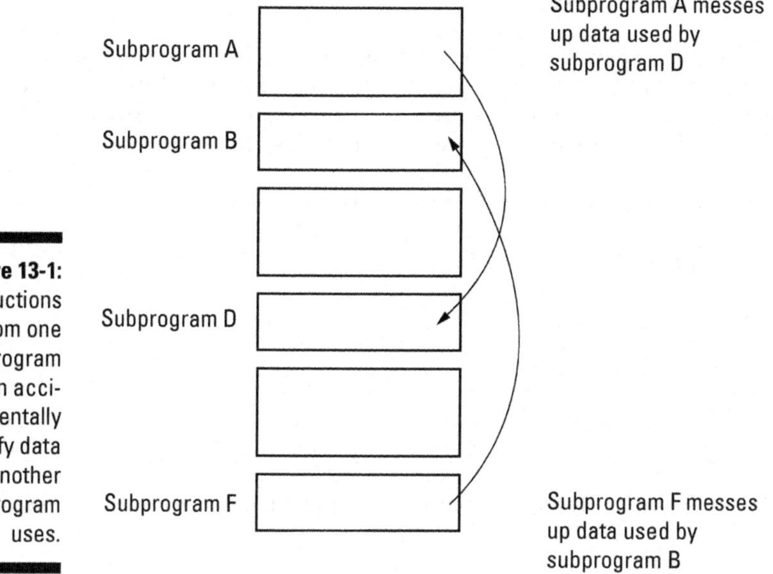

Figure 13-1: Instructions from one subprogram can accidentally modify data that another subprogram uses.

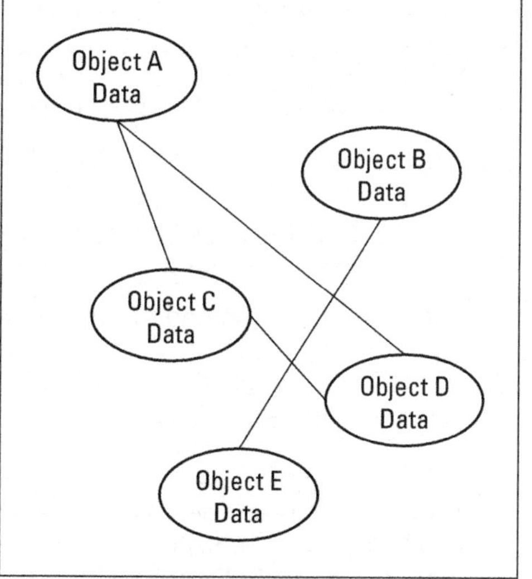

Figure 13-2: In object-oriented programs, objects isolate data and instructions from other objects.

Creating a class

The first step to creating an object is to define a *class*. A class defines the data stored in an object along with any instructions that manipulate that data. A class acts like a blueprint that defines an object. After you create a class, you can create one or more objects based on that class to use in your program.

The following example shows how to create a class in C++:

```
class monster                              →1
{                                          →2
public:                                    →3
 int x_coordinate;                         →4
 int y_coordinate;                         →5
 void moveme(int, int);                    →6
 void initialize(int, int);                →7
};                                         →8
```

This simple C++ code tells the computer to perform the following tasks:

- →1 Creates a new class called `monster`.
- →2 Defines the start of the class definition.
- →3 The `public` command defines the properties (data) and methods (subprograms) as accessible to any part of the program.
- →4 Creates the integer variable `x_coordinate`.
- →5 Creates the integer variable `y_coordinate`.
- →6 Tells the computer that the object contains a subprogram (or method), `moveme`, which accepts two integer values.
- →7 Tells the computer that the object contains a subprogram, `initialize`, which accepts two integer values.
- →8 Defines the end of the class definition.

A *class* isn't an object. To create an object, you must define a variable that represents your defined class.

When you create a class in C++, you have to type every line of code. In REALbasic, you just have to define the properties (data) and methods (subprograms), and REALbasic types and organizes the details of your class in a window, as shown in Figure 13-3.

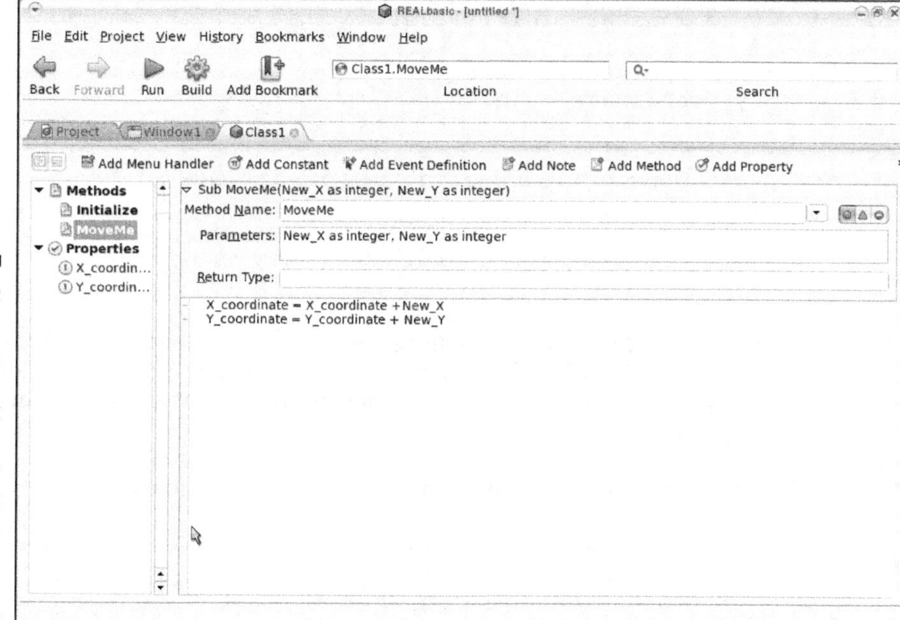

Figure 13-3: REALbasic organizes a class in a window that lets you selectively view its properties and methods.

Writing an object's methods

After you declare the subprograms (or methods) that you want to store in a class, you still need to write the actual instructions that make that subprogram work. Suppose you want to use the class definition defined in the preceding section in the following example:

```
class monster
{
public:
 int x_coordinate;
 int y_coordinate;
 void moveme(int, int);
 void initialize(int, int);
};
```

This class defines two subprograms (or methods): `moveme` and `initialize`. To make these methods actually do something, you must write the complete methods directly below the class definition, as the following C++ code demonstrates:

```
void monster::initialize(int init_x, int init_y)
{
 x_coordinate = init_x;
 y_coordinate = init_y;
}

void monster::moveme(int new_x, int new_y)
{
 x_coordinate = x_coordinate + new_x;
 y_coordinate = y_coordinate + new_y;
}
```

The `initialize` method defines the X coordinate and Y coordinate of any object that you derive from the `monster` class. The `moveme` method moves an object's position a certain distance in the X (right and left) direction and Y (up and down) direction.

In REALbasic, the equivalent methods appear as follows:

```
Sub Initialize(Init_X as Integer, Init_Y as Integer)
  X_coordinate = Init_X
  Y_coordinate = Init_Y
End Sub

Sub MoveMe(New_X as Integer, New_Y as Integer)
  X_coordinate = X_coordinate + New_X
  Y_coordinate = Y_coordinate + New_Y
End Sub
```

Creating an object from a class

After you define a class and write any methods that you declare within that class, you still need to define a variable to represent that class. This variable represents the actual object in object-oriented programming.

In C++, you just have to define the class name and variable, as shown here:

```
className objectName;
```

If you want to create an object named `zombie` based on the `monster` class, use the following:

```
monster zombie;
```

To create an object, you declare a variable to represent that object. The C++ program in Listing 13-1 defines an object named `zombie` to represent the `monster` class definition.

Listing 13-1: A C++ Program That Demonstrates How to Create an Object

```
#include <iostream.h>

class monster
{
public:
 int x_coordinate;
 int y_coordinate;
 void moveme(int, int);
 void initialize(int, int);
};

void monster::initialize(int init_x, int init_y)
{
 x_coordinate = init_x;
 y_coordinate = init_y;
}

void monster::moveme(int new_x, int new_y)
{
 x_coordinate = x_coordinate + new_x;
 y_coordinate = y_coordinate + new_y;
}

int main()                                              →24
{                                                       →25
 monster zombie;                                        →26
 zombie.initialize(12, 15);                             →27
 cout << "The X-location of the zombie is " <<
         zombie.x_coordinate << "\n";                   →28
 cout << "The Y-location of the zombie is " <<
         zombie.y_coordinate << "\n";                   →29
 zombie.moveme (34, 9);                                 →30
 cout << "The new X-location of the zombie is " <<
         zombie.x_coordinate << "\n";                   →31
 cout << "The new Y-location of the zombie is " <<
         zombie.y_coordinate << "\n";                   →32
cout << "\nPress ENTER to continue..." << endl;
getchar();
return 0;                                               →33
}                                                       →34
```

This C++ program is stored in the C++ Sample Programs folder as `Chapter 13 - Objects.cpp`.

The main C++ program starts with the `int main()` line. This portion, line by line, makes the computer do the following:

- **→24** Starts the C++ program.
- **→25** Defines the start of all instructions inside the main C++ program.

- →26 Creates the object `zombie` and bases it on the class definition `monster`.
- →27 Runs the method `initialize` (stored in the `monster` class), which defines the X coordinate (12) and Y coordinate (15) of the `zombie` object.
- →28 Prints the message `The X-location of the zombie is 12.`
- →29 Prints the message `The Y-location of the zombie is 15.`
- →30 Runs the `moveme` method, which moves the `zombie` object 34 units of measurement in the X direction and 9 units in the Y direction.
- →31 Prints the message `The new X-location of the zombie is 46.` (That's 12, the original `X-location` of the zombie as line 24 defines, plus 34 as line 30 defines, which equals 46.)
- →32 Prints the message `The new Y-location of the zombie is 24.` (That's 15, the original `Y-location` of the zombie as line 27 defines, plus 9 as line 30 defines, which equals 24.)
- →33 Prints the message `Press ENTER to continue.`
- →34 Runs the `getchar()` command to wait for the user to press the Enter key.
- →35 Returns the value of `0` when the program finishes running. (You can safely ignore the purpose of this line because the program doesn't use this value of `0` for anything.)
- →36 The right curly bracket defines the end of the main C++ program.

The two main points to remember about creating an object are

- You must define a class first.
- A class contains data and instructions (methods) for manipulating the object's data.

To create an object from a class in REALbasic, you need to accomplish two steps. For the first step, you must define an object name as a class, like this:

```
Dim objectName As className
```

For the second step, you must use the `new` command to create a new object, as shown here:

```
objectName = new className
```

So if you want to create a `Zombie` object based on the `Monster` class file, use the following lines:

```
Dim Zombie As Monster
Zombie = new Monster
```

Hiding and exposing data in an object

In the `Zombie` class example in this chapter, both the data and methods are declared public, which means that any part of the program can access that object's data and run that object's methods. Objects can also classify their data and instructions as *private* or *protected*.

If an object defines data and instructions as private, only that particular object can use that data and instructions. No other object can ever use private data and instructions. (That's why you call them private.)

On the other hand, other objects can use public data and instructions. Objects use public data and instructions to communicate and share data with other objects.

Protected data and instructions work the same as private data and instructions, with one important exception: If you use inheritance to copy an existing object and create a new object, the new object inherits only public and protected data and instructions. Any private data and instructions remain with the old object.

The equivalent REALbasic program looks like this:

```
Sub Action()
  Dim Zombie as Monster
  Zombie = new Monster
  Zombie.Initialize(12,15)
  MsgBox "The X-location of the zombie is " +
         Str(Zombie.X_coordinate)
  MsgBox "The Y-location of the zombie is " +
         Str(Zombie.Y_coordinate)
  Zombie.MoveMe(34,9)
  MsgBox "The new X-location of the zombie is " +
         Str(Zombie.X_coordinate)
  MsgBox "The new Y-location of the zombie is " +
         Str(Zombie.Y_coordinate)
End Sub
```

This REALbasic program creates an object called `Zombie`, which is based on the `Monster` class. Then it uses the `Initialize` method to store the values of `12` and `15` into the `Zombie` object's `X_coordinate` and `Y_coordinate` properties.

The `MoveMe` method changes the values of the `Zombie` object's `X_cooordinate` and `Y_coordinate` properties.

This REALbasic program is stored in the REALbasic Sample Programs folder as `Chapter 13 - Objects.rb`.

Inheritance: Reusing Code

Inheritance allows you to reuse code from an existing object without physically copying that code.

In the old days of programming, you could divide a large program into several subprograms. After studying one of your subprograms, you may realize that, with a little modification, you can adapt it to work in a second program. Unfortunately, any time that you modify a program, you take the risk of messing it up so that it doesn't work at all.

To help you modify an existing subprogram without wrecking it by mistake, objects use inheritance. Inheritance enables you to copy an existing object and then add new code to this new copy without ever modifying any of the existing code inside. Thus the new copy of your object inherits all the old data and code while still enabling you to tack on new code to modify the object for a slightly different purpose.

Inheritance not only protects you from ruining a perfectly good chunk of code by mistake, but also helps you create programs faster. Copying and modifying an existing object is easier than creating a brand-new object from scratch.

To create a new class in C++ that inherits all the data and methods of an existing class, you need to define a new class followed by a colon and the name of the existing class that you want to inherit data and methods from. Take a look at the structure:

```
class className : public existingClassName
  {
  // Additional properties declared here
  // Additional methods declared here
  };
```

So if you want to create a new class that inherits the `monster` class, add the bold code to the previous C++ program in Listing 13-1, as shown in Listing 13-2.

Listing 13-2: Inheriting a Class by Using C++

```
#include <iostream.h>

class monster
{
public:
 int x_coordinate;
 int y_coordinate;
```

```
 void moveme(int, int);
 void initialize(int, int);
};

void monster::initialize(int init_x, int init_y)
{
 x_coordinate = init_x;
 y_coordinate = init_y;
}

void monster::moveme(int new_x, int new_y)
{
 x_coordinate = x_coordinate + new_x;
 y_coordinate = y_coordinate + new_y;
}

class person : public monster
{
public:
 int ammo;
 void shoot(int);
};

void person::shoot(int bullets)
{
 ammo = ammo - bullets;
}

int main()
{
 monster zombie;
 zombie.initialize (12, 15);
 cout << "The X-location of the zombie is " <<
          zombie.x_coordinate << "\n";
 cout << "The Y-location of the zombie is " <<
          zombie.y_coordinate << "\n";
 zombie.moveme (34, 9);
 cout << "The new X-location of the zombie is " <<
          zombie.x_coordinate << "\n";
 cout << "The new Y-location of the zombie is " <<
          zombie.y_coordinate << "\n";

 person hero;
 hero.initialize (97,52);
 hero.ammo = 5;
 hero.moveme (49,71);
 cout << "The new X-location of the hero is " <<
          hero.x_coordinate << "\n";
 cout << "The new Y-location of the hero is " <<
          hero.y_coordinate << "\n";
```

(continued)

Listing 13-2 *(continued)*

```
  cout << "The number of bullets initially is " <<
           hero.ammo << "\n";
  hero.shoot(3);
  cout << "The number of bullets left is " << hero.ammo <<
           "\n";
  cout << "\nPress ENTER to continue..." << endl;
  getchar();
  return 0;
}
```

This C++ program is stored in the C++ Sample Programs folder as `Chapter 13 - Inheritance.cpp`.

The `person` class inherits from the `monster` class. From the computer's point of view, the `person` class looks like the following code. The bold code identifies the properties and methods inherited from the `monster` class:

```
class person
{
public:
  int x_coordinate;
  int y_coordinate;
  void moveme(int, int);
  void initialize(int, int);
  int ammo;
  void shoot(int);
};
```

Rather than type the bold code, inheritance lets you type just the following equivalent class definition, which is much shorter:

```
class person : public monster
{
public:
  int ammo;
  void shoot(int);
};
```

The `: public monster` portion of the first line tells the computer to inherit all the public properties and methods from the `monster` class and use them in the `person` class.

When you create a class in REALbasic, you can specify another class to inherit through the Super list box, as shown in Figure 13-4.

After you create a `Person` class that inherits from the `Monster` class, you can add a `Shoot` method, like so:

```
Sub Shoot(Bullets as Integer)
  Ammo = Ammo - Bullets
End Sub
```

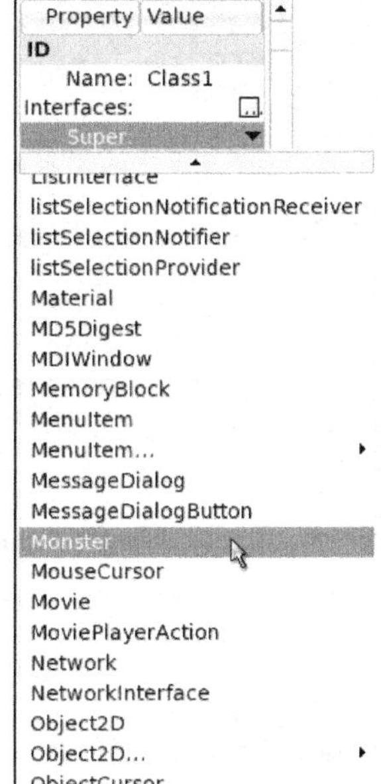

Figure 13-4: The Super list box lets you define the name of another class to inherit.

The complete REALbasic program looks like Listing 13-3.

Listing 13-3: Using an Inherited Class in REALbasic

```
Sub Action()
  Dim Zombie as Monster
  Zombie = new Monster
  Zombie.Initialize(12,15)
  MsgBox "The X-location of the zombie is " +
         Str(Zombie.X_coordinate)
  MsgBox "The Y-location of the zombie is " +
         Str(Zombie.Y_coordinate)
  Zombie.MoveMe(34,9)
  MsgBox "The new X-location of the zombie is " +
         Str(Zombie.X_coordinate)
  MsgBox "The new Y-location of the zombie is " +
         Str(Zombie.Y_coordinate)

  Dim Hero as Person
  Hero = new Person
  Hero.Initialize (97,52)
  Hero.Ammo = 5
  Hero.MoveMe (49, 71)
  MsgBox "The new X-location of the hero is " +
         Str(Hero.X_coordinate)
```

(continued)

Listing 13-3 *(continued)*

```
  MsgBox "The new Y-location of the hero is " +
         Str(Hero.Y_coordinate)
  MsgBox "The number of bullets initially is " +
         Str(Hero.Ammo)
  Hero.Shoot(3)
  MsgBox "The number of bullets left is " + Str(Hero.Ammo)
End Sub
```

The preceding REALbasic program is equivalent to the C++ code shown in Listing 13-2. The important point the REALbasic code demonstrates is that the Hero object (which inherits properties and methods from the Person class) includes a new Ammo property and a Shoot method.

This REALbasic program is stored in the REALbasic Sample Programs folder as Chapter 13 - Inheritance.rb.

Polymorphism: Rewriting Code

The whole idea behind polymorphism is to allow you to rewrite code in one object without physically changing the code stored in another object.

In the previous inheritance program example, the Monster class defines an Initialize method, which is also inherited and used by the Person class. For the Monster class, the Initialize method just accepts an X and Y value for the Monster position.

However, for the Person class, you can rewrite the Initialize method to accept an X and Y value for the Person class as well as accept an initial value for the Ammo property. In this case, the Initialize method remains the same between the Monster and Person class, but the code within each Initialize method can be different.

To allow polymorphism, you must use the virtual command in front of any method that you want to allow other objects to inherit and modify. So to allow polymorphism on the Initialize method, the original Monster class could look like the following code with the added virtual command:

```
class monster
{
public:
 int x_coordinate;
 int y_coordinate;
 void moveme(int, int);
 virtual void initialize(int, int);
};
```

When you create a new class that inherits the `Initialize` method, you must use the `virtual` command once more to define the `Initialize` method, as shown here:

```
class person : public monster
{
public:
 int ammo;
 void shoot(int);
 virtual void initialize(int, int, int);
};
```

The entire C++ program now looks like Listing 13-4.

Listing 13-4: Using Polymorphism in C++

```
#include <iostream.h>

class monster
{
public:
 int x_coordinate;
 int y_coordinate;
 void moveme(int, int);
 virtual void initialize(int, int);
};

void monster::initialize(int init_x, int init_y)
{
 x_coordinate = init_x;
 y_coordinate = init_y;
}

void monster::moveme(int new_x, int new_y)
{
 x_coordinate = x_coordinate + new_x;
 y_coordinate = y_coordinate + new_y;
}

class person : public monster
{
public:
 int ammo;
 void shoot(int);
 virtual void initialize(int, int, int);
};

void person::shoot(int bullets)
{
 ammo = ammo - bullets;
```

(continued)

Listing 13-4 *(continued)*

```
}

void person::initialize (int init_x, int init_y, int
          bulletsupply)
{
 x_coordinate = init_x;
 y_coordinate = init_y;
 ammo = bulletsupply;
}

int main()
{
 monster zombie;
 zombie.initialize (12, 15);
 cout << "The X-location of the zombie is " <<
          zombie.x_coordinate << "\n";
 cout << "The Y-location of the zombie is " <<
          zombie.y_coordinate << "\n";
 zombie.moveme (34, 9);
 cout << "The new X-location of the zombie is " <<
          zombie.x_coordinate << "\n";
 cout << "The new Y-location of the zombie is " <<
          zombie.y_coordinate << "\n";

 person hero;
 hero.initialize (97,52,5);
 // hero.ammo = 5;
 hero.moveme (49,71);
 cout << "The new X-location of the hero is " <<
          hero.x_coordinate << "\n";
 cout << "The new Y-location of the hero is " <<
          hero.y_coordinate << "\n";
 cout << "The number of bullets initially is " <<
          hero.ammo << "\n";
 hero.shoot(3);
 cout << "The number of bullets left is " << hero.ammo <<
          "\n";
 cout << "\nPress ENTER to continue..." << endl;
 getchar();
 return 0;
}
```

This C++ program is stored in the C++ Sample Programs folder as `Chapter 13 - Polymophism.cpp`.

Notice that the `zombie.initialize` command accepts only two integers (12 and 15) whereas the `hero.initialize` command accepts three integers (97, 52, and 5). The third integer is used to set an initial value to the `ammo` property of the `person` class.

Choosing an object-oriented language

Not all object-oriented programming languages are alike. The two types of object-oriented programming languages are

- Hybrid object-oriented languages
- True (or pure) object-oriented languages

A *hybrid object-oriented language* simply takes an existing language and slaps object-oriented features on top of it. Some of the more popular hybrid languages are Delphi (based on Pascal), REALbasic (based on BASIC), and C++ (based on C).

The main advantage of using a hybrid language is that if you already know how to use a language such as Pascal, BASIC, or C, you can quickly learn to use the object-oriented features of these languages with a minimum of training, anguish, and experimentation. If you're not quite sure about the benefits of object-oriented programming, you can write a small part of your program with objects and write the bulk of your program with old-fashioned programming methods.

The main disadvantage of hybrid languages is that they enable programmers to mix traditional and object-oriented programming techniques, which can become an untidy mess. Hybrid languages enable programmers to use none, some, or all object-oriented programming techniques. As a result, using hybrid languages often creates programs that don't take full advantage of objects, destroying the advantage of using objects and making the program harder to read and understand.

That's why many people prefer pure object-oriented languages that force you to use objects right from the start. Some popular pure object-oriented languages are

- SmallTalk
- C#
- Java

Whether you decide to stick to a conventional language (and use its object-oriented hybrid) or jump straight into a pure object-oriented language, get used to the idea behind breaking your program into objects. Object-oriented programming techniques alone don't make software easier to write or more reliable, but they can make you more aware of the problems in writing software and how object-oriented programming can solve those problems.

In the long run, nobody really cares what language you use, whether you use any object-oriented programming techniques, or whether you write software while sitting in your underwear and listening to Barry Manilow albums at 3 a.m. The important point is to write software that works and to finish it in a timely manner. If you can do that, you can focus on producing results and leave trivial details (such as wearing a tie, dealing with corporate politics, and fighting others for a cubicle near a window) for your coworkers to worry about.

By defining a method as polymorphic with the `virtual` command, one class can rewrite the code for a method without physically changing the original code. Both `Initialize` methods exist in separate objects.

In REALbasic, every method can be polymorphic. All you have to do is create a new method, with the same name, in another class file. The `Person` class includes a new `Initialize` method that looks like this:

```
Sub Initialize(Init_X as Integer, Init_Y as Integer,
          BulletSupply as Integer)
  X_coordinate = Init_X
  Y_coordinate = Init_Y
  Ammo = BulletSupply
End Sub
```

The equivalent REALbasic program now looks like Listing 13-5.

Listing 13-5: Using Polymorphism in REALbasic

```
Sub Action ()
  Dim Zombie as Monster
  Zombie = new Monster
  Zombie.Initialize(12,15)
  MsgBox "The X-location of the zombie is " +
          Str(Zombie.X_coordinate)
  MsgBox "The Y-location of the zombie is " +
          Str(Zombie.Y_coordinate)
  Zombie.MoveMe(34,9)
  MsgBox "The new X-location of the zombie is " +
          Str(Zombie.X_coordinate)
  MsgBox "The new Y-location of the zombie is " +
          Str(Zombie.Y_coordinate)

  Dim Hero as Person
  Hero = new Person
  Hero.Initialize (97,52,5)
  Hero.MoveMe (49, 71)
  MsgBox "The new X-location of the hero is " +
          Str(Hero.X_coordinate)
  MsgBox "The new Y-location of the hero is " +
          Str(Hero.Y_coordinate)
  MsgBox "The number of bullets initially is " +
          Str(Hero.Ammo)
  Hero.Shoot(3)
  MsgBox "The number of bullets left is " + Str(Hero.Ammo)
End Sub
```

The preceding REALbasic program is equivalent to the C++ code in Listing 13-4. The important feature of the REALbasic code is that it demonstrates how two objects can have the same method name (`Initialize`) but each `Initialize` method works differently.

In the REALbasic example, the `Zombie.Initialize` method accepts two numbers, but the `Hero.Initialize` method accepts three numbers.

This REALbasic program is stored in the REALbasic Sample Programs folder as `Chapter 13 - Polymophism.rb`.

Part III

Advanced Programming Topics

In this part . . .

Programming is more than just writing code in your favorite programming language. After you finish writing a program, you need to make sure it works properly, a process known as debugging.

Language compilers provide various ways to test and debug your program, from exhaustively stepping through your entire program, line-by-line, to watching when a particular variable suddenly stores the wrong data.

Debugging a program can ensure that it works. After you get a program working, you may want to go one step further and optimize your program to make it run faster or take up less memory or hard drive space. Optimization is like tuning up your program: It's not necessary (which explains why so many programs gobble up memory and run slowly), but it can turn a slow, working program into a fast and responsive working program.

Finally, this part of the book covers designing a user interface. Every program needs a way to respond and display information, so the easier your user interface is for users to understand, the easier your program will be to use. A great program with a lousy user interface is no different than a lousy program.

By making sure your programs work, run as quickly as possible, and are as easy to use as possible, you can create programs that people will actually find useful, which is a task that often eludes even companies like IBM, Microsoft, and Apple Computers.

Chapter 14

Sorting and Searching Algorithms

In This Chapter

- Sorting data in many ways
- Performing a sequential search
- Performing a binary search
- Picking a sorting and searching algorithm

Programs typically accept data from the outside world (such as someone typing on the keyboard), manipulate that data somehow, and spit it back out in a format that someone finds useful.

Somewhere between accepting data and spitting it back out, the program must store the data in its memory by using a variable or a data structure like an array (see Chapter 12 for more information about arrays). Before the program can spit out its useful result, it may need to sort and search the data first.

A database is fairly useless if it won't let you find a specific name or sort through the names and addresses that you've stored. You may want to rearrange your data alphabetically by last name, numerically by telephone area code, or by some other criterion, such as by those people who are single and earn $75,000 or more every year. To do this, your program needs to know how to sort data.

Although sorting may seem like a fairly mundane topic, it can actually get rather complex. That's because whenever a program sorts data, it needs to sort the information as quickly as possible. After all, a program that sorts names and addresses is useless if it takes three hours just to sort 15 names.

Part of computer science centers on studying and developing the most efficient sorting and searching methods (known as *algorithms*). Because many types of programs need to sort and search data, nearly every programmer needs to know the different sorting and searching algorithms available and how they work.

Measuring efficiency with Big-O notation

To measure the efficiency of specific algorithms, computer scientists created something known as *Big-O notation.* Essentially, Big-O notation measures the speed of a particular algorithm (such as a sorting algorithm) based on the number of items it must manage.

If you have an algorithm that sorts a list of names alphabetically, for example, the speed of that algorithm depends on the number of names to search. In Big-O notation, you express this relationship as `O(N)`, where `O` stands for order of magnitude and `N` stands for the total number of items the algorithm must manage.

The way that programmers determine the Big-O notation of a particular algorithm depends on that algorithm's speed of execution and the number of items it must handle. For example, if an algorithm's speed of execution and number of items (`N`) it can handle is expressed as `N2 + N + 1`, the Big-O notation for this algorithm is `O(N2)`.

In calculating the Big-O notation for an algorithm, you choose the fastest-growing item (in this case, `N2`) and ignore the rest of the expression. (Naturally, if you use the wrong expression to represent your algorithm, your Big-O notation is wrong as well.)

Programmers often use Big-O notation to measure the average and worst-case scenarios as they study how an algorithm behaves while managing a typical number of items and how that same algorithm behaves while managing an extremely large number of items.

Not surprisingly, some algorithms are fast at managing relatively small numbers of items but slow down rapidly if you force them to manage a large number of items. Curiously, other algorithms are very fast and efficient in sorting items that are almost correctly sorted initially but slow if sorting items that you randomly scatter in the list.

Programmers study the average and worst-case scenarios of an algorithm by using Big-O notation to help them choose the algorithm that's best suited for their particular program.

Computer scientists have created a variety of sorting and searching algorithms — but no single, perfect algorithm exists that you should use all the time. The most efficient algorithm depends partly on the data that you want to sort and partly on the data structures that your program uses to store data.

This chapter shows code examples only for Liberty BASIC and C++, but you can also sort and search with other programs.

Insertion Sort

Imagine that you're playing cards and the dealer deals the cards to you. As soon as you get two cards, your first inclination is probably to sort those two cards in relation to one another (perhaps by suit or by number). After the dealer gives you a third card, you sort that card in relation to your previous two cards. When you sort each additional card that you receive in relation to your previously sorted cards, you're using an insertion-sort algorithm (see Figure 14-1). From the computer's point of view, the insertion-sort algorithm works as follows:

1. It compares the first two items in the list and sorts those two items.
2. It looks at the next item in the list and sorts that item in relation to the previously sorted items.
3. It repeats Step 2 for each additional item in the list until it finishes sorting the entire list.

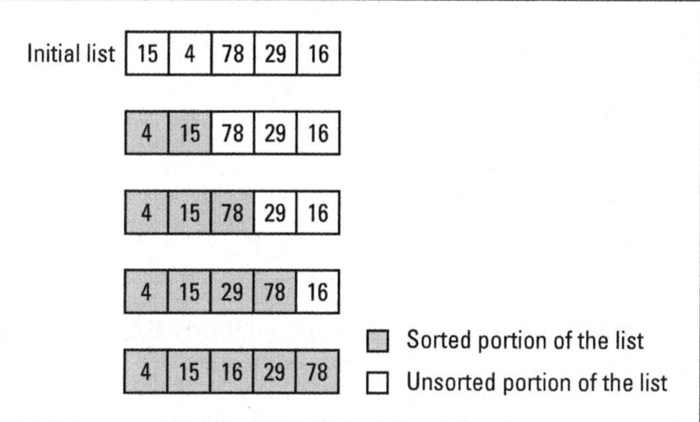

Figure 14-1: An insertion sort removes one item at a time and sorts it in relation to the previous sorted items in the list.

To see for yourself how the insertion-sort algorithm works, try the Liberty BASIC program in Listing 14-1.

Listing 14-1: An Insertion-Sort Algorithm in Liberty BASIC

```
MaxSize = 5
REDIM MyArray(MaxSize)

FOR I = 1 TO MaxSize
 MyArray(I) = INT(RND(1) * 100) + 1
 PRINT MyArray(I); SPACE$(1);
NEXT I
PRINT "(Initial array)"

FOR ArrayPos = 2 TO MaxSize
 TempValue = MyArray(ArrayPos)
 StopNow = 0
 Count = 1
```

(continued)

Listing 14-1 ***(continued)***

```
 Time2Stop = 0
 WHILE (Time2Stop = 0)
   IF TempValue < MyArray(Count) THEN
     FOR J = ArrayPos TO Count STEP -1
       MyArray(J) = MyArray(J - 1)
     NEXT J
     MyArray(Count) = TempValue
     StopNow = 1
     FOR I = 1 TO MaxSize
       PRINT MyArray(I); SPACE$(1);
     NEXT I
     PRINT
   END IF
   Count = Count + 1
   IF (StopNow = 1) OR (Count = ArrayPos) THEN
     Time2Stop = 1
   END IF
 WEND
NEXT ArrayPos

FOR I = 1 TO MaxSize
 PRINT MyArray(I); SPACE$(1);
NEXT I
PRINT "(Sorted array)"
END
```

This Liberty BASIC program is stored in the Liberty BASIC Sample Programs folder as `Chapter 14 - Insertion Sort.bas`.

A typical output for this program appears as follows:

```
57 89 77 3 21 (Initial array)
57 77 89 3 21
3 57 77 89 21
3 21 57 77 89
3 21 57 77 89 (Sorted array)
```

Listing 14-2 shows the equivalent C++ program.

Listing 14-2: An Insertion-Sort Algorithm in C++

```
#include <cstdlib>
#include <ctime>
#include <iostream>

using namespace std;

int main()
  {
  const int MAXSIZE = 5;
  int myArray[MAXSIZE+1];
```

```
  srand((unsigned)time(0));
  for(int i=1; i<MAXSIZE+1; i++)
    {
    myArray[i] = (rand()%100)+1;
    cout << myArray[i] << "  ";
    }
  cout << "(Initial array)" << "\n";

  int tempValue;
  int stopNow;
  int count;
  int time2stop;
  for(int arrayPos=2; arrayPos<=MAXSIZE; arrayPos++)
    {
    tempValue = myArray[arrayPos];
    stopNow = 0;
     count = 1;
     time2stop = 0;
     while (time2stop == 0)
       {
       if (tempValue < myArray[count])
         {
        for (int j=arrayPos; j>=count; j--)
          {
          myArray[j] = myArray[j-1];
          }
        myArray[count] = tempValue;
        stopNow = 1;
        for (int i = 1; i<= MAXSIZE; i++)
          {
          cout << myArray[i] << "  ";
          }
        cout << "\n";
        }
     count = count + 1;
     if ((stopNow == 1) || (count == arrayPos))
       {
       time2stop = 1;
       }
     }

    }
    for(int i=1; i<MAXSIZE+1; i++)
      {
      cout << myArray[i] << "  ";
      }
    cout << "(Sorted array)" << "\n";
    cout << "\nPress ENTER to continue..." << endl;
    getchar();
}
```

This C++ program is stored in the C++ Sample Programs folder as `Chapter 14 - Insertion Sort.cpp`.

Bubble Sort

The *bubble-sort algorithm* bears its name because individual items in a list appear to "bubble up" to their correct locations. The bubble-sort algorithm examines a list of items repeatedly and sorts adjacent items until it sorts the entire list, as shown in Figure 14-2. Your computer handles a bubble-sort algorithm in the following way:

1. It compares the first two items in the list and sorts those two items.
2. It moves to the next item in the list and sorts that item with the last item of the previously sorted pair.
3. It repeats Step 2 for each additional item in the list until the entire list is examined.
4. It repeats Steps 1 through 3 until the entire list is sorted.

Initial list	15	4	78	29	16
	4	15	78	29	16
	4	15	78	29	16
	4	15	29	78	16
	4	15	29	16	78
	4	15	29	16	78
	4	15	29	16	78
	4	15	16	29	78
Sorted list	4	15	16	29	78

☐ Sorts these two items

Figure 14-2: The bubble sort examines each item in a list and sorts it in relation to its neighbor.

One drawback to the bubble-sort algorithm is that it often must reexamine a list two or more times before it correctly sorts all items (refer to Figure 14-2).

To see for yourself how the bubble-sort algorithm works, look at the Liberty BASIC program in Listing 14-3.

Listing 14-3: A Bubble-Sort Algorithm in Liberty BASIC

```
MaxSize = 5
REDIM MyArray(MaxSize)
FOR I = 1 TO MaxSize
 MyArray(I) = INT(RND(1) * 100) + 1
 PRINT MyArray(I); SPACE$(1);
```

```
NEXT I
PRINT "(Initial array)"

Pass = 1
Time2Stop = 0
WHILE (Time2Stop = 0)
  NoSwaps = 1
  FOR I = 1 TO (MaxSize - Pass)
    IF MyArray(I) > MyArray(I + 1) THEN
      TempValue = MyArray(I)
      MyArray(I) = MyArray(I + 1)
      MyArray(I + 1) = TempValue
      NoSwaps = 0
      FOR J = 1 TO MaxSize
        PRINT MyArray(J); SPACE$(1);
      NEXT J
      PRINT
    END IF
  NEXT I
  IF NoSwaps = 1 THEN
    Time2Stop = 1
  END IF
WEND

FOR I = 1 TO MaxSize
 PRINT MyArray(I); SPACE$(1);
NEXT I
PRINT "(Sorted array)"
END
```

This Liberty BASIC program is stored in the Liberty BASIC Sample Programs folder as `Chapter 14 - Bubble Sort.bas`.

A typical output for this program looks like this:

```
5 19 61 26 27 (Initial array)
5 19 26 61 27
5 19 26 27 61
5 19 26 27 61 (Sorted array)
```

For sorting small lists, the bubble-sort algorithm is fairly fast, but it's extremely slow if you need to sort a large number of items. Even worse, the bubble-sort algorithm takes a long time to sort if one or more low values are near the end of the array, which means that the bubble-sort algorithm must run multiple times.

Listing 14-4 shows the equivalent C++ program.

Listing 14-4: A Bubble-Sort Algorithm in C++

```
#include <cstdlib>
#include <ctime>
#include <iostream>

using namespace std;

int main()
  {
  const int MAXSIZE = 5;
  int myArray[MAXSIZE+1];
  srand((unsigned)time(0));
  for(int i=1; i<MAXSIZE+1; i++)
    {
    myArray[i] = (rand()%100)+1;
    cout << myArray[i] << "  ";
    }
  cout << "(Initial array)" << "\n";

  int pass;
  int tempValue;
  int noSwaps;
  int time2stop;
  pass = 1;
  time2stop = 0;
  while (time2stop == 0)
   {
   noSwaps = 1;
   for (int i=1; i<=(MAXSIZE-pass); i++)
     {
     if (myArray[i] > myArray[i+1])
       {
      tempValue = myArray[i];
      myArray[i] = myArray[i+1];
      myArray[i+1] = tempValue;
      noSwaps = 0;
      for (int j=1; j<=MAXSIZE; j++)
        {
        cout << myArray[j] << "  ";
        }
      cout << "\n";
      }
     }
    if (noSwaps == 1)
     {
     time2stop = 1;
     }
    }

   for(int i=1; i<MAXSIZE+1; i++)
      {
      cout << myArray[i] << "  ";
      }
```

```
    cout << "(Sorted array)" << "\n";
    cout << "\nPress ENTER to continue..." << endl;
    getchar();
  }
```

This C++ program is stored in the C++ Sample Programs folder as `Chapter 14 - Bubble Sort.cpp`.

Shell Sort

One problem with insertion-sort and bubble-sort algorithms is that they often must move an item from the far end of a list to the front, which is an especially serious drawback for the bubble-sort algorithm. The *shell-sort algorithm* presents a simple solution to make sorting faster.

The shell-sort algorithm works by the principle of divide and conquer. Instead of trying to sort an entire list at a time, the shell-sort algorithm divides a larger list into multiple smaller lists. After it sorts these smaller lists, it combines them into a final sorted list.

The shell-sort algorithm doesn't actually do any sorting; it works with an existing sorting algorithm (such as insertion sort or bubble sort) to speed up the overall sorting process.

Basically, the shell sort follows these steps:

1. It divides a long list into multiple smaller lists. Figure 14-3 shows a list divided into three smaller lists. In this case, the shell-sort algorithm is taking every third item in the list to create three separate smaller lists.

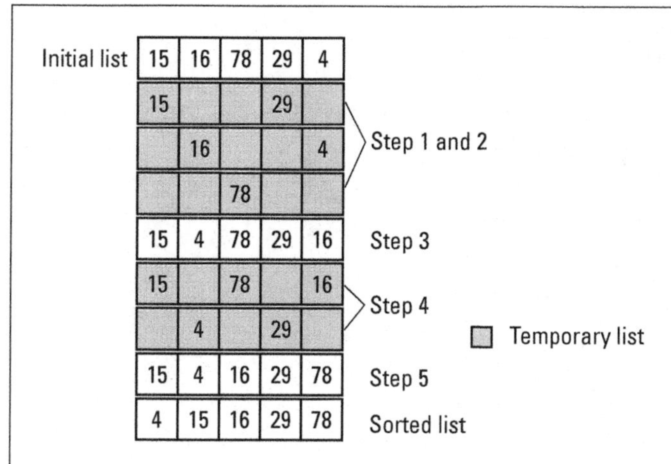

Figure 14-3: The shell sort breaks a large list into smaller lists and sorts those smaller lists.

2. It sorts each smaller list by using an algorithm such as insertion sort or bubble sort. In the example shown in Figure 14-3, the first mini-list contains the numbers 15 and 29, which don't need sorting. The second mini-list contains the numbers 16 and 4, so it sorts their positions. The third mini-list contains just the number 78.
3. It smashes all the smaller lists back into a large list. In Figure 14-3, notice that the numbers 4 and 16 are sorted.
4. It divides the long list into multiple smaller lists again but into fewer smaller lists than in Step 1. In Figure 14-3, the shell-sort algorithm divides the list into two small lists, taking every second item to create two smaller lists.
5. It repeats Steps 2 through 4 (if necessary) until a single sorted list remains. Notice that after it sorts the numbers 16 and 78, the entire list is completely sorted.

To see how the shell-sort algorithm works, run the Liberty BASIC program in Listing 14-5, which uses shell sort to initially sort items and then uses the bubble-sort method to actually sort the items in the list.

Listing 14-5: A Shell-Sort Algorithm in Liberty BASIC

```
MaxSize = 5
REDIM MyArray(MaxSize)
FOR I = 1 TO MaxSize
  MyArray(I) = INT(RND(1) * 100) + 1
  PRINT MyArray(I); SPACE$(1);
NEXT I
PRINT "(Initial array)"

X = INT(MaxSize / 2)
WHILE X > 0
  Time2Stop = 0
  Limit = MaxSize - X
  WHILE (Time2Stop = 0)
    Switch = 0
    FOR K = 1 TO Limit
      IF MyArray(K) > MyArray(K + X) THEN
        TempX = MyArray(K)
        MyArray(K) = MyArray(K + X)
        MyArray(K + X) = TempX
        Switch = K
      END IF
    NEXT K
    Limit = Switch - X
    IF Switch = 0 THEN
      Time2Stop = 1
```

```
    END IF
  WEND

  FOR I = 1 TO MaxSize
    PRINT MyArray(I); SPACE$(1);
  NEXT I
  PRINT
  X = INT(X / 2)
WEND

FOR I = 1 TO MaxSize
  PRINT MyArray(I); SPACE$(1);
NEXT I
PRINT "(Sorted array)"
END
```

This Liberty BASIC program is stored in the Liberty BASIC Sample Programs folder as `Chapter 14 - Shell Sort.bas`.

A typical output for this program looks like this:

```
94 17 70 90 62 (Initial array)
62 17 70 90 94
17 62 70 90 94
17 62 70 90 94 (Sorted array)
```

The first time that the program runs, the shell-sort algorithm compares the numbers that locations 1, 3, and 5 of the array stores (94, 70, and 62, respectively). After sorting this list, it sorts the numbers in locations 2 and 4 of the array (17 and 90). Then it sorts the entire list.

Listing 14-6 shows the equivalent C++ program.

Listing 14-6: A Shell-Sort Algorithm in C++

```
#include <cstdlib>
#include <ctime>
#include <iostream>

using namespace std;

int main()
  {
  const int MAXSIZE = 5;
  int myArray[MAXSIZE+1];
  srand((unsigned)time(0));
  for(int i=1; i<MAXSIZE+1; i++)
    {
    myArray[i] = (rand()%100)+1;
    cout << myArray[i] << "  ";
```

(continued)

Listing 14-6 *(continued)*

```
 }
cout << "(Initial array)" << "\n";

int x;
int limit;
int switchme;
int time2stop;
int tempX;
x = int(MAXSIZE / 2);
while (x > 0)
 {
 time2stop = 0;
 limit = MAXSIZE - x;
 while (time2stop == 0)
   {
   switchme = 0;
   for (int k=1; k<=limit; k++)
     {
     if (myArray[k] > myArray[k+x])
       {
       tempX = myArray[k];
       myArray[k] = myArray[k+x];
       myArray[k+x] = tempX;
       switchme = k;
       }
 }
   limit = switchme - x;
   if (switchme == 0)
     {
     time2stop = 1;
     }
   }
 for (int i=1; i<=MAXSIZE; i++)
   {
   cout << myArray[i] << "  ";
   }
 cout << "\n";
 x = int(x / 2);
 }

 for(int i=1; i<MAXSIZE+1; i++)
     {
     cout << myArray[i] << "  ";
     }
 cout << "(Sorted array)" << "\n";
 cout << "\nPress ENTER to continue..." << endl;
 getchar();
}
```

This C++ program is stored in the C++ Sample Programs folder as `Chapter 14 - Shell Sort.cpp`.

Quicksort

One of the more popular sorting algorithms is known as *quicksort.* The quicksort method works by picking a number from the middle of the list and then sorting the remaining numbers to the left and right of the picked number, as shown in Figure 14-4.

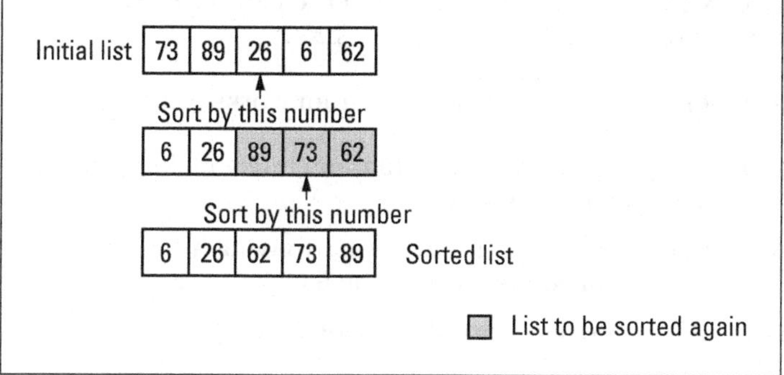

Figure 14-4: The quicksort divides a larger list into small lists based on a number chosen from the middle of that list.

The quicksort method works as follows:

1. It picks a number from the middle of the list and uses that number to divide the long list in half. All numbers less than the randomly picked number get moved to the left, and all numbers greater than the randomly picked number get moved to the right.
2. It repeats Step 1 for each half of the list that a randomly picked number divides until it sorts all items in a bunch of smaller lists.
3. It smashes all the smaller lists back into a large list.

Because the quicksort algorithm repeats the same steps for smaller and smaller lists, it uses a technique known as *recursion.* Recursion simply means that a subprogram repeatedly runs itself.

Because the quicksort algorithm needs to use recursion, you must store the actual quicksort algorithm in a separate subprogram. Thus the complete quicksort program consists of a main program and a subprogram, as in the following Liberty BASIC example:

```
MaxSize = 5                                          →1
REDIM MyArray(MaxSize)
FOR I = 1 TO MaxSize
  MyArray(I) = INT(RND(1)*10) + 1
  PRINT MyArray(I); " ";
NEXT I
```

```
PRINT "(Initial array)"                                    →7

CALL QSort 1, MaxSize                                      →8

FOR I = 1 TO MaxSize                                       →9
  PRINT MyArray(I); " ";
NEXT I
PRINT "(Sorted array)"
END                                                        →13
```

This Liberty BASIC program is stored in the Liberty BASIC Sample Programs folder as `Chapter 14 - Quicksort.bas`.

The main portion of the quicksort program works as follows:

- **→1-7** Creates an array of five random integers and prints the array on-screen for you to see.
- **→8** Calls the `QSort` subprogram by giving it the front of the list (1) and the maximum size of the list (`MaxSize`).
- **→9-12** Prints the final sorted array on-screen.
- **→13** Tells the computer that the program is at an end.

The subprogram `QSort` looks like this:

```
SUB QSort Start, Finish
  I = Start
  J = Finish
  X = MyArray(INT((I+J)/2))
  WHILE I <= J
    WHILE MyArray(I) < X
      I = I + 1
    WEND
    WHILE MyArray(J) > X
      J = J - 1
    WEND
    IF I <= J THEN
      A = MyArray(I)
      MyArray(I) = MyArray(J)
      MyArray(J) = A
      I = I + 1
      J = J - 1
    END IF
  WEND
  FOR K = 1 TO Finish
    PRINT MyArray(K); " ";
  NEXT K
  PRINT
  IF J > Start THEN CALL QSort Start, J
  IF I < Finish THEN CALL QSort I, Finish
END SUB
```

Here's a typical output for this program:

```
27 62 5 79 14 (Initial array)                              →1
5 62 27 79 14                                              →2
5 14 27 79 62                                              →3
5 14 27 62 79                                              →4
5 14 27 62 79 (Sorted array)                               →5
```

Examining the preceding program output, this is how the quicksort algorithm worked:

- →1 The first time that the program runs, the quicksort algorithm chooses the third number (5) in the array. Then it sorts the remaining numbers depending on whether they're less than or greater than 5.
- →2 Because all the numbers in the array are greater than 5, the quicksort algorithm stores them to the right of the array.
- →3 Out of the four remaining numbers to the right of 5, the program picks the number 27 and sorts this smaller list, depending on whether the numbers are less than or greater than 27.
- →4 Now a third smaller list remains, consisting of 79 and 62.
- →5 The algorithm sorts this short list and then combines it with all the other small lists to make up the entire sorted list.

Listing 14-7 shows the equivalent C++ program.

Listing 14-7: A Quicksort Algorithm in C++

```
#include <cstdlib>
#include <ctime>
#include <iostream>

using namespace std;

const int MAXSIZE = 5;
int myArray[MAXSIZE+1];

void QuickSort (int start, int finish)
  {
  int i;
  int j;
  int x;
  int a;
  i = start;
  j = finish;
  x = myArray[int(i+j)/2];
  while (i <= j)
    {
```

(continued)

Listing 14-7 *(continued)*

```
    while (myArray[i] < x)
      {
      i = i + 1;
      }
    while (myArray[j] > x)
      {
      j = j - 1;
      }
    if (i <= j)
      {
      a = myArray[i];
      myArray[i] = myArray[j];
      myArray[j] = a;
      i = i + 1;
      j = j - 1;
      }
    }
    for (int k=1; k<=finish; k++)
      {
      cout << myArray[k] << " ";
      }
    cout << "\n";
    if (j > start)
      {
      QuickSort (start, j);
      }
    if (i < finish)
      {
      QuickSort (i, finish);
      }
  }

int main()
  {
  srand((unsigned)time(0));
  for(int i=1; i<MAXSIZE+1; i++)
    {
    myArray[i] = (rand()%100)+1;
    cout << myArray[i] << " ";
    }
  cout << "(Initial array)" << "\n";

  QuickSort (1, MAXSIZE);

  for(int i=1; i<MAXSIZE+1; i++)
    {
    cout << myArray[i] << "  ";
    }
   cout << "(Sorted array)" << "\n";
   cout << "\nPress ENTER to continue..." << endl;
   getchar();
  }
```

This C++ program is stored in the C++ Sample Programs folder as `Chapter 14 - Quicksort.cpp`.

Choosing a Sorting Algorithm

The insertion-sort, bubble-sort, shell-sort, and Quicksort algorithms show you the variety of methods that programs can use to sort data. Naturally, computer scientists keep inventing additional sorting algorithms with their own advantages and disadvantages, so choose your sorting algorithms carefully. Pick the right sorting algorithm, and your program can run quickly. Pick the wrong sorting algorithm, and your program may seem unbearably slow to the user.

As a general rule, insertion sort is best for small lists, bubble sort is best for lists that are already almost sorted, and quicksort is usually fastest for everyday use. To speed up either insertion sort or bubble sort, consider first sorting a list by using the shell-sort algorithm and then sorting it a second time with either insertion sort or bubble sort.

Using a Built-In Sorting Algorithm

No matter what sorting algorithm you choose, the biggest problem is taking the time to write all the instructions to implement a particular sorting algorithm. To save you time, many programming languages include built-in sorting commands. By using a built-in sorting command, you can save time because you don't have to write (and test) your own sorting algorithm.

Although built-in sorting commands may not necessarily be the fastest way to sort data, they're much easier to use in comparison to writing your own sorting algorithm. In Liberty BASIC, the built-in sorting command is simply `SORT`, and it looks like this:

```
SORT ArrayName, FirstArrayElement, LastArrayElement
```

To use the `SORT` command, you just have to specify the name of the array you want to sort along with the `FirstArrayElement` and `LastArrayElement` to sort. If you want to sort an entire array, the value of `FirstArrayElement` would be `0`, and the value of `LastArrayElement` would be the length of the array, such as `5`.

If you want to sort only part of an array, the value of `FirstArrayElement` would be any number other than `1`, such as `4`, and the value of `LastArray`

Element would be any number greater than FirstArrayElement but less than or equal to the total length of the array.

The following Liberty BASIC example shows how to use the SORT command to sort an array that consists of six (6) elements:

```
MaxSize = 5
REDIM MyArray(MaxSize)
MyArray(1) = INT(RND(1) * 100) + 1
PRINT MyArray(1); SPACE$(1);
FOR I = 2 TO MaxSize
  MyArray(I) = INT(RND(1) * 100) + 1
  PRINT MyArray(I); SPACE$(1);
NEXT I
PRINT

SORT MyArray() 1, MaxSize
PRINT
PRINT "This is the sorted list."
FOR I = 1 TO MaxSize
  PRINT MyArray(I); SPACE$(1);
NEXT
END
```

This Liberty BASIC program is stored in the Liberty BASIC Sample Programs folder as Chapter 14 - Sort Command.bas.

If your programming language offers a built-in sorting command, use it. If it turns out to be way too slow for your particular data, take the time to write your own sorting algorithm.

Searching Algorithms

Searching for data is the second most common activity (after sorting data) necessary for creating many types of programs. A program that stores names and addresses, for example, needs to sort data and then use a search algorithm to find the data that you want (such as all people who live in Los Angeles and whose last names begin with the letter *M*).

To make searching easier, programs usually sort the data before trying to search it.

An *algorithm* is just a fancy way of giving the computer specific types of instructions to accomplish a task. Choosing the right sorting and searching algorithms can make your program run quickly and efficiently. Choose the wrong sorting and searching algorithms, and your program may run sluggishly, even for small amounts of data.

Searching sequentially

A *sequential search* examines every possible item in a data structure (such as an array) until it finds what it's looking for. This type of search is like looking for your car keys in your apartment by going through room by room, looking in every conceivable location until you find your car keys. Although such a sequential search eventually turns up your car keys (assuming that they're in your apartment in the first place), it may take a long time.

For small lists, a sequential search is simple to use and fast. But if you need to search large amounts of data, the sequential search is slow and cumbersome. Imagine the futility of trying to find your car keys somewhere in the city of New York. That's the type of task that a sequential search must face in searching through huge amounts of data.

A sequential search can start at the beginning or end of a list. It then proceeds to examine every item in the list until it finds the one item that it's searching for. Then it stops. To see how a sequential search works, try running the Liberty BASIC program in Listing 14-8.

Listing 14-8: Searching Sequentially with Liberty BASIC

```
MaxSize = 5
REDIM MyArray(MaxSize)
MyArray(1) = INT(RND(1) * 10) + 1
PRINT MyArray(1); SPACE$(1);

FOR I = 2 TO MaxSize
  MyArray(I) = MyArray(I - 1) + INT(RND(1) * 10) + 1
  PRINT MyArray(I); SPACE$(1);
NEXT I
PRINT
INPUT "Which number do you want to find: "; FindMe

FoundIt = 0
FOR J = 1 TO MaxSize
  IF FoundIt = 0 THEN
    PRINT "Checking array location "; J
    IF MyArray(J) = FindMe THEN
      FoundIt = 1
    END IF
  END IF
NEXT J

IF FoundIt = 1 THEN
  PRINT "Found it!"
ELSE
  PRINT "The number you want is not in the list."
END IF
END
```

This Liberty BASIC program is stored in the Liberty BASIC Sample Programs folder as `Chapter 14 - Sequential Search.bas`.

One advantage of a sequential search is that you can use it on both sorted and unsorted lists.

Listing 14-9 shows the equivalent C++ program that searches an array sequentially.

Listing 14-9: Searching Sequentially in C++

```
#include <cstdlib>
#include <ctime>
#include <iostream>

using namespace std;

int main()
  {
  int findme;
  int foundit;
  const int MAXSIZE = 5;
  int myArray[MAXSIZE+1];
  srand((unsigned)time(0));
  myArray[1] = (rand()%10)+1;
  cout << myArray[1] << "  ";

  for(int i=2; i<MAXSIZE+1; i++)
    {
    myArray[i] = myArray[i-1] + (rand()%10)+1;
    cout << myArray[i] << "  ";
    }
  cout << "\n";
  cout << "Which number do you want to find: ";
  cin >> findme;

  foundit = 0;
  for(int j=1; j<=MAXSIZE; j++)
    {
     if (foundit == 0)
     {
       cout << "Checking array location " << j << "\n";
      if (myArray[j] == findme)
      {
      foundit = 1;
                                                         }
      }
   }
  cout << "\n";

  if (foundit == 1)
    {
```

```
    cout << "Found it!";
  }
else
  {
    cout << "The number you want is not in the list.";
  }
 cout << "\nPress ENTER to continue..." << endl;
 getchar();
}
```

This C++ program is stored in the C++ Sample Programs folder as `Chapter 14 - Sequential Search.cpp`.

Performing a binary search

A sequential search starts from the beginning or end of a list and keeps trudging through the entire list from start to finish until it finds what it's looking for. But if a list is already sorted, you can shorten the search by using a *binary search*.

A binary search divides a long (previously sorted) list in half. If the list that you want to sort contains ten numbers that it arranges from smallest (on the left) to largest (on the right), the computer looks to see which half of the list (five numbers on the left and five numbers on the right) contains the number for which it's searching.

Figure 14-5 shows a binary search trying to find the number 37 in a list containing ten numbers. The search goes like this:

1. The binary search algorithm cuts the long list in half and examines the number in the middle of the list.

   Because the list contains ten numbers, the binary search examines the fifth number in the list. In this case, the middle (fifth) number is 30, which tells the binary search algorithm that the number that it wants (37) must lie in the right half of the list.

2. The binary search takes the right half of the list (consisting of five numbers) and cuts this list in half, which points to the third number in the list (59).

   Because 59 is larger than 37 (the number that it's trying to find), the binary-search algorithm determines that the number 37 must lie in the left side of this part of the list.

3. The binary search algorithm looks at the two numbers in the left part of the list.

   Fortunately, the first number is 37 and is the number the binary search is looking for. So the search is over.

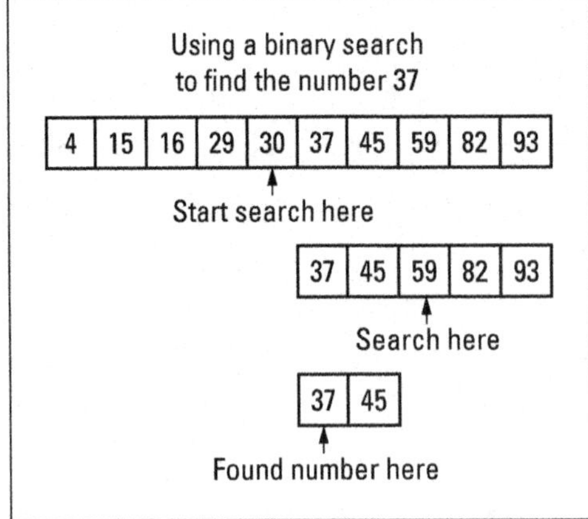

Figure 14-5: A binary search cuts a list in half until it finds what it's looking for.

To see how the binary-search algorithm works, try the Liberty BASIC program in Listing 14-10.

Listing 14-10: Binary Searching in Liberty BASIC

```
MaxSize = 5
REDIM MyArray(MaxSize)
MyArray(1) = INT(RND(1) * 10) + 1
PRINT MyArray(1); SPACE$(1);
FOR I = 2 TO MaxSize
  MyArray(I) = MyArray(I - 1) + INT(RND(1) * 10) + 1
  PRINT MyArray(I); SPACE$(1);
NEXT I
PRINT

INPUT "Which number do you want to find: "; FindMe
Left = 1
Right = MaxSize
Time2Stop = 0
WHILE Time2Stop = 0
  Half = INT((Left + Right) / 2)
  IF FindMe < MyArray(Half) THEN
    Right = Half - 1
  ELSE
    Left = Half + 1
  END IF
  IF (FindMe = MyArray(Half) OR Left > Right) THEN
    Time2Stop = 1
  END IF
WEND
```

```
IF FindMe = MyArray(Half) THEN
  PRINT "Found it in location "; Half
ELSE
  PRINT "The number you want is not in the list."
END IF
END
```

This Liberty BASIC program is stored in the Liberty BASIC Sample Programs folder as `Chapter 14 - Binary Search.bas`.

The binary-search algorithm can work only on a list that has already been sorted.

The equivalent C++ for doing a binary search appears in Listing 14-11.

Listing 14-11: Binary Searching in C++

```
#include <cstdlib>
#include <ctime>
#include <iostream>

using namespace std;

int main()
  {
  int left;
  int right;
  int time2stop;
  int half;
  int findme;
  const int MAXSIZE = 5;
  int myArray[MAXSIZE+1];
  srand((unsigned)time(0));
  myArray[1] = (rand()%10)+1;
  cout << myArray[1] << "  ";

  for(int i=2; i<MAXSIZE+1; i++)
    {
    myArray[i] = myArray[i-1] + (rand()%10)+1;
    cout << myArray[i] << "  ";
    }
  cout << "\n";

  cout << "Which number do you want to find: ";
  cin >> findme;

  left = 1;
  right = MAXSIZE;
```

(continued)

Listing 14-11 *(continued)*

```
    time2stop = 0;
    while (time2stop == 0)
      {
        half = int((left+right)/2);
        if (findme<myArray[half])
        {
          right = half - 1;
        }
        else
        {
          left = half + 1;
        }
        if ((findme == myArray[half]) || (left > right))
        {
        time2stop = 1;
        }
        }

    if (findme == myArray[half])
      {
       cout << "Found it in location " << half << "\n";
     }
    else
      {
       cout << "The number you want is not in the list.";
     }
     cout << "\nPress ENTER to continue..." << endl;
     getchar();
    }
```

This C++ program is stored in the C++ Sample Programs folder as `Chapter 14 - Binary Search.cpp`.

Picking a Searching Algorithm

Sequential searching is the easiest search method to implement and is the fastest for small lists, but for larger lists, sequential searching takes too long. For general use, binary searching is usually faster than sequential searching. The main drawback is that binary searching works only on data that's already sorted.

As a general rule, use sequential searching for small lists or unsorted lists and binary searching for larger, sorted lists.

Chapter 15

Debugging Programs

In This Chapter

- Understanding computer bugs
- Finding syntax errors
- Discovering run-time errors
- Figuring out logic errors

Nobody writes programs that work 100 percent correctly all the time. The problem is that programming means giving the computer extremely detailed instructions. If you give the computer one wrong instruction or one misplaced instruction, make one wrong assumption, or omit one necessary instruction, the computer has no idea what to do next, which can cause your program to fail or, in programming lingo, to *crash*.

If a program doesn't work correctly, programmers never say, "My program has a problem." Instead, programmers use their own lingo and say, "My program has a *bug*." Most people find bugs distasteful, so the idea of a bug infesting your program creates more visually effective imagery than simply saying, "My program has a problem." When programmers try to find bugs in a program, the process is known as *debugging*.

No matter how large or small your programs are, you always need to look for bugs that may keep your program from working correctly. Although eliminating all bugs from a program is impossible, most language compilers provide special features to help you track down the obvious bugs and wipe them out so that your program works well enough for people to actually use it.

Anatomy of a Computer Bug

Computer bugs tend to fall into the following three categories:

- **Syntax errors:** This type of error occurs if you type a command incorrectly, such as misspelling `PRINT` as `PRRINT` or if you forget to type a semicolon at the end of each line in a C++ program.
- **Run-time errors:** These errors occur if your program runs into something unexpected, such as if you ask the user to input an age, the user types a negative number, and your program expects a positive number.
- **Logic errors:** These bugs occur when your instructions work but don't do exactly what you expected, creating unpredictable results.

Although bugs riddle every program, most bugs are relatively harmless or cause only minor problems, such as displaying a menu incorrectly at unpredictable times. Bugs that keep a program from working at all are more serious. Any bug that keeps a company from shipping (and selling) a program is known as a *showstopper.*

Syntax Errors

Syntax errors are often misspellings of valid commands or omissions (or misplacement) of crucial characters such as a comma or a left parenthesis. If you misspell a command such as `PRINTT`, most compilers are smart enough to highlight the line where the syntax error occurs so that you can fix it later, as shown in Figure 15-1.

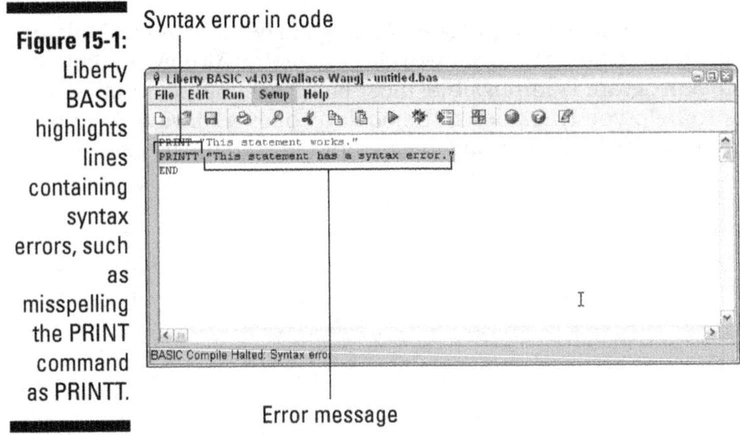

Figure 15-1: Liberty BASIC highlights lines containing syntax errors, such as misspelling the PRINT command as PRINTT.

Although syntax errors usually prevent a program from working at all, watch out for your own misspellings because the computer assumes that you know what you're doing, even if you make a mistake. Especially troublesome are those times that you misspell a variable name. Consider, for example, the following program:

```
PROMPT "How many times do I need to tell you no"; Answeer$
PRINT "Your reply = "; Answer$
END
```

The preceding program asks the user, `"How many times do I need to tell you no?"` Then the program stores whatever the user types into the variable `Answeer$` (the misspelling of `Answer$`). Because Liberty BASIC considers `Answer$` and `Answeer$` to be two completely different variable names, the `Answer$` variable doesn't contain any data. If you run this program, it doesn't print what the user types, simply because of a single misspelling.

Most compilers can detect syntax errors in misspelled commands, but they cannot always detect misspelled variable names.

Besides misspelling a variable name, watch out for mixing upper- and lowercase letters in variable names. Languages such as Liberty BASIC and C++ consider the variable `Answer$` to be completely different from the variable `answer$` simply because one starts with an uppercase letter *A* and the other doesn't.

The destruction of Mariner 1

Syntax errors are usually caught because they give an invalid command to the computer, which immediately keeps the program from running at all. The worst syntax errors, however, are those that somehow give a valid but unintended command to the computer. Thus, the program keeps working — but not the way you want it to.

Back in 1962, NASA sent the Mariner 1 probe to study Venus, but before the rocket carrying the probe could make its way into outer space, it veered off course, and NASA had to prematurely detonate the rocket. According to one story, the program was supposed to contain a `FOR-NEXT` loop that told the computer to loop three times, as in the following example:

```
FOR I = 1, 3
```

But rather than a comma, the programmer had accidentally typed a period, as follows:

```
FOR I = 1.3
```

So instead of telling the computer to loop three times, this command told the computer to set the value of the variable `I` to `1.3`. The end result was that this error managed to give the computer a valid but incorrect command, causing NASA to lose a multimillion-dollar rocket and payload as a result.

Because a single misspelling of a variable name can mess up your program, many programmers take shortcuts and choose short, cryptic variable names. Don't take this route! The time that you save in using short variable names is lost in comparison with the time that you need to decipher what those short variable names represent.

Such errors can prove hard to detect because a misspelling can still allow the program to run, albeit incorrectly. Anytime that your program runs but doesn't seem to work right, start looking for misspellings or incorrectly capitalized variable names.

Run-Time Errors

Run-time errors are sneaky little bugs that hide in programs. A program may work correctly right up until it receives data that the programmer never expected, such as a negative number that the user types for his year of birth. Unfortunately, the only time that you can find run-time errors is after they cause the program to crash.

That's why software companies always test their programs with the general public by releasing beta copies of the program. A *beta copy* is a version of the program that the company hopes to sell soon, but the company wants special people (known as *beta testers*) to play with the program and see whether they can find bugs that the company's internal testers missed.

Death from the Therac-25

The Therac-25 was a radiation-therapy machine designed to administer radiation doses to patients. To prevent excessive doses of radiation, the Therac-25 included a safety mechanism that relied completely on its software to prevent any problems — but the software contained a fatal run-time error.

The Therac-25 offered two modes of operation: X-ray and electron beam. If the technician accidentally selected the X-ray mode first, the Therac-25 would select a high-intensity energy level. If the technician then switched to electron-beam mode right away without completing the X-ray mode, the Therac-25 would maintain its higher energy intensity level for electron-mode operation, which meant delivering a fatal radiation burn to any unlucky patient lying underneath.

Only after several people suffered severe radiation burns at the hands of the Therac-25 did someone finally discover this hidden run-time error, but by then, it was too late for all the people who'd already been irreparably burned by the Therac-25 and its supposedly fail-safe software safety mechanism.

Because run-time errors occur only after your program receives data that it doesn't know how to handle, the best way to hunt down run-time errors is to run your program over and over, feeding the program extreme values of different data each time.

If your program asks the user to input an age, for example, type a huge number (such as 60,000). Then type zero. Finally, type a negative number such as –9,489. By testing extreme ranges of values, you can often smoke out run-time errors before you release your program for actual use.

Fun with Logic Errors

Of all the types of bugs that can infest your program, none is more insidious than a *logic error.* Syntax errors can prove fairly easy to find because you just need to look for misspellings or places where you've forgotten to type a character, such as a closing parenthesis. Similarly, you can often find run-time errors by testing your program with extreme values of data.

Logic errors, however, occur even after you write your instructions perfectly — except for the fact that they're the *wrong* instructions. Because you assume that the instructions you write are correct, to find and correct a logic error, you must examine these instructions line by line to see whether they're missing a step or simply solving the wrong problem altogether.

The sinking of the *H.M.S. Sheffield*

The trouble with eradicating all logic bugs from a program is that you must examine your entire program for mistaken assumptions. Although programs may work perfectly fine during testing, they may encounter unexpected situations in the real world, causing the programs to fail catastrophically.

One prominent example of a logic bug occurred during the Falkland Islands War between Great Britain and Argentina. The *H.M.S. Sheffield,* a British destroyer, used an advanced computer air-defense system designed to protect the ship from air and missile attack. To prevent this air-defense system from shooting down its own missiles, the computers were programmed to allow certain "friendly" missiles to fly unmolested through its defenses. These "friendly" missiles included all the types of missiles that the British Navy used, which included the French-built Exocet antiship missile.

Unfortunately for the British, Argentina had also bought Exocet antiship missiles from the French, so when the *Sheffield's* computers detected the incoming Exocet missiles, they assumed the missiles were "friendly" and allowed them to pass uncontested through the *Sheffield's* air-defense system — and right into the *Sheffield,* sinking the ship with several direct hits.

Because logic errors can prove so difficult to find, language compilers provide special debugging features to help make this task a little easier. The two main ways to examine a program for logic errors are by *stepping* and *watching*.

The following examples use Liberty BASIC, but most language compilers work the same way, letting you step through your code, line by line, and then watch to see how your variables change.

Stepping line by line

Stepping involves running through your program line by line and watching to see how your program works. The moment that you spot the program doing something wrong, you know exactly which line in your program is making the mistake.

To step through a Liberty BASIC program, follow these steps:

1. **Load the program that you want to step through line by line.**
2. **Choose Run⇨Debug, press Alt+F5, or click the Debug icon on the toolbar.**

   A Debugging window appears, as shown in Figure 15-2. If the main window also appears, you need to close it or move it out of the way to see the Debugging window.

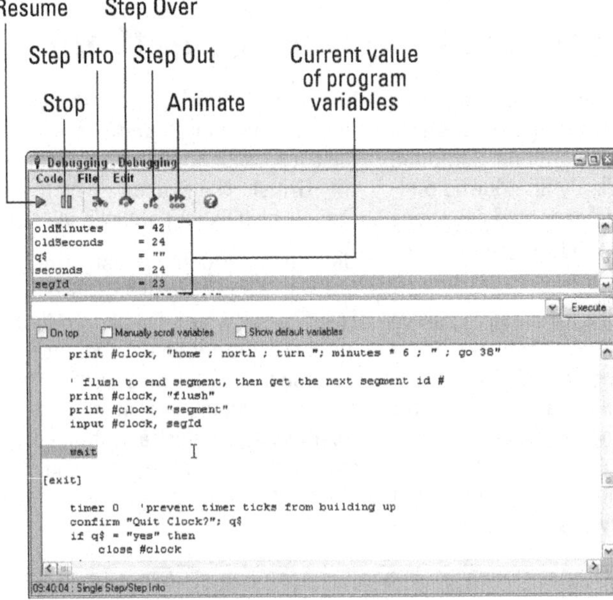

Figure 15-2: The Debugging window enables you to examine your program for bugs.

3. **Click one of the following icons:**

   - **Step Into:** Runs your program line by line so you can see what it's doing at each instruction.
   - **Step Over:** Runs your program line by line but doesn't highlight any lines buried inside subroutines or functions.
   - **Step Out:** In case you used the Step Into command to view code inside a subroutine or function, the Step Out command lets you quickly jump out of a subroutine or function without having to go through every single line in that particular subroutine or function.
   - **Animate:** Runs your entire program, line by line. You can halt at any time by clicking the Stop icon. To start running your program again, click the Resume icon.

To help you study how a small chunk of your program works, click a line in your program and then choose Code⇨Run to Line. Liberty BASIC runs all the instructions up to the line that you selected and shows you the values of all your variables in the top pane of the Debugging window.

Tracing through your program

Stepping through an entire program line by line can prove tedious and time-consuming, especially if you already have an idea of which part of your program may hide a bug. Instead of stepping through your whole program from the beginning, you can step through your program at any point, such as in the middle or near the end.

To use tracing in Liberty BASIC, follow these steps:

1. **Open the program that you want to debug.**
2. **Type** TRACE **at the point in your program where you want to start debugging.**

   When using the `TRACE` command, you have the following three options:

   - `TRACE 0` runs your program from start to finish and stops only if you're fast enough to click the Stop button in the Debugging window.
   - `TRACE 1` runs your program line by line, giving you a chance to click the Stop button in the Debugging window at any time.
   - `TRACE 2` runs your program line by line in the Debugging window.
3. **Choose Run⇨Debug or press Alt+F5.**

   The Debugging window appears. Depending on the `TRACE` command you typed in your program (such as `TRACE 0` or `TRACE 2`), your program may run quickly or wait for you to click one of the Step icons to examine your program line by line.

4. **When you're done studying your program, click the Run icon in the Debugging window.**

   Liberty BASIC runs your program until it finds another `TRACE` command.

You can add multiple `TRACE` commands anywhere you need to put them in your program. The `TRACE` commands have no effect on the running of your program. Use `TRACE` commands only if you're debugging a program.

One problem with typing a `TRACE` command directly in your code is that you have to delete that `TRACE` command when you no longer need it. Instead of the tracing approach, most language compilers offer something called *breakpoints.* A breakpoint lets you highlight an existing line of code that tells the computer, "Run the entire program from the beginning but stop when you reach the line of code designated as a breakpoint." When the program stops at a breakpoint, you can step through your code, line by line, to look for errors.

Watching your variables

When you step through a program line by line, you can often watch the contents of different variables so you can see exactly when the contents of a variable suddenly change. As soon as you see the variable change, you know exactly which line of code is causing the change, as shown in Figure 15-3.

Stepping through each line of code...

...shows you how any variables may change.

Figure 15-3: Combining stepping with watching lets you see exactly which line changes the contents of a variable.

For example, if a variable is supposed to hold a positive number but, as you step through your code, you suddenly see which line stores a negative number in a variable, you know which line is causing the bug in your program.

Creating secure software

In the old days, programmers just worried about getting their programs to work. Nowadays, programmers have to worry about getting their programs to work and making sure their programs don't have any security flaws that could allow hackers to break through. If you're designing a program to display your cat's head on-screen, you probably don't care about security, but if you're designing a program to store thousands of credit card numbers for a bank, you had better be worried about security.

Writing secure code means that your program not only does what you want it to do, but doesn't do anything else you don't want it to do. Many programs, such as firewalls and operating systems, actually work perfectly well. The problem occurs when hackers probe a program and find a flaw in a program, which can be manipulated in some unexpected way. One of the most popular flaws in programs is something called a *buffer overflow*.

To exploit a buffer overflow, hackers typically send a program useless data along with a command or executable program. When faced with large amounts of data, the program gets confused and runs the command or executable program, allowing a hacker to break into a computer.

So the next time you write a program, make sure it does what it's supposed to do and nothing more. Otherwise, you may find yourself rushing to fix (or *patch*) any holes that may turn your program into a security risk.

Chapter 16

Optimizing Your Code

In This Chapter

- Selecting the right data structure
- Choosing the best algorithm
- Tuning up the source code
- Writing with a faster language
- Optimizing your compiler

Getting a program to work correctly is often a miracle in itself. But after you do get it to work and eliminate as many bugs as possible, the next question is whether to use (or release) the program right away or take some time to optimize it.

Optimization means trying to meet the following three goals (without introducing bugs into the program in the process):

- Make the program faster.
- Make the program smaller.
- Make the program require less memory to run.

As a general rule, software companies rush the new version (such as version 1.0 or version 4.0) of any program out the door just to grab market share. Within a few months, companies usually release slightly modified versions (such as version 1.01 or version 4.1), which fix some bugs (and usually introduce some new ones, as well) and optimize the program in some way. In the commercial software market, optimization is usually a luxury, which is why so many programs are known as *bloatware* — they require globs of memory and hard drive space.

Choosing the Right Data Structure

Every program needs to store data, so you need to choose the right data structure for holding information in your program. An array may seem easy to create, but you must know the number of items that the array needs to hold ahead of time. If you make an array too small, your program runs out of space to store additional data, possibly crashing your program. If you make an array too large, you risk allocating space for storage that you don't need, which can cause your program to gobble up more memory than necessary.

For example, if you create a large two-dimensional array but store only a small number of items in it, you waste a large amount of space. If you replace the two-dimensional array with two dynamic, one-dimensional arrays, you waste no space (although you now have the problem of writing additional instructions to create and manage the dynamic arrays).

Ultimately, the data structure you choose can determine the performance of your entire program. If you choose the wrong data structure, your program may still work, but it may run slower and require more memory than necessary.

Sometimes software that works is worse than software that doesn't work

Apple Computer had a unique idea. Following the success of the new Intel-based Macintosh computers and the famous ease-of-use of the Mac OS X operating system and its accompanying programs (dubbed iLife), Apple decided to create a new digital photography program geared just for professional and hardcore amateur photographers, called Aperture.

The idea behind Aperture was simple: Provide a program for professional photographers to organize, store, search, edit, and print their digital images. Apple succeeded and cheerfully rushed the program to market.

Then the problems began. Aperture worked correctly, but it didn't work very well. Even on the fastest computers, Aperture ran slowly and needed at least 1GB of memory just to display and edit still images. (In comparison, Apple had released a program, called Final Cut, which edited video, and that program needed a minimum of 512MB of memory to run while displaying and editing both sound and video.)

To appease unhappy customers, Apple dropped the price of Aperture from its original $499 to $299 and offered $200 rebates to anyone who had purchased the program at its original higher price.

So Apple had a dilemma on its hands. Does it stop further development of Aperture and admit a mistake, or does it sink more time and money into rewriting and optimizing the entire Aperture program from top to bottom in an effort to make the program responsive and less of a memory hog?

In this case, Apple would have been better off if Aperture had never worked in the first place. Now that it's released, Apple is stuck with two equally distasteful options — all because the original programmers didn't correctly design and optimize Aperture from the beginning.

Choosing the Right Algorithm

An *algorithm* tells the computer how to accomplish a specific task. Think about all the different ways you can tell your friends to get to your house from downtown. You can tell them to take the highway, which is easier but may take longer. Or you can tell them to take a variety of side streets that ultimately make the trip shorter but make your directions harder to follow.

Deciding which set of directions to give someone is much like deciding which algorithm to use in your program. If you need to sort a list of 30,000 names, for example, the bubble-sort algorithm sorts that list much slower than the Quicksort algorithm does. After you sort 30,000 names, using a sequential-search algorithm to find a name is much slower than using a binary-search algorithm. (See Chapter 14 for explanations on the bubble-sort, quicksort, sequential-search, and binary-search algorithms.)

For another example of choosing the right algorithm, think of a video game that displays the ten highest scores. Before anyone plays the game, the ten highest scores are all zero. The first time that a person plays the game, the video game lists that person's score as number one. Each time that someone plays the game again, the video game must sort the scores to display the highest to lowest ten scores.

For this video game example, the insertion-sort algorithm is most efficient. After the video game shows two scores, the insertion-sort algorithm sorts those two scores from highest to lowest. The third time that someone plays the video game, the insertion-sort algorithm compares the third score with the previous two scores and inserts the third score in its correct place. Each additional time that someone plays the video game, the insertion-sort algorithm compares the new score with the previous high scores to determine where to insert the new score in the top-ten list (assuming that it ranks that high, of course).

If you use a bubble-sort algorithm to sort the top-ten scores, the bubble-sort algorithm needs to examine the list multiple times and compare each score with its neighbor — taking more time than the insertion-sort algorithm as a result. In this particular case, you can see how the insertion-sort algorithm is more efficient than the bubble-sort algorithm.

As you write your own programs, remember that different algorithms are available for you to use to accomplish identical tasks for your program. Choose the algorithm that runs the fastest for your program.

Fine-Tuning the Source Code

Even if you choose data structures and algorithms with care, you can still optimize your program by fine-tuning the source code. Fine-tuning involves you rewriting portions of your program to make it run faster or require less memory.

Putting the condition most likely to be false first

When you use the AND operator in an IF-THEN statement, you combine two or more conditions, as follows:

```
IF (Boolean expression 1) AND (Boolean expression 2) THEN
  ' Follow one or more instructions listed here
END IF
```

This IF-THEN statement runs only after the computer takes time to verify that both *Boolean expression 1* and *Boolean expression 2* are true. If either one of these Boolean expressions is false, the instructions inside the IF-THEN statement don't run.

So if you intend to use the AND operator, put the expression that's most likely false in the first part of the AND operation. For example, if *Boolean expression 1* is false, the computer doesn't bother checking to see whether *Boolean expression 2* is true because one false Boolean expression always makes the entire AND operation false.

The moment that the computer determines that the first Boolean expression in an AND operation is false, it doesn't check the second Boolean expression, thus saving time and helping make your program run just a little bit faster.

See Chapter 9 for more information about Boolean expressions.

Putting the condition most likely to be true first

The IF-THEN-ELSEIF and SELECT CASE statements often need to check several conditions to make a decision, as the following code shows:

```
IF (Boolean expression 1) THEN
  ' Follow one or more instructions listed here
```

```
ELSEIF (Boolean expression 2) THEN
  ' Follow one or more instructions listed here
END IF
```

In this `IF-THEN-ELSEIF` statement, the computer first checks to see whether *`Boolean expression 1`* is true. If not, it checks to see whether *`Boolean expression 2`* is true.

But what if *`Boolean expression 1`* is false most of the time and *`Boolean expression 2`* is true most of the time? Then the program wastes time always checking *`Boolean expression 1`* (which is usually false) before it can get to *`Boolean expression 2`* (which is usually true).

To keep your program from wasting time checking a Boolean expression that's usually false, put the Boolean expression that's most likely true at the front and the Boolean expression that's least likely true at the end of the `IF-THEN-ELSEIF` statement, as follows:

```
IF (Boolean expression 2) THEN
  ' Follow one or more instructions listed here
ELSEIF (Boolean expression 1) THEN
  ' Follow one or more instructions listed here
END IF
```

By placing the Boolean expression that's most likely true at the beginning, you save the computer from wasting time checking one or more additional Boolean expressions that are usually going to prove false anyway.

Liberty BASIC doesn't support the `IF-THEN-ELSEIF` or `SELECT CASE` statements but other languages, such as REALbasic, do.

This technique also works for `SELECT CASE` statements, as in the following example:

```
SELECT CASE Variable
CASE Value1
  ' Follow these instructions if the Variable = Value1
CASE Value2
  ' Follow these instructions if the Variable = Value2
END SELECT
```

`SELECT CASE` statements check to see whether a variable equals one value (such as *`Value1`*). If you put the values most likely to match the `SELECT CASE` variable up front, you avoid forcing the computer to check a long list of values that are least likely to match anyway.

Although the technique of putting the conditions that are most likely true first may seem trivial, every little bit of time that you save can add up to make a faster and more responsive program.

Don't run a FOR-NEXT loop needlessly

Loops can gobble up time, so make sure that you choose the right loop. If you're using a sequential search to find an item in an array, for example, you can use a FOR-NEXT loop. The FOR-NEXT loop can count to make the computer check every position in the array to look for a specific item.

The FOR-NEXT loop runs a specific number of times. What do you think happens if it finds the item that it's looking for on the first try? The FOR-NEXT loop doesn't care; it continues looping a fixed number of times anyway, thereby wasting time. The following code examines an array that contains 5,000 elements and searches for the number 55:

```
FOR J = 1 TO 5000
  IF MyArray(J) = 55 THEN
     PRINT MyArray(J)
  END IF
NEXT J
```

If the loop finds the number 55 in the first element of the array, it continues looping anyway for another 4999 times, wasting time. If you don't absolutely need to loop and repeat a set of instructions a fixed number of times, use a Boolean expression and a WHILE loop instead as the following code demonstrates:

```
J = 1
WHILE (MyArray(J) <> 55) AND (J <= 5000)
    J = J + 1
WEND
PRINT MyArray(J)
```

The moment the WHILE loop finds the number 55 in the array named MyArray, it immediately stops looping.

Cleaning out your loops

To make your loops work, you must place all the instructions inside the loop. When you put an unneeded instruction inside a loop, you force the computer to keep running that instruction repeatedly, thereby slowing down your loop and ultimately your program as well.

Consider the following loop:

```
FOR J = 1 TO 5000
  I = 0
  IF MyArray(J) = 55 THEN
     PRINT MyArray(J)
  END IF
NEXT J
```

The preceding `FOR-NEXT` loop repeats itself 5,000 times, but the program never uses the `I = 0` instruction inside the `FOR-NEXT` loop. It forces the computer to run the `I = 0` instruction 5,000 times for no reason. To avoid this problem, simply remove the `I = 0` instruction from the loop, as follows:

```
I = 0
FOR J = 1 TO 5000
  IF MyArray(J) = 55 THEN
    PRINT MyArray(J)
  END IF
NEXT J
```

In the programming world, *nesting* occurs if you cram one type of control or loop structure inside another one. In the preceding Liberty BASIC program example, an `IF-THEN` statement nests inside a `FOR-NEXT` loop.

Why C++ programs can be hard to understand

Programs that you write in C++ usually run faster and more efficiently than equivalent programs written in other languages, such as BASIC. But C++ has developed a well-deserved reputation for creating cryptic code. One reason is that C++ allows a variety of shortcuts that can make your program run faster — but at the sacrifice of readability.

Rather than type **x = x + 5** or **y = y – 23**, for example, C++ enables you to use shortcuts, as in the following examples:

```
x += 5; /* equivalent to x=x+5 */
y -= 23; /* equivalent to y=y-23 */
```

C++ also includes something called a *prefix* or *postfix* operator that can increment or decrement a variable by one. The following are examples of postfix operators:

```
x++; /* equivalent to x=x+1 */
y--; /* equivalent to y=y-1 */
```

The prefix operators that are equivalent to the preceding postfix operators are as follows:

```
++x; /* equivalent to x=x+1 */
--y; /* equivalent to y=y-1 */
```

If you think they look and act alike, you're almost right. The big difference occurs if you combine postfix or prefix operators into a formula, as follows:

```
x=y+z++
```

The preceding formula is actually equivalent to the following two instructions:

```
x=y+z
z=z+1
```

You can use the following prefix operator instead:

```
a=b+--c
```

(continued)

(continued)

This line is equivalent to the following two instructions:

```
c=c-1
a=b+c
```

C++ even offers a strange shortcut for an `IF-ELSE` statement that uses a combination of a question mark and a colon, as follows:

```
printf("This number is bigger = %d\n", (x > y) ? x : y);
```

This line is equivalent to the following normal-looking `IF-ELSE` statement:

```
if (x > y)
 printf("This number is bigger = %d\n", x);
else
 printf("This number is bigger = %d\n", y);
```

The shorter, more cryptic version of the `IF-ELSE` statement may take up less space and run faster, but it's harder to understand at first glance. In using shortcuts, be aware that they can make your program harder to read.

Be especially wary of nested loops. If you nest one loop inside another, the inner loop runs more often than the outer loop. By ridding the inner loop of any instructions that don't need to be inside that loop, you avoid forcing the computer to repeat an instruction needlessly.

Using the correct data types

To save memory, use the correct data types. Many versions of BASIC, such as Visual Basic, allow you to declare your variables as integers (as in `DIM Num AS INTEGER`) or as long integers (as in `DIM Num AS LONG`). Long integers can range in value from –2,147,483,648 to 2,147,483,647, whereas ordinary integers can range in value only from –32,768 to 32,767.

A long integer variable, however, gobbles up more memory if you need to stuff a really large number into it, such as 2,147,483,647. If your variables never need to hold such a large number, a smaller data type (such as an integer) works just as well and requires less memory.

Using built-in commands whenever possible

Nearly every programming language includes special built-in commands that run faster than equivalent commands that you type yourself. If you have a variable (`MyNumber`) that you want to increment by 1, for example, you can use the following command:

```
MyNumber = MyNumber + 1
```

Nothing is wrong with this command, but languages offer shortcuts for incrementing a variable by 1. In C++, you can use the shortcut shown in the following example:

```
mynumber++
```

If you want to increment a variable in Delphi (which is based on the Pascal language), you can use the following bit of code:

```
Inc(MyNumber)
```

If you use built-in commands, you risk making your code more cryptic and harder to understand. That's because not all programmers know all the built-in commands (shortcuts) that a particular language offers. If a programmer encounters a built-in command, he may not understand how that particular command actually works.

Using a Faster Language

The fastest possible language in which you can write a program is machine code, followed by assembly language and C/C++, with the other languages (such as Pascal and BASIC) trailing slightly behind. If you want to speed up your program, consider switching to a different programming language.

Many programmers use a simple language such as Visual Basic to develop a prototype program that they can show to a client and to design the user interface. After you create a prototype program, you have two choices:

- **Dump the entire prototype program and rewrite the whole thing from scratch by using a faster language, such as C/C++.** Naturally, this process can take a long time and doesn't guarantee that the program works right (but at least it probably looks good).
- **Use the prototype of the program as the basis for your actual working program.** But instead of writing the entire program in a single language, you can write the parts of the program that you expect people to use most often in a faster language.

If you use two or more languages to create a single program, you can take advantage of each language's strengths. The drawback of this strategy is trying to make two or three different programming languages cooperate with one another.

Optimizing Your Compiler

As an alternative to using a faster language, you can use a faster compiler. If you put the identical program through different compilers, each compiler creates the same program, but one compiler's program may run faster than another compiler's program. Unfortunately, if you write a program in C++ for one compiler (such as Microsoft Visual C++), the program may not run at all in another C++ compiler (such as Borland C++ Builder) without extensive modifications.

To give you more control over your program, most compilers offer options for changing the way that the compiler works. You can change these options to fine-tune your compiler for your particular program, as shown in Figure 16-1.

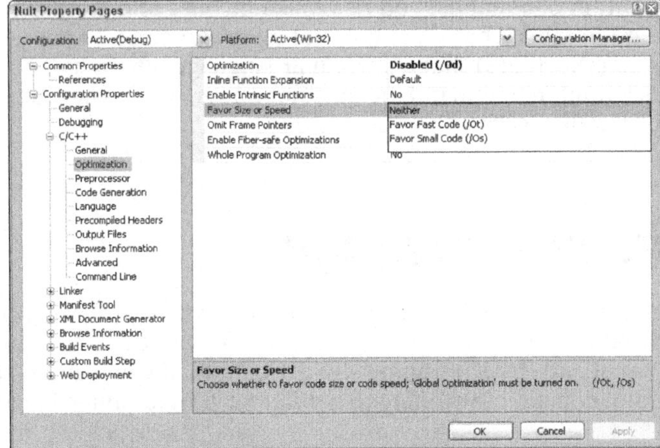

Figure 16-1: Optimization settings for the Visual C++ compiler.

Make sure that you know what you're doing before you change any of your compiler optimization settings. Most of these optimization settings can make your program run faster but at the expense of turning off the compiler's built-in error-checking feature, which can help you spot bugs in your program. If you turn off your compiler's error-checking capabilities, your program runs faster, but it may crash more often as a result of missed errors.

Chapter 17

Creating a User Interface

In This Chapter

- Creating a window
- Adding menus to a window
- Placing controls in a window

As the name implies, a *user interface* acts as the middleman between the user and your program. The user gives commands through your program's user interface, which passes those commands to the part of your program that actually does the work. Then your program passes data back to the user interface to display on-screen for the user to see.

In the old days, user interfaces were known as *command-line interfaces* because a program would display a message and wait for the user to type a reply. The area on-screen where the program expected the user to type a command was known as the command line.

In Liberty BASIC, you can create a simple command-line interface by using the `INPUT` and `PRINT` commands, as shown here:

```
INPUT "Enter your name: "; Name$
PRINT Name$ + ", why don't you take the day off?"
END
```

In C++, you can use the `cout` and `cin` commands to accept data from the user and display it on-screen like this:

```
#include <iostream>

using namespace std;

int main()
  {
  string name;
```

```
cout << "Enter your name: ";
cin >> name;
cout << name + ", why don't you take the day off?";
cout << "\nPress ENTER to continue..." << endl;
getchar();
return 0;
}
```

Besides looking ugly, the biggest drawback of a command-line interface is that it forces the user to type data, which can lead to misspellings. If the user doesn't type a valid command, the command-line interface doesn't do a thing to help. (Until the user knows the proper command to ask for help, the command-line interface won't offer any help either.)

Not surprisingly, few programs rely on command-line interfaces any more because not many people want to use them. Instead, most programs now offer graphical user interfaces (abbreviated as GUI and pronounced as *gooey*). A typical GUI offers windows and pull-down menus, so instead of forcing a user to type data, a GUI displays options that the user can choose by pointing the cursor and clicking the mouse button.

This chapter focuses exclusively on showing you how to create a GUI in REALbasic and Revolution while also showing you all the extra code you need to write just to create a similar user interface in Liberty BASIC.

The birth of GUI operating systems

In the old days, writing a program meant writing code that made your program work and then writing additional code to create a user interface. Writing a program and designing a user interface essentially doubled the size and complexity of writing a program.

Even worse, every program used a different user interface. In some programs, you gave commands by pressing the Esc key to see a menu. In other programs, you pressed the slash (/) key to display a menu, and in still other programs, you just had to memorize which commands you could give a program by pressing a certain function key, such as F7.

Obviously, having every program display a different user interface made using each program confusing and difficult. To solve this problem, companies started designing operating systems that displayed a consistent user interface. Two of the earliest, and most popular, GUI operating systems were Apple's Macintosh and Microsoft Windows.

In some programming languages (such as Liberty BASIC and C++), you still have to write commands to design a user interface, but in newer languages (such as REALbasic and Revolution), you can design your user interface without writing any code at all.

By letting the language compiler help you design a user interface, you can create bug-free user interfaces in a minimal amount of time. Now all you have to do is concentrate on getting your program to work.

Designing a Window

A window looks like a rectangle that you can move and resize on-screen, as shown in Figure 17-1. Most programs use windows for two purposes:

- To display your program's commands, such as pull-down menus or command buttons, so that the user can use them to make selections or input information into the program
- To display information on-screen for the user to see, such as a graph of a stock price or text that the user needs to see

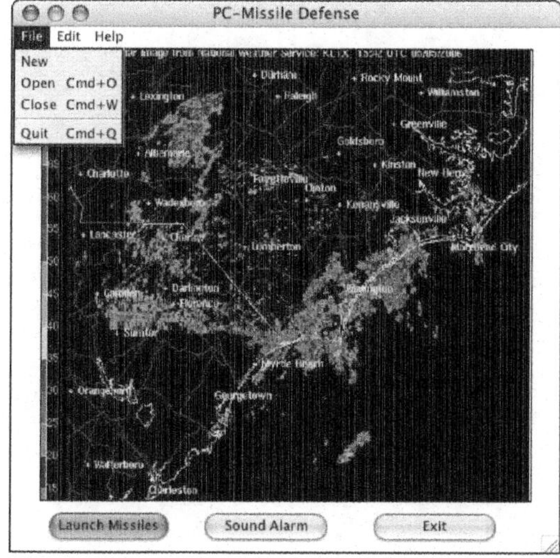

Figure 17-1: A window can display information on-screen along with buttons and pull-down menus so you can give the program a command.

To see how clumsy and troublesome it is to create a user interface by writing instructions in a programming language, consider the following Liberty BASIC program, which does nothing but create and display a window on-screen:

```
NOMAINWIN
OPEN "Titlebar text" FOR Window AS #1
PRINT #1, "trapclose [quit]"
WAIT

[quit]
CONFIRM "Are you sure that you want to quit?"; quit$
IF quit$ = "no" THEN WAIT
CLOSE #1
END
```

This Liberty BASIC program is stored in the Liberty BASIC Sample Programs folder as `Chapter 17 - Window.bas`.

The first four lines create and display the actual window, as shown in Figure 17-2. The last five lines contain commands that tell the window what to do when the user clicks the window's Close button.

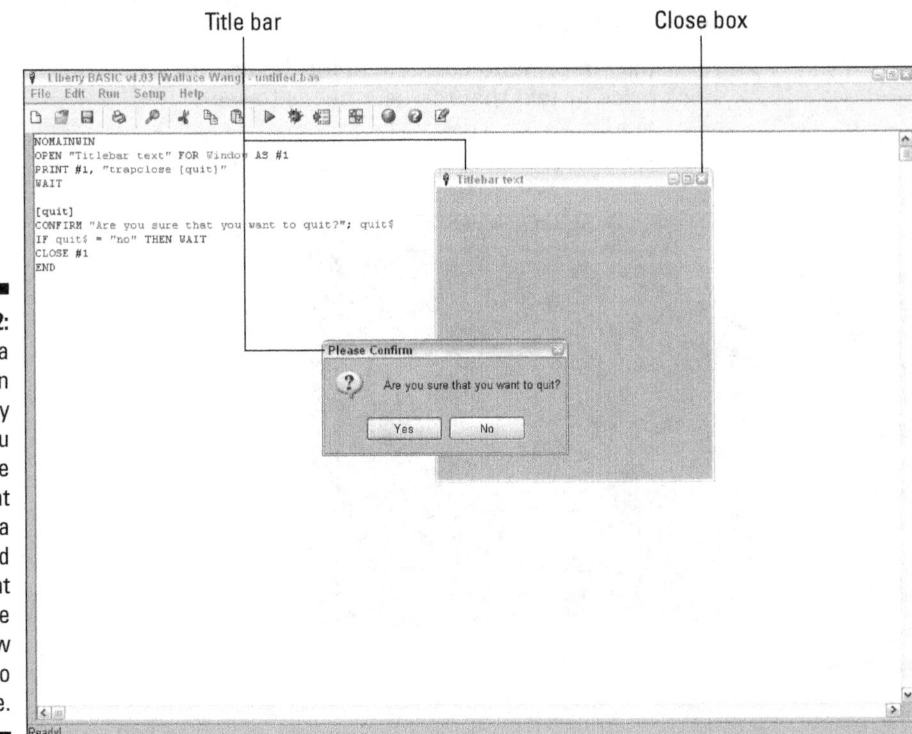

Figure 17-2: To display a window in Liberty BASIC, you must write code that creates a window and code that tells the window how to close.

So not only do you have to write code to create a user interface, but you also have to write code that tells your user interface how to work (in addition to your code that makes your program do something useful).

Because of the added complexity of writing your own user interface from scratch, most programmers rely on a language compiler to create a user interface.

To create a window in REALbasic, you don't have to write any code at all to display the window or make it work. Given the choice between writing code (that you may need to debug later) to create a user interface or writing no code at all to create a bug-free user interface, which option do you think makes programming easier and faster?

Putting Pull-Down Menus in a Window

Most windows provide *pull-down menus* so that users can pick a command. Most pull-down menus include the following:

- A menu title (typical menu titles are File, Edit, and Help)
- One or more menu commands that appear on the menu (such as Edit, Print, or Cut)

With languages like Liberty BASIC and C++, you have to write code to display a pull-down menu and then write additional code to make your pull-down menu actually respond to the user.

To see how Liberty BASIC can create a pull-down menu, take a look at the program in Listing 17-1.

Listing 17-1: Creating a Pull-Down Menu in Liberty BASIC

```
NOMAINWIN
MENU #1, "&File", "&Open", [asOpen], "&Print", [asPrint],
         "E&xit", [quit]
MENU #1, "&Help", "&Contents", [asContents], "&About",
         [asAbout]
OPEN "Menu Example" FOR Window AS #1
PRINT #1, "trapclose [quit]"
WAIT

[quit]
CONFIRM "Are you sure that you want to quit?"; quit$
IF quit$ = "no" THEN WAIT
CLOSE #1
END

[asOpen]
NOTICE "Open command chosen"
WAIT

[asPrint]
NOTICE "Print command chosen"
WAIT

[asContents]
```

(continued)

Listing 17-1 *(continued)*

```
NOTICE "Contents command chosen"
WAIT

[asAbout]
NOTICE "About command chosen"
WAIT
```

This Liberty BASIC program is stored in the Liberty BASIC Sample Programs folder as `Chapter 17 - Pulldown Menus.bas`.

Creating pull-down menus from scratch involves writing code to display the menus and then writing additional code to make the pull-down menus work.

In comparison, creating pull-down menus in a program like REALbasic or Revolution simply requires typing the menu titles and commands you want and then writing code to make your program respond to the menu commands the user picks, as shown in Figure 17-3.

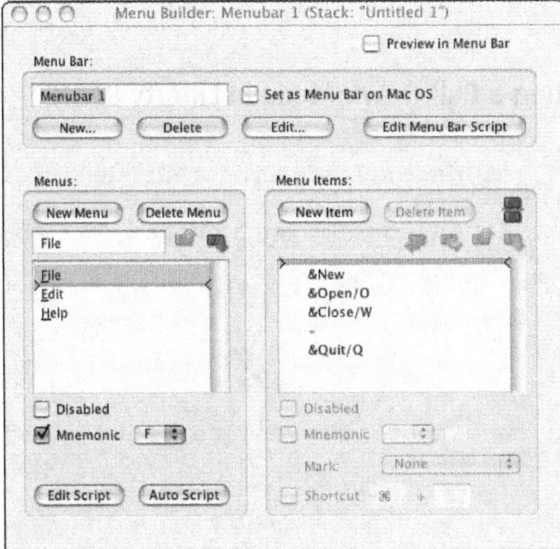

Figure 17-3: The Menu Builder dialog box in Revolution lets you create a pull-down menu just by typing the menu titles and commands.

Displaying Controls

Pull-down menus let users give a command to a program, but they don't let users give any data to the program. To get data from the user, your program needs to display additional controls on-screen. Common types of controls that a program can display include

- Command buttons
- Check boxes and radio buttons
- List boxes and combo boxes
- Text boxes

To create a user interface in REALbasic and Revolution, you can just choose the user interface controls you want and drag them onto a window, as shown in Figure 17-4.

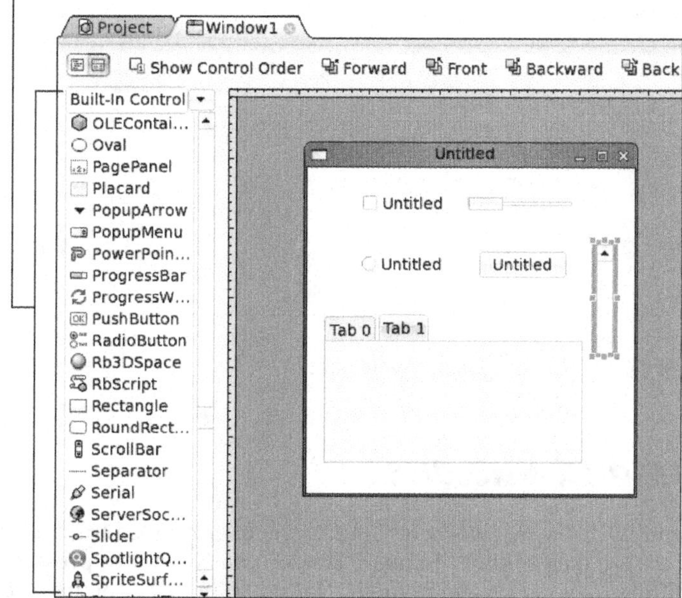

Figure 17-4: To create a user interface in REALbasic, you just have to choose the control you want and drag it onto a window.

The first step to creating a user interface is designing its appearance. The second step is writing code to make your user interface actually work.

To make your user interface work, you need to write subprograms that run when a certain event occurs, such as when the user clicks the mouse button. In REALbasic, you can create an event subprogram just by double-clicking a control, as shown in Figure 17-5.

In Revolution, you can create an event subprogram by clicking a control and then clicking the Script icon. A Script Editor displays, as shown in Figure 17-6, where you can write a subprogram that runs whenever the user clicks the mouse button.

Double-clicking this control...

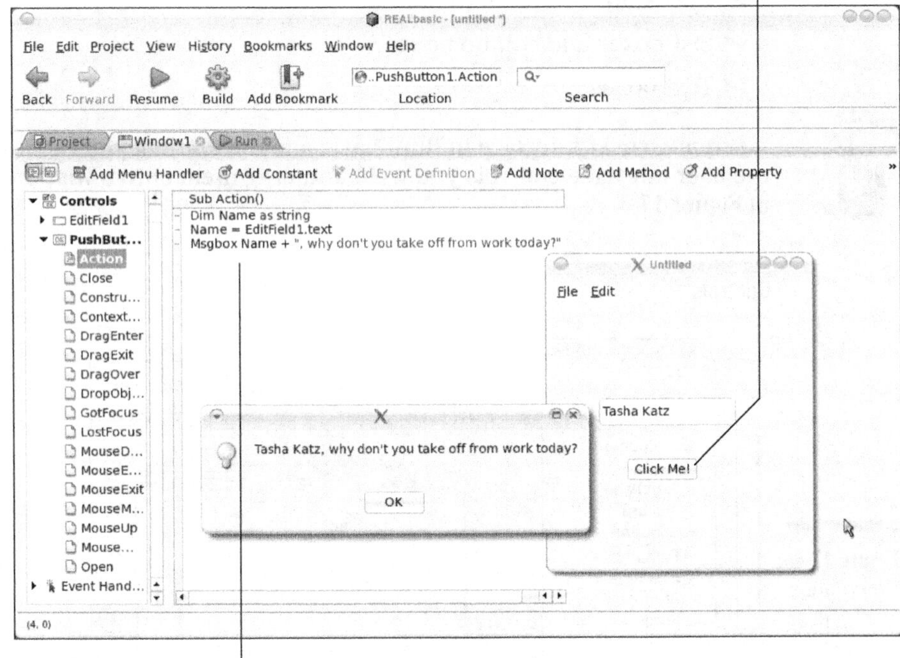

...displays the editor where you can write code.

Figure 17-5: Double-clicking a control in REALbasic opens a blank subprogram for writing code so the control can respond to the user.

Command buttons

Command buttons are handy for letting the user choose from a limited range of options, such as asking the user "Do you really want to press the button and annihilate all life on the planet?" Rather than force the user to type Yes or No (or Y or N), your program can display two command buttons labeled Yes and No, as shown in Figure 17-7.

The following REALbasic program displays two command buttons. If the user clicks the Yes button, the program displays the word `BOOM!` on-screen. If the user clicks the No button, the program displays the phrase `Nothing happens` on-screen.

The Yes button contains the following subprogram:

```
Sub Action()
  MsgBox "BOOM!"
End Sub
```

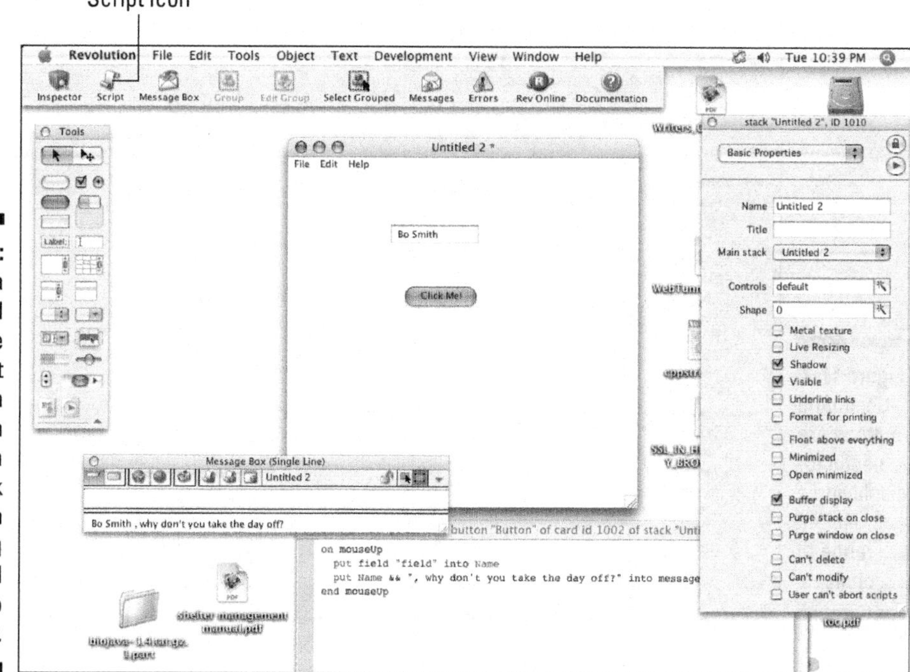

Figure 17-6: Clicking a control and clicking the Script icon in Revolution displays a blank subprogram for making the control respond to the user.

The No button contains the following subprogram:

```
Sub Action()
  MsgBox "Nothing happens"
End Sub
```

In Revolution, the Yes button subprogram looks like this:

```
on mouseUp
  put "BOOM!" into message
end mouseUp
```

The No button subprogram in Revolution looks like this:

```
on mouseUp
  put "Nothing happens" into message
end mouseUp
```

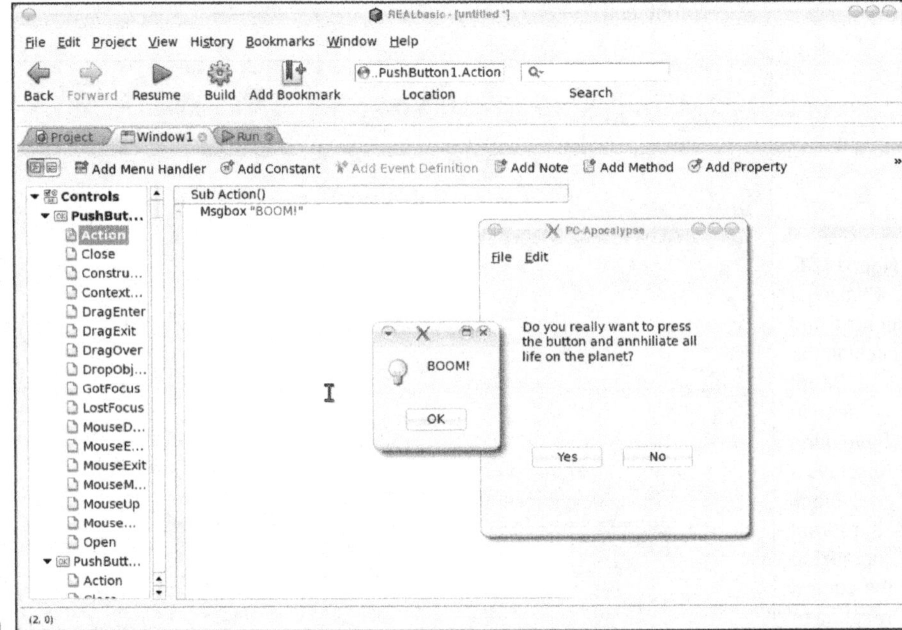

Figure 17-7: Command buttons are useful for displaying a limited range of choices.

Check boxes and radio buttons

One problem with command buttons is that each button represents a single option. If you want the user to choose from multiple options, your program can look cluttered with multiple command buttons.

To avoid this problem, user interfaces typically display either check boxes or radio buttons. Check boxes are useful for giving users the option of choosing one or more options. Radio buttons are useful for displaying a group of options but only allowing the user to select one at a time, as shown in Figure 17-8.

Using REALbasic

In REALbasic, check boxes and radio buttons have a property called `Value`, which can be set to either `True` or `False`. A `True` value means that the user selected the check box or radio button. A `False` value means that the check box or radio button is blank.

You can check the `Value` property of a check box or radio button by specifying the check box or radio button name followed by the `Value` property, as shown here:

```
objectName.Value
```

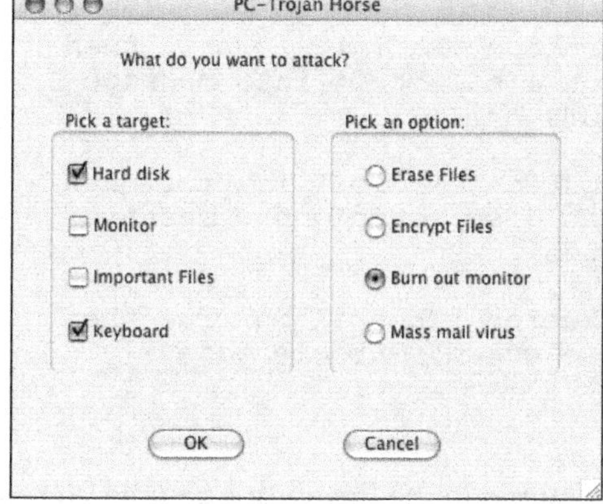

Figure 17-8: Check boxes and radio buttons can replace multiple command buttons.

The following REALbasic program checks whether a check box (named `CheckBox1`) or one of two radio buttons (named `RadioButton1` and `RadioButton2`) have been selected by the user:

```
Sub Action()
  If RadioButton1.value = True Then
    MsgBox "Radio button 1 selected"
  End If
  If RadioButton2.value = True Then
    MsgBox "Radio button 2 selected"
  End If
  If CheckBox1.value = True Then
    MsgBox "Check box selected"
  End If
End Sub
```

This REALbasic program is stored in the REALbasic Sample Programs folder as `Chapter 17 - Check Box.rb`.

A user can select only one radio button at a time.

Using Revolution

In Revolution, check boxes and radio buttons have a property called `hilite`, which can be set to `True` or `False`. A `True` value means that the user selected the check box or radio button. A `False` value means that the check box or radio button is blank.

To tell whether a check box (named `Check1`) or one of two radio buttons (named `Radio1` and `Radio2`) is selected, you have to check its `hilite` property, as the following Revolution program demonstrates:

```
on mouseUp
  if the hilite of button "Radio1" is true then
    put "Radio button 1 selected" into message
    wait for 3 seconds
  end if
  if the hilite of button "Radio2" is true then
    put "Radio button 2 selected" into message
    wait for 3 seconds
  end if
  if the hilite of button "Check1" is true then
    put "Check box selected" into message
  end if
end mouseUp
```

This Revolution program is stored in the Revolution Sample Programs folder as `Chapter 17 - Check Box.rev`.

In Revolution, a radio button and a check box are objects created (inherited) from a `button` class. That's why the preceding Revolution code checks the `hilite` property of a button, but then you have to specify the name of the button, such as `Radio2` or `Check1`.

List boxes and combo boxes

Although check boxes and radio buttons may be smaller than command buttons, they still represent a single option. If you want to offer multiple options to the user, you have to clutter the screen with multiple check boxes or radio buttons.

To offer many choices in a small amount of space, programs offer list boxes and combo boxes. A list box simply displays a long list of options for the user to select. For example, many word processors and desktop publishing programs use a list box to display the available fonts you can choose for text.

Combo boxes represent a combination of a list box and a text box. Like a list box, a combo box can display a long list of options, but like a text box, a combo box also lets the user type data that may not be offered in the combo box's list, as shown in Figure 17-9.

Using REALbasic

To use a list box or combo box, you need to store and retrieve information stored in the list box and combo box's properties. In REALbasic, list boxes and combo boxes store their choices in the `InitialValue` property, which you can edit in a dialog box, as shown in Figure 17-10.

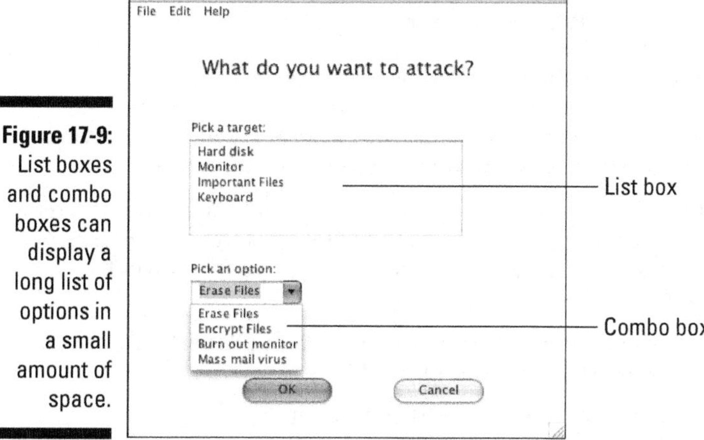

Figure 17-9: List boxes and combo boxes can display a long list of options in a small amount of space.

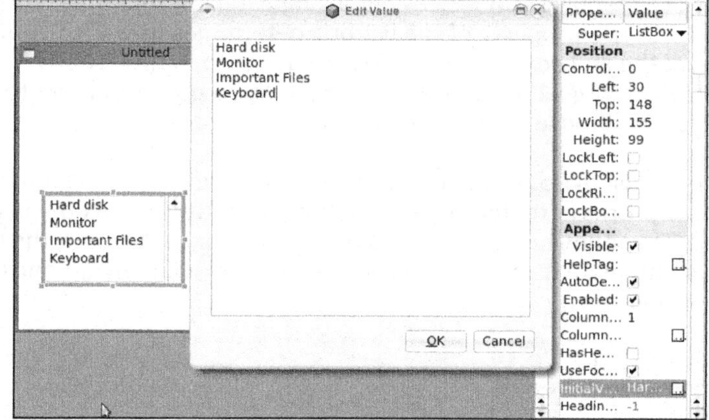

Figure 17-10: In REALbasic, you can edit the contents of a list box or combo box by editing its InitialValue property in a dialog box.

When the user clicks a list box or combo box, REALbasic stores the clicked item in the `Text` property of the list box or combo box. The following REALbasic subprogram runs whenever the user clicks an item in a list box:

```
Sub Change ()                                              →1
  If ListBox1.SelectionType = 0 then 'Single selection     →2
     MsgBox "This is the item selected = " +
            Listbox1.text                                   →3
  End if                                                    →4
End Sub                                                     →5
```

This REALbasic program is stored in the REALbasic Sample Programs folder as `Chapter 17 - List Box Single.rb`.

The preceding REALbasic subprogram works as follows:

- →1 Defines the start of the `Change` subprogram, which runs every time the user clicks an item displayed in a list box.
- →2 Checks the `SelectionType` property to make sure that the user can select only a single item in the list box. If the `SelectionType` property is `0`, the `MsgBox` command displays the currently selected item.
- →3 Displays the contents of the list box's `Text` property, which contains the item that the user clicked.
- →4 Marks the end of the `IF-THEN` statement.
- →5 Marks the end of the `Change` subprogram (method).

A list box can let users choose either a single item or multiple items. The `SelectionType` property of the list box determines how the list box behaves. If the `SelectionType` property is set to `0`, the list box lets users choose only a single item. If the `SelectionType` property is set to `1`, the list box lets users choose multiple items.

If a list box has its `SelectionType` property set to `1`, you must use the `Selected` property to determine which items in the list box the user has selected. The following REALbasic subprogram runs whenever the user selects multiple items in a list box and then clicks a command button to run the following:

```
Sub Action()                                                    →1
  Dim I as integer                                              →2
  Dim FoundItems as string
  FoundItems = ""                                               →4
  For I = 0 to (ListBox1.ListCount - 1)                         →5
    If (ListBox1.Selected(I) = true)  then
      FoundItems= FoundItems + ListBox1.List(I) + ", "
    End if
  Next                                                          →9
  FoundItems = Left(FoundItems, Len(FoundItems) - 2)           →10
  MsgBox "FoundItems = " + FoundItems                          →11
End Sub                                                        →12
```

This REALbasic program is stored in the REALbasic Sample Programs folder as `Chapter 17 - List Box Multiple.rb`.

The REALbasic subprogram works as follows:

- →1 Defines the start of the `Action` subprogram, which runs every time the user clicks a command button.
- →2-4 Creates two variables called `I` and `FoundItems`. The `I` variable can hold only integers, and the `FoundItems` variable can hold only strings. Line 4 initially stores a blank in the `FoundItems` variable.
- →5-9 The first item in a list box is numbered 0, the second is numbered `1`, and so on. So line 5 creates a `FOR-NEXT` loop that checks each item in the list box to see whether the user has selected the item. If an item's `Selected` property is `True`, line 7 stores the item in the `FoundItems` variable and adds a comma and a space to separate each selected item so that the `FoundItems` variable contains a string such as

  ```
  Item1, Item2, Item3, Item4,
  ```
- →10 The `Left` function removes the last two characters from the end of the `FoundItems` variable, which removes the last comma and extra space at the end of the string in the `FoundItems` variable.
- →11 The `MsgBox` command displays all the items selected in the list box where each item is separated by a comma and a space.
- →12 Marks the end of the `Action` subprogram.

A combo box contains an initial list of choices stored in its `InitialValue` property. When the user either clicks an item or types data in the combo box, the combo box stores the user's selection in its `Text` property.

The following code retrieves the `Text` value of a combo box:

```
Sub Action()
   MsgBox "This is the item selected = " + Combobox1.text
End Sub
```

This REALbasic program is stored in the REALbasic Sample Programs folder as `Chapter 17 - Combo Box.rb`.

Using Revolution

In Revolution, a list box (called a List Field) stores its initial list of items in the `Contents` property, but a combo box stores its initial list of items in the `Menu Items` property, as shown in Figure 17-11.

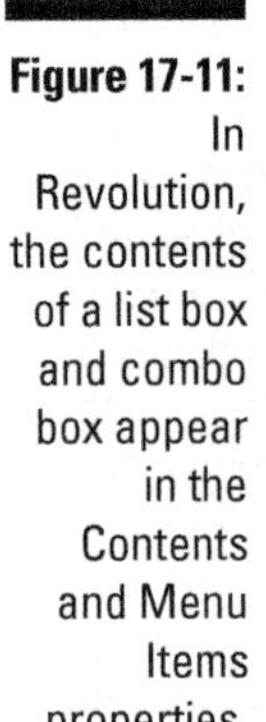

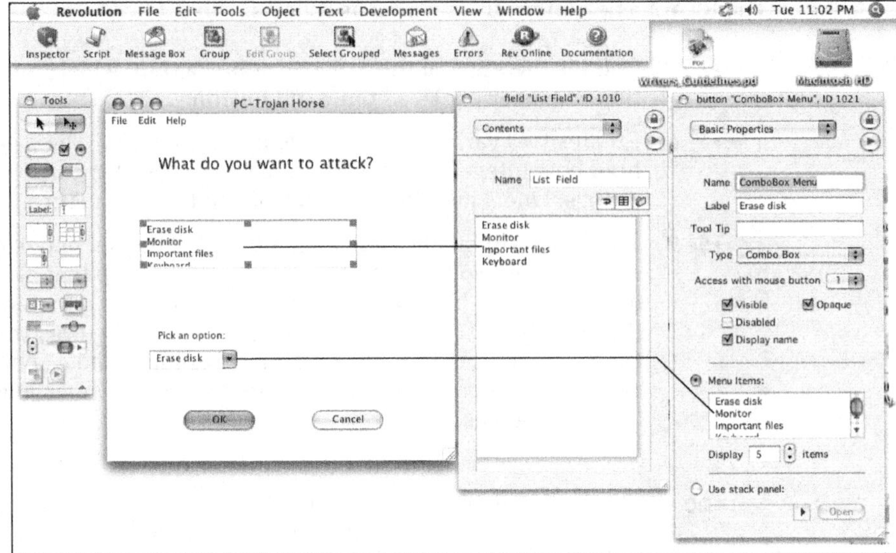

Figure 17-11: In Revolution, the contents of a list box and combo box appear in the Contents and Menu Items properties.

To retrieve the list box item the user has clicked, you need to retrieve the contents of the `clickText` variable. The following subprogram does the job, and it runs whenever the user clicks a list box:

```
on mouseup
   put the clickText into message
end mouseup
```

This Revolution program is stored in the Revolution Sample Programs folder as `Chapter 17 - List Field Single.rev`.

If you want a Revolution list box to allow the user to select multiple items, you need to select one or more of the following check boxes displayed in the list box's Basic Properties, as shown in Figure 17-12:

- **Multi-Line:** Lets the user select multiple items in the list box.
- **Non-Contiguous:** Lets the user press Ctrl (Windows) or ⌘ (Mac) to select multiple items. If this check box is not selected but the Multi-Line check box is selected, then the user can select a range of multiple items by pressing Shift.
- **Click to Toggle:** Lets the user select or deselect an item by clicking it. If this check box is not selected, clicking an item only selects it but never deselects it.

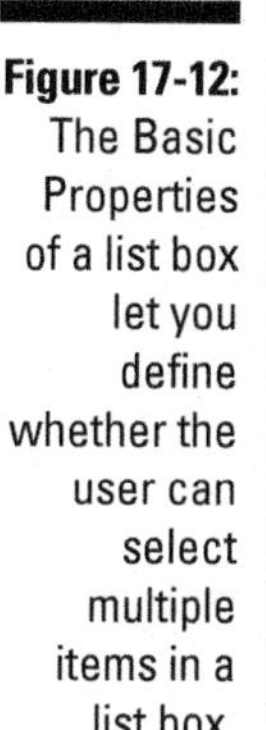

Figure 17-12: The Basic Properties of a list box let you define whether the user can select multiple items in a list box.

After you select the Multi-Line, Non-Contiguous, or Click to Toggle check boxes under a List Field's Basic Properties, you can use the following code:

```
on mouseUp
  put the selectedText of field 1 into field "Label Field"
end mouseUp
```

The `mouseUp` handler belongs to a command button. When the user clicks this command button, Revolution uses the `selectedText` command to copy all the items selected in the List Field identified as `field 1`. Then it copies all these selected items into a label called `"Label Field"`, as shown in Figure 17-13.

When using a combo box, the list of initial values appears in the `Menu Items` property of the combo box's Basic Properties. When the user clicks or types an item in the combo box, the combo box stores this text in its `Label` property, which you can retrieve by using the following code:

```
on mouseUp
  put the label of button "ComboBox Menu" into message
end mouseUp
```

The `Label` property contains the selected item in the combo box, and the combo box is a button identified by its name, which in this example happens to be `"ComboBox Menu"`.

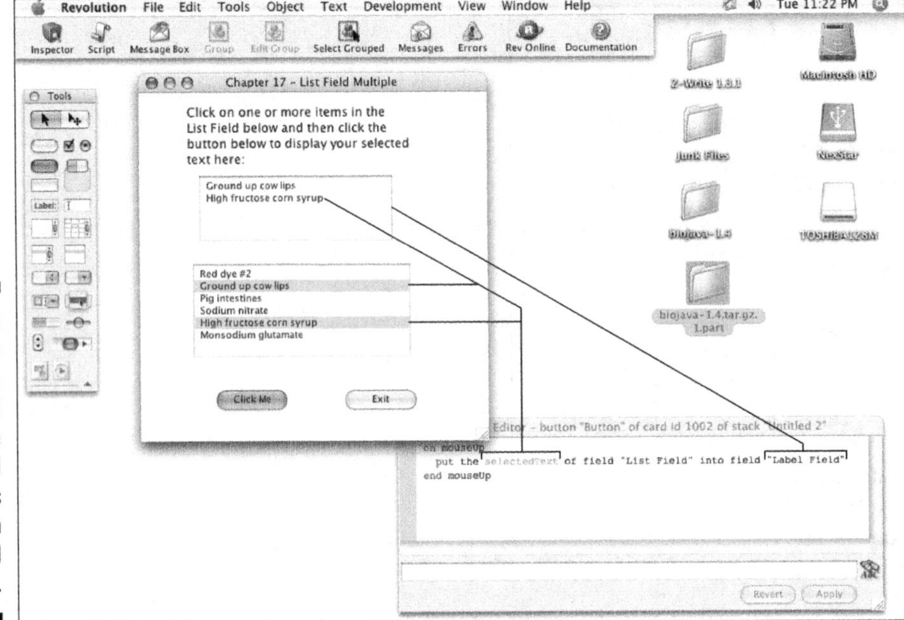

Figure 17-13: When the user clicks a command button, the selected text gets stored in a label control.

Text boxes and labels

Text boxes let the user type a large amount of text from a single letter or number to an entire paragraph. Text boxes are most useful for accepting data that can't be restricted to a limited number of choices (for example, names or passwords).

Although text boxes can display and accept text, labels are used just for displaying text on-screen.

Using REALbasic

In REALbasic, you can create a label by using a `StaticText` control and a text box by using the `EditField` control, as shown in Figure 17-14. To store text in a `StaticText` or `Text Box` control, you just need to modify the `Text` property of the control.

If a user types data into a text box, you can retrieve the contents by accessing the text box's `Text` property, as in this example:

```
Password = EditFieldName.Text
```

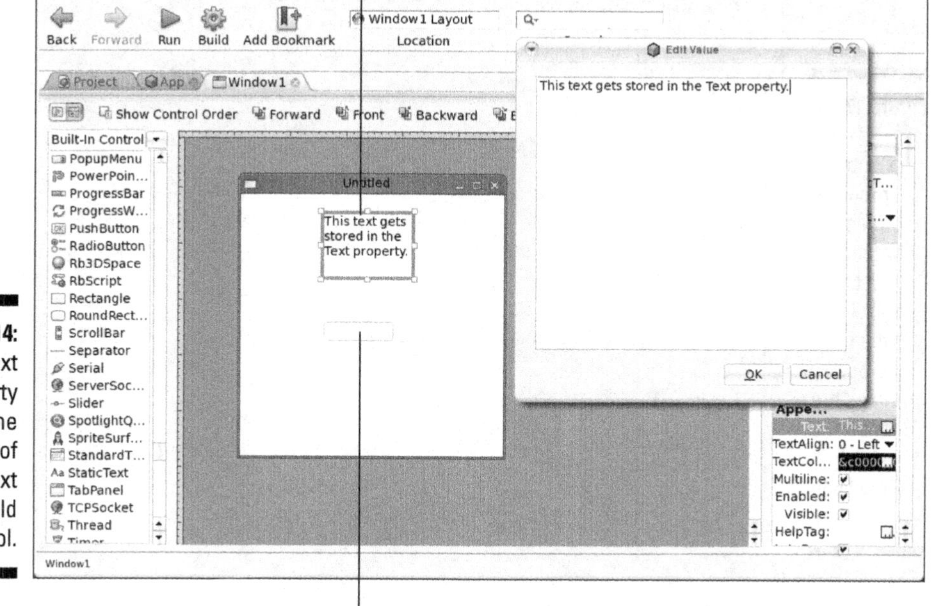

Figure 17-14: The Text property defines the contents of a StaticText and EditField control.

The following REALbasic method (subprogram) runs when the user clicks a command button. The code simply retrieves the contents of the `EditField` control (text box) where the user typed something and displays those contents in a dialog box by using the `MsgBox` command:

```
Sub Action()
  MsgBox "The user typed = " + EditField1.Text
End Sub
```

This REALbasic program is stored in the REALbasic Sample Programs folder as `Chapter 17 - Text Box.rb`.

Using Revolution

In Revolution, you can create a label by using a `Label` control and a text box by using the `Text Entry Field` control, as shown in Figure 17-15. To store text in a `Label` control, you need to modify the `Contents` property. To store text in a `Text Entry Field` control, you have to modify the `Field` property.

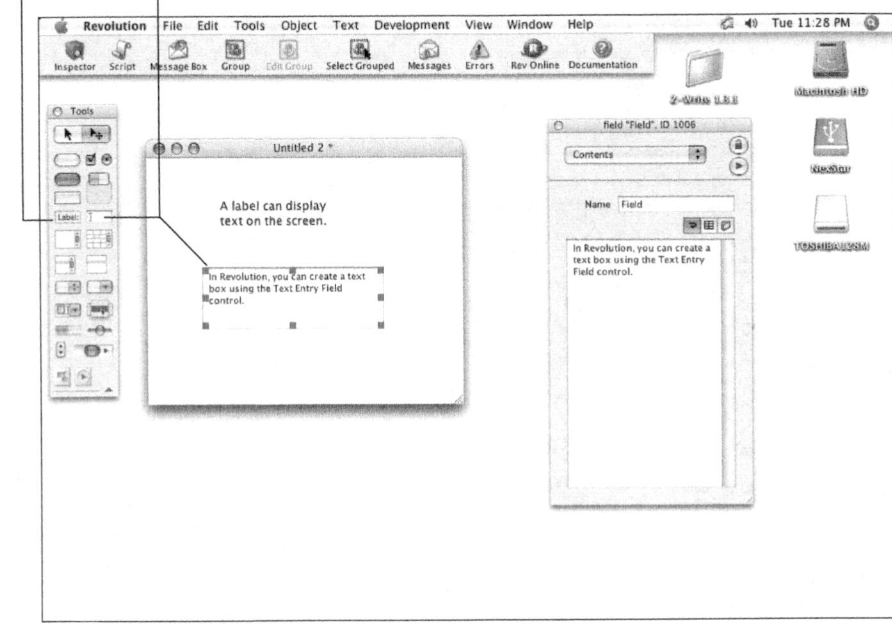

Figure 17-15: The Contents property defines the contents of a Label control and the Field property defines the contents of the Text Entry Field control.

If a user types data into a text box, you can retrieve the contents by accessing the text box's `Field` property as shown here:

```
put field "EntryFieldName" into Password
```

The following Revolution subprogram runs when the user clicks a command button. The code simply retrieves the contents of the `Text Entry Field` control (text box) where the user typed something and displays those contents in a dialog box by using the `message` command:

```
on mouseUp
  put field "TextEntryFieldName" into message
end mouseUp
```

This Revolution program is stored in the Revolution Sample Programs folder as `Chapter 17 - Text Box.rev`.

Part IV

Internet Programming

In this part . . .

Computer programming used to mean writing a program that ran on a single computer at a time. But with the introduction of the Internet, you can now store a program on a single computer and run that program on multiple computers located all over the world.

This part of the book offers a brief and gentle introduction to the world of writing programs for the Internet. The most common Internet programming language is HyperText Markup Language (HTML), which contains the magic code that defines how Web pages appear within a browser.

Although HTML forms the foundation of Internet programming, many other Internet programming languages are designed to turn your static Web pages into interactive programs. Two of the most popular Internet programming languages are JavaScript and Java.

You can find entire books devoted to teaching you JavaScript or Java programming, so consider this part of the book a brief introduction that shows you how to create interesting Web pages by using the programming skills that you developed with C++, BASIC, and Revolution.

Chapter 18

Playing with HTML

In This Chapter

- Understanding the basics of HTML
- Using tags to define text
- Using tag attributes
- Making lists
- Creating hyperlinks
- Using graphics
- Creating a user interface

The World Wide Web adds a graphical user interface to the Internet. Initially, the World Wide Web consisted of text, *hyperlinks* (text references that point to other documents stored on the Web), and graphics, although now many Web sites include other multimedia elements, such as animation, audio, and video.

Because any computer can access the Internet, Web pages consist of a special code or language that each computer (whether it's running Windows or Mac OS X) must translate to display the graphical interface of a Web page. The language of Web pages is called *HyperText Markup Language,* or *HTML.*

At the simplest level, a Web page consists of nothing but HTML codes stored in an ASCII file, which usually ends with the file extension `.htm` or `.html`. If another computer wants to view the Web site, it uses a special program known as a *browser* that translates the HTML code into a pretty graphical interface.

Using programs like Microsoft FrontPage, Apple iWeb, or Macromedia Dreamweaver, you can design a Web page without knowing any HTML at all. However, if you want to tweak or customize your Web page, you may need to know how HTML works.

Grasping the Basics of HTML

HTML code defines the way that text and graphics appear in a browser. HTML code consists of *tags,* which appear in brackets. Most (but not all) tags appear in pairs, where the first tag defines the start of something and the second tag defines the end of something, such as defining italic text, as in the following example:

```
<I>This text appears in italic.</I>
```

You can write HTML tags in UPPERCASE or lowercase (or any combination of the two). Generally, typing HTML tags in uppercase makes them stand out so they're easier to read.

An ASCII file contains nothing but characters without any formatting such as fonts or underlining. Because all computers can understand characters (such as letters, numbers, and symbols that you can type from a keyboard), you can transfer text from one computer to another by using ASCII files.

Ending tags always use a slash (/) character, as in `</I>` or `</BODY>`.

You can enclose tags within other tags, as in the following line:

```
<B>This <I>text</I> appears in bold.</B>
```

The preceding two tags display the entire line in bold and display the word *text* in both bold and italic, which looks like this:

This *text* appears in bold.

Tags act as containers for text. Think of tags as marking the beginning and ending of a container. Make sure that you don't mix up your tags, or you may get unpredictable formatting of text, as in the following example:

```
<B>This <I>text appears</B> in bold. </I>
```

If you use the mixed-up tags, your text looks like this:

This *text appears* *in bold.*

Ideally, you want to locate tags completely inside the beginning and ending of other tags, as shown in Figure 18-1.

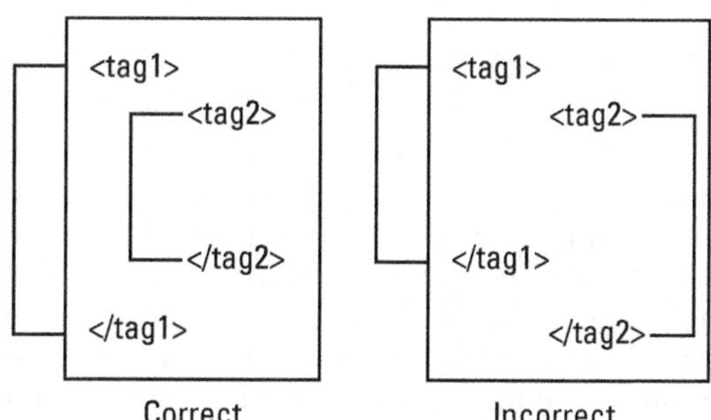

Figure 18-1: The correct (left) and incorrect (right) ways to use HTML tags.

HTML codes can look cryptic if you cram them together, so feel free to use plenty of blank lines and spaces to make your HTML code look halfway readable. Remember that when a browser interprets your HTML code into a Web page, it ignores blank lines and spaces.

You can write HTML code in any text editor, such as Windows Notepad or even the Liberty BASIC editor. Just remember to save your file with the HTM file extension. After you create an HTML file, you can load that file into your browser by choosing File⇨Open from the browser's menu bar.

Grasping the most important HTML tags

The following are the first HTML tags that every Web page needs:

```
<HTML>
</HTML>
```

These two tags simply define a blank Web page. Anything that appears inside these two tags appears on the Web page. Nothing should appear before the `<HTML>` tag or after the `</HTML>` tag. If anything does appear in these locations in your text editor, it doesn't appear on-screen when you view the page in a Web browser.

Creating a header and title

Next, you need to define anything that you want to appear in the header (the top) of your Web page by using the `<HEAD>` tag, which looks like this:

```
<HTML>
<HEAD>
</HEAD>
</HTML>
```

The most common item to place between the <HEAD> and </HEAD> tags is a title. If someone decides to bookmark your Web page, the title is the text that the browser stores in that person's bookmark list. Without a title, the user's bookmark list contains the actual filename, which is often cryptic and confusing. After all, what's easier to read in a bookmark listing — an actual Web page name, such as `Web Site Containing American Nuclear Secrets`, or a filename, such as `NK2007.HTM`?

To define a title for your Web page, you shove the title tags between the header tags, as follows:

```
<HTML>
<HEAD>
 <TITLE>Document title</TITLE>
</HEAD>
</HTML>
```

A Web page needs only one title.

Defining the bulk of your Web page

After you define a header and title for your Web page, you need to define the remainder of your page by using the <BODY> and </BODY> tags, as follows:

```
<HTML>
<HEAD>
 <TITLE>Document title</TITLE>
</HEAD>
<BODY>
</BODY>
</HTML>
```

Adding comments

In ordinary programming languages, you can insert comments that explain what your program is doing, when you last changed the program, and who last modified the program. (See Chapter 7 for information about commenting programs.) HTML code also lets you add comments directly in the HTML code that defines your Web pages.

Comments don't appear in a browser; they appear only if you're viewing the HTML code. A comment must appear inside brackets, as follows:

```
<!-- A comment: Your mother is ugly, and so are you. -->
```

The `<!--` marks the beginning of the comment tag, and the `-->` marks the end of the comment tag.

Defining Text with Tags

The basic HTML tags define your Web page as a whole, but you need to add text to provide something useful for viewers to read. HTML provides special tags for creating the following elements:

- **Headings** separate sections of text and categorize blocks of text under a single topic (similar to the way that headings in this chapter separate and categorize text).
- **Paragraphs** are blocks of text consisting of one or more sentences.
- **Quotes** are similar to paragraphs, but the HTML tags for quotes indent and surround them with more space than ordinary paragraphs.
- **Text emphasis** displays text in a certain format or style to highlight the text.

The following sections describe each of these different text tags.

Making a heading

HTML enables you to choose among six heading styles. Heading 1 signifies the most important heading, and Heading 6 signifies the least important heading. Figure 18-2 shows an example of each type of heading.

To create one of these six headings, use one of the following sets of HTML tags:

```
<H1>Heading 1</H1>
<H2>Heading 2</H2>
<H3>Heading 3</H3>
<H4>Heading 4</H4>
<H5>Heading 5</H5>
<H6>Heading 6</H6>
```

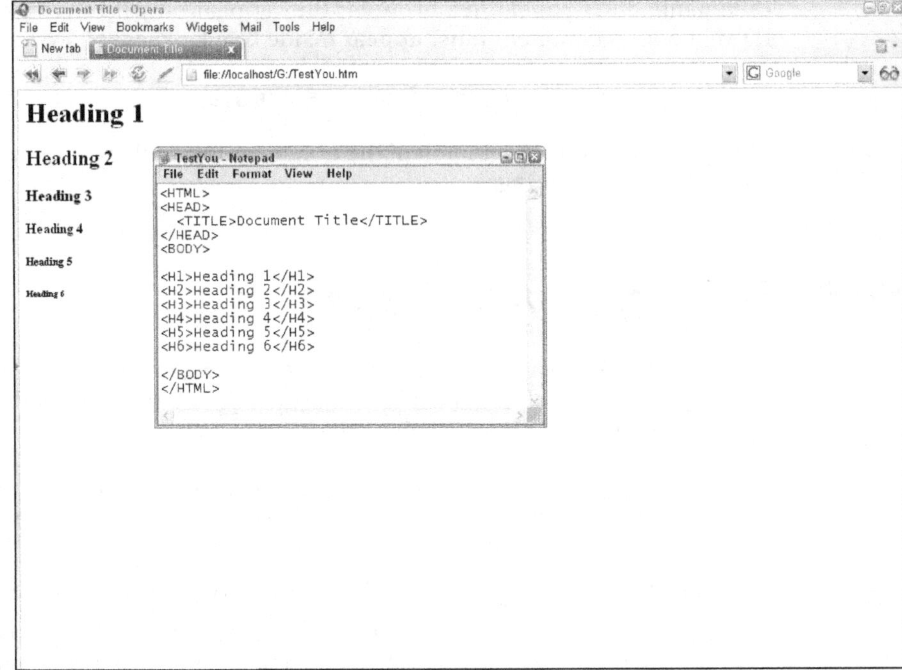

Figure 18-2: The six types of headings that you can create by using HTML tags.

Usually, you want at least two subheadings under each heading, such as two or more Heading 2s under a single Heading 1.

Defining a paragraph

A paragraph is a chunk of text that you separate from the surrounding text by a blank line (just as with the paragraphs that you see on this page). To define the start of a paragraph, you use the `<P>` tag, and to define the end of the paragraph, you use the `</P>` tag, as follows:

```
<P>
This text you can consider a paragraph.
</P>
```

If you add text inside a pair of paragraph tags, the entire paragraph can exist on a single line, extending from the left margin of the screen to beyond the right margin of the screen. The paragraph tags automatically take care of displaying text within the margins of the screen.

To make your paragraph text easier to read in the HTML file itself, you may want to press Enter to make paragraph lines appear on multiple lines rather than on a single line. Breaking lines in this manner has no effect on what your browser displays on-screen, however.

If you want to insert a line break in the middle of a paragraph, you can use a special line-break tag — the `<BR>` tag. Unlike other tags, the line-break tag appears by itself. Figure 18-3 shows how the paragraph tag `<P>` and the line-break tag `<BR>` can create a blank line between paragraphs.

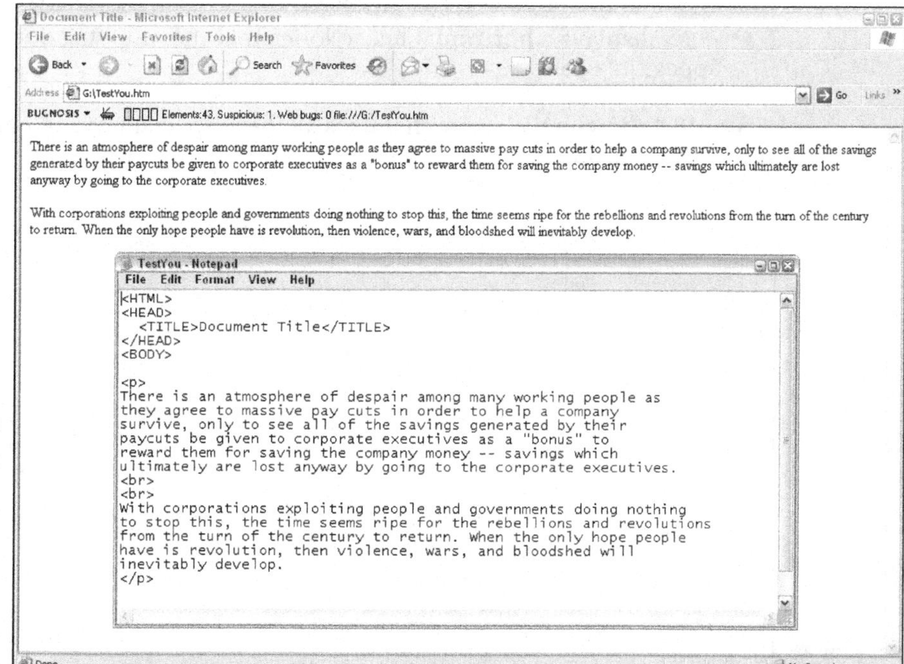

Figure 18-3: How a paragraph looks if you display it in a Web browser.

Highlighting a quote

If you want to make a paragraph stand out from the rest of your text, you can define it as a quote this way:

```
<BLOCKQUOTE>
This text appears indented.
</BLOCKQUOTE>
```

Adding emphasis to text

You may want to highlight specific words or phrases. To do so, you can use the following pairs of HTML tags:

- <B> and </B> display text in bold.
- <I> and </I> display text in italic.
- <U> and </U> display text underlined.
- <TT> and </TT> display text as if you're printing it from a typewriter.
- <HR> displays a horizontal line. (Notice that the <HR> tag doesn't appear in a pair.)

Figure 18-4 shows a Web page that uses all these special ways to emphasize text within a browser.

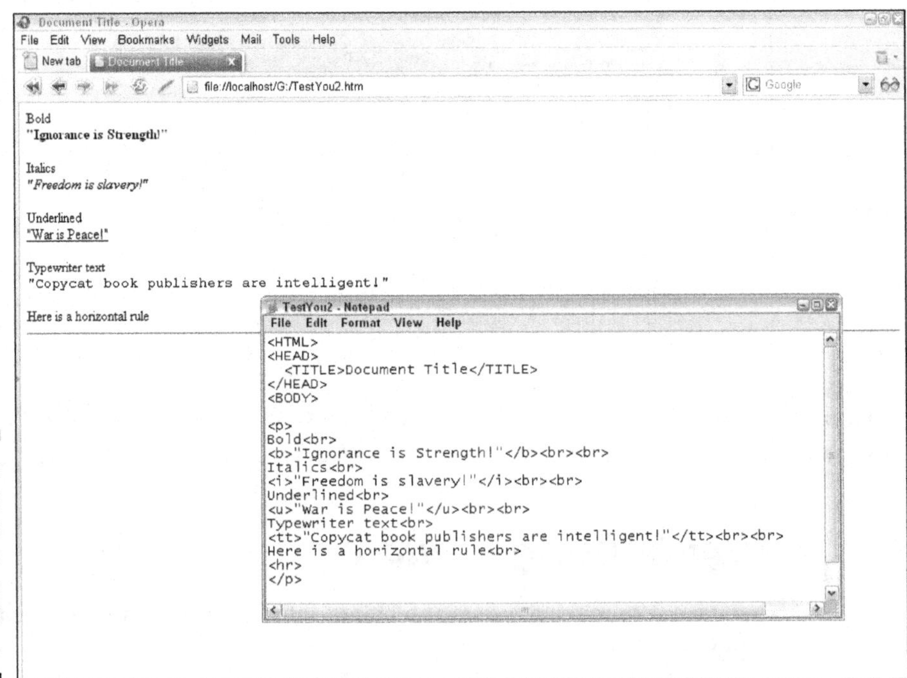

Figure 18-4: Displaying text to emphasize certain words and phrases.

Using Tag Attributes

To truly enhance the appearance of your text, you can use attributes. An *attribute* is a special command that you bury inside an HTML tag. An attribute modifies the behavior of the browser when it interprets the tag. For instance, you can use an attribute to change the appearance of text displayed by the `<P>` and `</P>` tags.

The following are some common attributes:

- `ALIGN` aligns paragraph or heading text to the right, center, or left.
- `BGCOLOR` changes the background color of a Web page.
- `TEXT` changes the color of text.
- `LINK` changes the color of hyperlinks.
- `VLINK` changes the color of hyperlinks that a user has already visited.

Aligning text

You normally left-align headings and paragraphs, but you can also right-align or center them by using the `ALIGN` attribute inside the first heading or paragraph tag.

To center-align text, you just need to use the word `"center"` with the `ALIGN` attribute, as in the following example:

```
<P ALIGN="center">
This text appears centered.
</P>
```

To align text to the right or left, use the word `"right"` or `"left"` with the `ALIGN` attribute, as follows:

```
<H1 ALIGN="right">
This text appears right-aligned.
</H1>
```

Playing with colors

To define the background and text colors, you must set the `BGCOLOR` and `TEXT` attributes to the color that you want to use. The latest versions of most browsers allow you to define colors by using names such as `red`, `blue`, or `yellow`. The following example displays black text on a white background:

```
<BODY BGCOLOR="white">
<BODY TEXT="black">
```

For greater flexibility, you can use a six-digit number that represents the *RGB* (Red-Green-Blue) value. An RGB value defines how much red, green, and blue appear in the resulting color. By altering the amount of red, green, or blue, you can create a variety of different colors such as purple, white, orange, yellow, and so on. The following code shows how to include the RGB values to display black text on a white background:

```
<BODY BGCOLOR="FFFFFF">
<BODY TEXT="000000">
```

You define RGB colors by using hexadecimal numbers, which range from 0 to F (0, 1, 2, 3, 4, 5, 6, 7, 8, 9, A, B, C, D, E, F). A zero (0) represents the absence of a color, whereas an F represents the maximum amount of a color. You can vary the values for red, blue, and green to create other colors.

The first two digits in the `BGCOLOR` and `TEXT` attributes represent the amount of red (`R`), the second two digits represent the amount of green (`G`), and the last two digits represent the amount of blue (`B`) in the color. If you want a completely red background, use the following command:

```
<BODY BGCOLOR="FF0000">
```

For a completely green background, use the following command:

```
<BODY BGCOLOR="00FF00">
```

And for a totally blue background, use the following command:

```
<BODY BGCOLOR="0000FF">
```

Coloring your hyperlinks

You may also want to adjust the colors for your hyperlinks. Most Web pages display hyperlinks in a bright color to make them obvious. After a user visits a hyperlink, that hyperlink can change colors to show the user that he or she has already been to that Web page. To change colors for your hyperlinks, use the following tags:

```
<BODY LINK="#hexadecimal_here">
<BODY VLINK="#hexadecimal_here">
```

The LINK attribute uses the same hexadecimal numbers as for text and backgrounds to define the color for a hyperlink. The VLINK attribute similarly defines the color to display a hyperlink that the user has already visited.

Making a List

Creating a Web page to inform people about something is like creating an attention-grabbing television advertisement. In both cases, you want to show the viewer as much information as possible in an attractive and easily digestible way. Many people find large chunks of text intimidating and hard to read, so consider separating your text into lists.

HTML provides the following three types of lists (and I'm using a list to show you those lists):

- **Unordered lists** display text with bullets in front of each line, such as the list you're reading right now.
- **Ordered lists** number each line of text.
- **Definition lists** indent each line of text.

Unordered lists

To create an unordered list, you need to use two types of HTML tags. The first HTML tags are <UL> and </UL>, which define the unordered list. The second tag, <LI> (which stands for List Item), marks each bulleted item. Following is an example:

```
<UL>
<LI>Take out the trash.</LI>
<LI>Develop a nuclear weapon. </LI>
<LI>Borrow an expensive appliance from the neighbor. </LI>
</UL>
```

The <LI> tag doesn't require an </LI> ending tag. However, some browsers may not display text correctly without the </LI> ending tag, so for consistency's sake and to insure compatibility, always use the </LI> ending tag.

You can also create a *nested* unordered list as follows:

```
<UL>
<LI>Take out the trash. </LI>
<LI>Develop a nuclear weapon. </LI>
```

```
 <UL>
 <LI>Steal military secrets</LI>
 <LI>Invade another country</LI>
 <LI>Export more MSG to the masses</LI>
 </UL>
<LI>Declare war on drugs</LI>
</UL>
```

Figure 18-5 shows how the preceding HTML code creates a nested unordered list. Notice that the nested unordered list uses unique bullets to differentiate it from the outer unordered list.

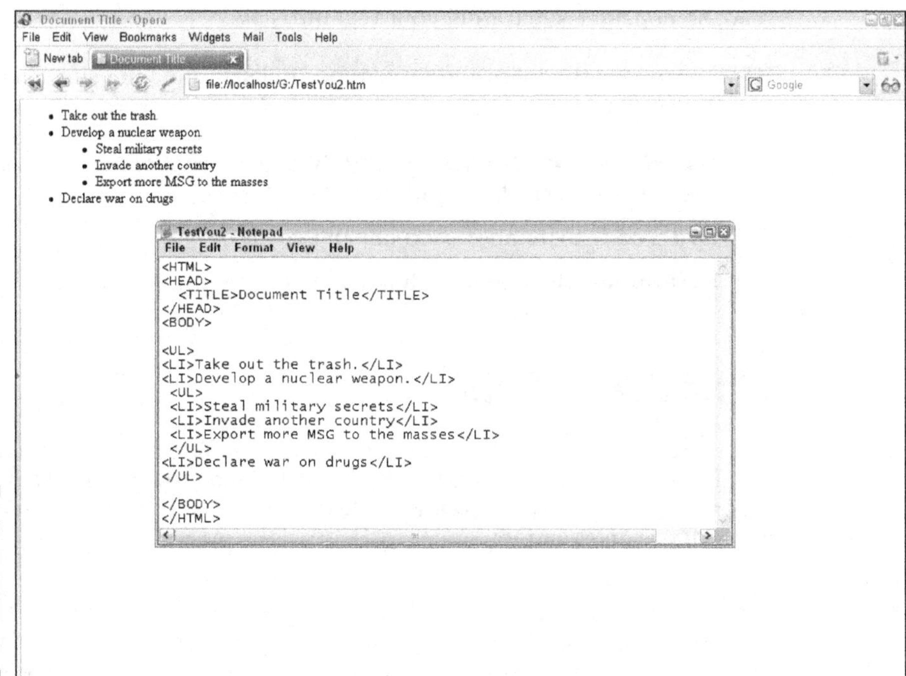

Figure 18-5: Creating a nested unordered list.

Ordered lists

Whereas an unordered list displays items with bullets, an ordered list displays items with numbers. The first list item is number 1; the second is number 2; and so on.

To create an ordered list, use the <OL> and </OL> tags to define the ordered list. Then use the <LI> tag to mark each numbered item. Following is an example:

```
<OL>
<LI>Turn left at the traffic light</LI>
<LI>Drive five blocks</LI>
<LI>Knock on the door and enter City Hall</LI>
</OL>
```

When you create an ordered list, the <OL> and </OL> HTML codes automatically number your list starting with 1. Although you can't change the type of numbers used (such as numbering your list starting with I, II, III, and so on), you can define a different starting number, as shown in the following code, which starts numbering your list with the number 4:

```
<OL START=4>
<LI>Turn left at the traffic light</LI>
<LI>Drive five blocks</LI>
<LI>Knock on the door and enter City Hall</LI>
</OL>
```

You can also create a *nested* ordered list as follows:

```
<OL>
<LI>Turn left at the traffic light. </LI>
<LI>Drive five blocks. </LI>
 <OL>
 <LI>Go past the burned out storefronts</LI>
 <LI>Turn right at the weed-choked abandoned lot</LI>
 <LI>Look for the building covered in graffiti</LI>
 </OL>
<LI>Knock on the door and enter City Hall</LI>
</OL>
```

Figure 18-6 shows a nested ordered list. Notice that the nested ordered list uses different numbering from the outer ordered list.

You can nest ordered and unordered lists inside one another, instead of nesting two unordered lists or two ordered lists. That way, you can have a bulleted list inside a numbered list or vice versa.

Definition lists

Definition lists get their name from the fact that people often use them in glossaries, where one line lists a term and a second line lists the definition of that term. To create a definition list, you need to use the following three types of HTML tags:

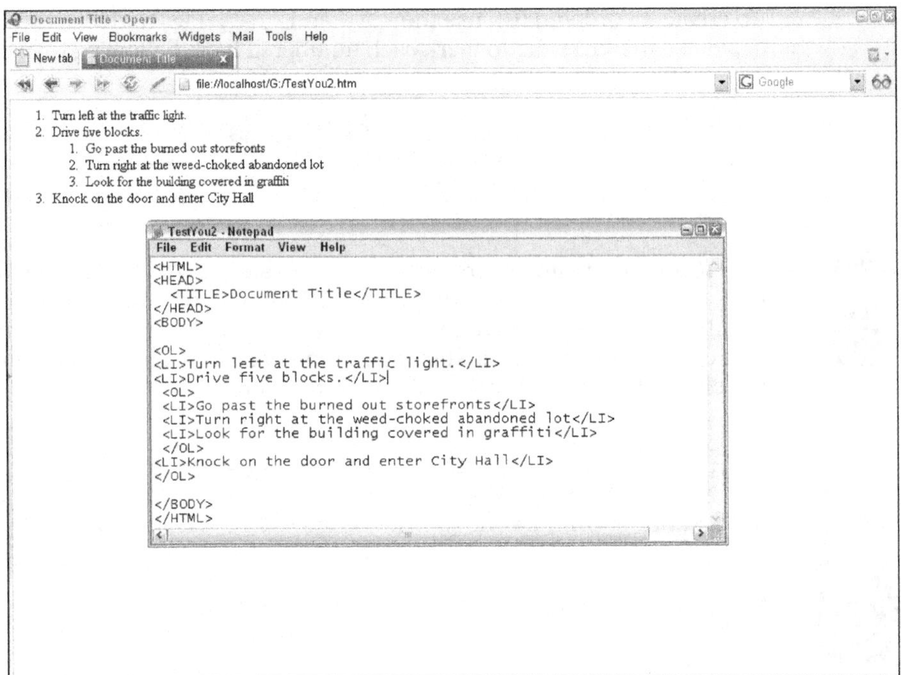

Figure 18-6: Creating a nested ordered list.

- The `<DL>` and `</DL>` tags define the start and end of a definition list.
- The `<DT>` tag displays a line of text, such as a single word or term.
- The `<DD>` tag displays a definition for the word or term that the preceding `<DT>` tag defines.

To see how to create a definition list, look at the following code and then take a look at Figure 18-7, which shows how the following HTML code looks in a browser:

```
<DL>
<DT>Cat
<DD>An animal that enslaves its owners
<DT>Liberal
<DD>A fanatic who wants to force everyone to change
<DT>Conservative
<DD>A fanatic who wants to force everyone not to change
</DL>
```

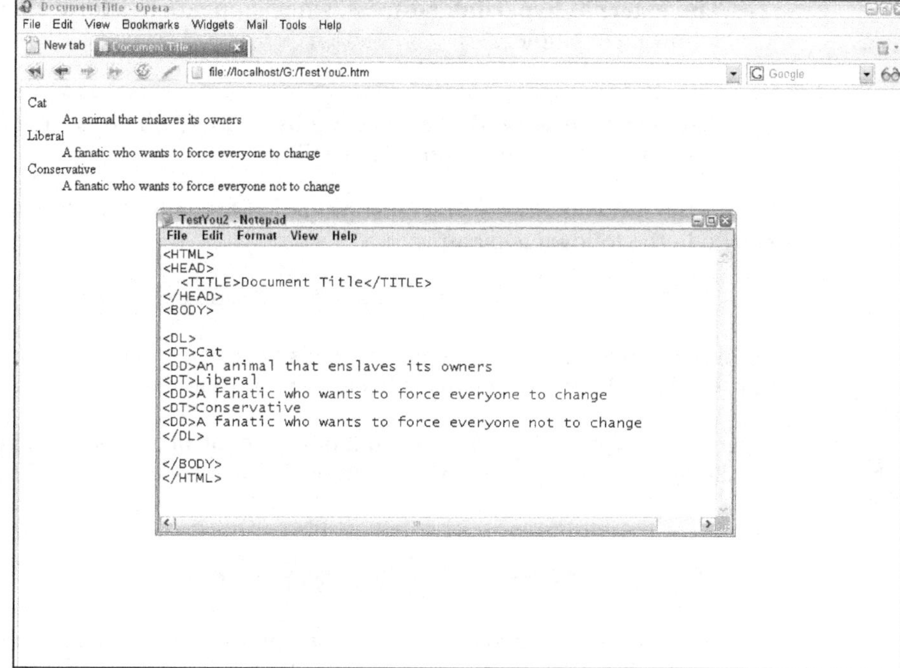

Figure 18-7: A definition list as it appears in a Web browser.

Creating Hyperlinks

Every good Web page needs two items: *information* (usually text) that provides some useful content and *hyperlinks* that link your Web page to a related Web page. A Web page usually offers the following two types of hyperlinks:

- **External hyperlinks** are links to other Web pages that typically reside on another server (and often in another geographical location).
- **Internal hyperlinks** are links to different pages of the same Web site or to a different part of the same Web page.

To create a hyperlink, you must use a pair of anchor tags, `<A>` and `</A>`. Inside the first anchor tag, you must specify either an external or internal hyperlink. Between the two anchor tags, you type the text or graphics that act as the hyperlink.

Making external hyperlinks

In defining an external hyperlink, the `HREF` (which stands for Hypertext REFerence) attribute defines the following two items:

- **The external hyperlink address,** which appears in a form similar to the following example:

  ```
  http://www.someaddress.com
  ```

- **The text or graphic that acts as the hyperlink,** which is what the user clicks to jump to the external hyperlink

To use the HREF attribute, you must put it inside the first anchor tag, as shown in the following example:

```
<A HREF="http://www.dummies.com">Dummies Web page</A>
```

In this example, the viewer sees the words Dummies Web page as the hyperlink. Clicking the hyperlink takes users to www.dummies.com.

External hyperlinks are completely out of your control, so if a Web site to which you link goes down, your Web page's hyperlink leads viewers to a dead end.

Making internal hyperlinks

To make a hyperlink to another Web page on your own site, use the HREF attribute — but instead of listing another Web site address, just type the filename of the Web page to which you want to link, as in the following example:

```
<A HREF="index.html">Index</A>
```

This code creates a hyperlink of the word Index. After users click this hyperlink, their browsers display the Web page that you store in the index.html file.

Linking to a specific spot on a Web page

One problem with linking to another Web page is that the user may need to scroll down the page to find specific information. To avoid this problem, you can create a hyperlink to a specific spot on a Web page, such as the middle or the bottom of the Web page. That way, the hyperlink directs the viewer to the exact information that you want to display.

Creating a hyperlink that connects to a particular spot on another Web page is a two-step process:

1. **Create an anchor in the spot on the Web page that you want a hyperlink to display.**

   If you want a hyperlink to direct a viewer to the bottom of a Web page, for example, you place an anchor at the bottom of that particular page.

2. **Create a hyperlink that directs a viewer to an anchor that you define.**

To create an anchor, you must use the NAME attribute, as follows:

```
<A NAME="TOC">Table of Contents</A>
```

This example displays the text Table of Contents on the Web page and assigns it the name "TOC". After you create an anchor, the next step is to create a hyperlink that points to that particular anchor.

Anchors are *case-sensitive,* which means that an anchor that you name TOC is completely different from an anchor that you name toc. If you forget this difference, your anchors won't work at all.

To make a hyperlink point to a predefined anchor, use the HREF attribute and include the Web page filename and the anchor name. Separate the anchor name from the Web page filename with the # character, as shown here:

```
<A HREF="index.html#TOC">Go to Page One</A>
```

The preceding code displays the Go to Page One hyperlink on-screen. After the user clicks this hyperlink, the browser jumps to the index.html page and displays the anchor that the name "TOC" defines. In this case, the browser displays the Table of Contents at the top of the page, regardless of whether the words Table of Contents appear in the middle or at the bottom of the Web page.

Displaying Graphics

Just displaying text on a Web page can get pretty boring, so HTML enables you to display graphic images on your Web pages to make everything look prettier. Graphics can appear as part of the Web page or in the background.

The two most popular picture formats that you can use for Web pages are *GIF* (Graphical Interchange Format) and *JPG* (also spelled *JPEG,* which stands for Joint Photographic Experts Group) files because every computer can display these formats. A third graphics standard, called PNG, is gaining popularity but still lags far behind GIF and JPEG files.

Putting a picture on a Web page

To display a picture on a Web page, you must use the image tag (<IMG>) and the source attribute (SRC) to tell the computer the specific filename of the graphic image that you want to display. Following is an example:

```
<IMG SRC="filename.gif">
```

To give you greater control over the placement of a picture in relation to any text that appears next to the picture, you can use the ALIGN attribute. This attribute defines whether text appears at the top, at the bottom, or to either side of the image, as follows:

```
<IMG SRC="filename.gif" ALIGN=middle>
```

Figure 18-8 shows examples of text aligning with graphic images in a browser.

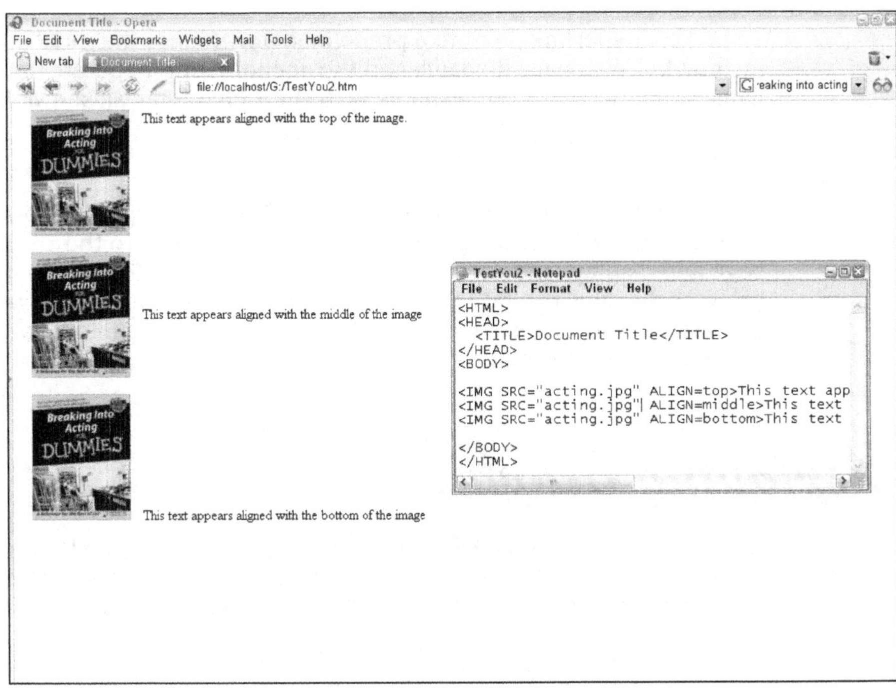

Figure 18-8: The three positions for aligning text with a graphic image.

Adding a background picture

In addition to adding colors to a Web page, you may also want to display a picture in the background. To add a picture to a Web page, use the BACKGROUND attribute inside the <BODY> tag, as in the following example:

```
<BODY BACKGROUND ="filename.GIF">
```

Creating a User Interface on a Form

Although you can use HTML to display text on-screen, you may want to create something more flexible — what's known as a *form.* A form enables you to display *text boxes*, *command buttons*, and *check boxes* on-screen. To define a form, you use the <FORM> and </FORM> tags, which you sandwich between the <BODY> and </BODY> tags, as follows:

```
<HTML>
<BODY>
<FORM>
</FORM>
</BODY>
</HTML>
```

Make sure that you sandwich the <FORM> and </FORM> tags inside the <BODY> and </BODY> tags; otherwise, your form doesn't appear on-screen.

Of course, the <FORM> and </FORM> tags simply define a form, so you still must add your user interface items on the form, as shown in Figure 18-9. The following are some common user interface items that you may want to include on a form:

- **Text boxes** are boxes in which users can type data.
- **Buttons** are command buttons that users can click.
- **Check boxes** are boxes that users can select or clear to choose or deactivate an option.
- **Radio buttons** are buttons that users can select to choose an option. You can select only one radio button at a time.

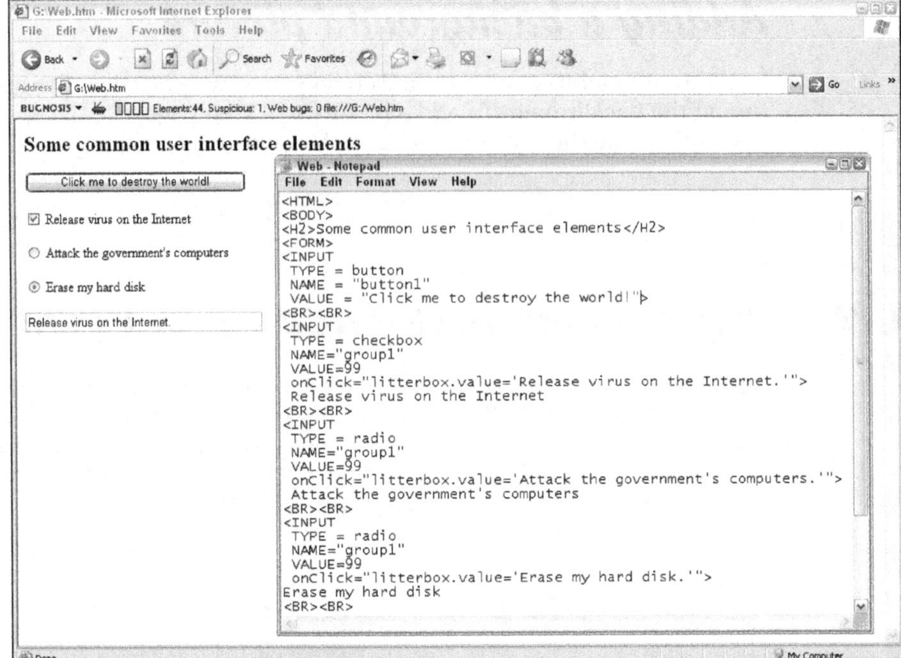

Figure 18-9: Common user interface elements that you can display on a form.

Handling events

Every user interface element displays information to the user. Any time that the user does something to a user interface item, such as clicking a command button, the action is known as an *event.*

After an event occurs on a specific user interface item, such as a command button, your form can respond by displaying text, opening a window, and so on. The following are the HTML codes for some common events:

- `onAbort` occurs after the user stops loading an image, either by clicking a link or clicking the Stop button.
- `onBlur` occurs after an item, such as a text box or command button, loses focus. This event usually occurs after the user clicks another item.
- `onChange` occurs after the contents of an item, such as a text box, change.
- `onClick` occurs after the user clicks a specific item, such as a radio button or a command button.

- `onFocus` occurs after the user clicks an object or highlights an object by pressing the Tab key.
- `onMouseOut` occurs after the mouse pointer no longer appears over a certain item.
- `onMouseOver` occurs after the mouse pointer moves over a certain item.
- `onSelect` occurs after the user selects text within a text box.

Events link to a specific user interface item, such as a command button or a check box. A single user interface item can respond to more than one type of event.

Creating a text box

A text box can display text and enable the user to type text. To create a text box, type the following command inside the `<FORM>` and `</FORM>` tags:

```
<FORM>
<INPUT
 TYPE=text                                    →3
 NAME="textboxName"                           →4
 VALUE="Text inside the text box"             →5
 SIZE=integer                                 →6
 [onBlur="command"]
 [onChange="command"]
 [onFocus="command"]
 [onSelect="command"]>                        →10
</FORM>
```

This text box event works like this:

- →3 Tells the computer to create a text box on-screen.
- →4 Assigns any name that you choose to represent your text box.
- →5 Displays text inside your text box.
- →6 Defines how many characters the text box can display without scrolling.
- →10 A text box can respond to four different events: `onBlur`, `onChange`, `onFocus`, and `onSelect`.

The following shows how to create a text box that displays the message `"Ow! You click too hard!"` after you click inside the text box:

```
<HTML>
<BODY>
<FORM>
<INPUT
 TYPE=text
 NAME="textboxName"
 VALUE="This appears inside the text box"
 SIZE=30
 onFocus="textboxName.value='Ow! You click too hard!'">
</FORM>
</BODY>
</HTML>
```

Notice the use of single and double quotation marks following the `onFocus` event. The double quotation marks enclose the entire command that you want the computer to follow after the `onFocus` event occurs. Any command inside the double quotation marks must use single quotation marks, or the entire command won't work.

Creating a command button

A user can click a command button to perform a specific action. To create a command button, use the following code inside the `<FORM>` and `</FORM>` tags:

```
<FORM>
<INPUT
 TYPE=button                                          →3
 NAME="buttonName"                                    →4
 VALUE="Text that appears on the button"              →5
 [onBlur="handlerText"]                               →6
 [onClick="handlerText"]
 [onFocus="handlerText"]>                             →8
</FORM>
```

The command button event works like this:

- →3 Creates a command button on-screen.
- →4 Assigns a name to represent your command button.
- →5 Displays the text that appears inside the command button, such as `OK` or `Click Me`.
- →6-8 Command buttons can respond to three different events: `onBlur`, `onClick`, and `onFocus`.

The following example shows how to create two command buttons — one that opens a window to display the Web page that you store in the `index.html` file and one that closes the window:

```
<HTML>
<BODY>
<FORM>
<INPUT
 TYPE=button
 NAME="open"
 VALUE="Open window"
 onClick="mywindow=window.open('index.html')">
<INPUT
 TYPE=button
 NAME="close"
 VALUE="Close window"
 onClick="mywindow.close()">
</FORM>
</BODY>
</HTML>
```

Notice that the command that the `onClick` event defines uses double quotation marks to enclose the entire command. Anything that appears inside must use single quotation marks or the entire command won't work.

Creating a check box

Check boxes display options that the user can choose by clicking the check box to add or remove a check mark. To make a check box, put the following command inside the `<FORM>` and `</FORM>` tags:

```
<FORM>
<INPUT
 TYPE=checkbox                         →3
 NAME="checkboxName"                   →4
 VALUE="checkboxValue"                 →5
 [CHECKED]                             →6
 [onBlur="handlerText"]                →7
 [onClick="handlerText"]
 [onFocus="handlerText"]>              →9
 textToDisplay                         →10
</FORM>
```

The check box event works like this:

- →3 Creates a check box on-screen.
- →4 Assigns a name to represent that check box.
- →5 Specifies a number or string that the check box represents if the user chooses it.
- →6 Displays a check mark in the check box.
- →7-9 A check box can respond to three different events: `onBlur`, `onClick`, and `onFocus`.
- →10 The `textToDisplay` variable represents any text that you want to display next to the check box.

The example in Listing 18-1 creates three check boxes.

Listing 18-1: Creating Check Boxes with HTML Code

```
<HTML>
<BODY>
<H2>Where do you want your computer to go today?</H2>
<FORM>
<INPUT
 TYPE = checkbox
 NAME="check1"
 VALUE=99
 onClick="litterbox.value='Throw the computer in the
          trash.'">
 In the trash can
<BR><BR>
<INPUT
 TYPE = checkbox
 NAME="check2"
 VALUE=99
 onClick="litterbox.value='Toss the computer outside.'">
 Out the window
<BR><BR>
<INPUT
 TYPE = checkbox
 NAME="check3"
 VALUE=99
 onClick="litterbox.value='Wreck it, and then throw it
          away.'">
 Smash it to pieces
<BR><BR>
<INPUT
 TYPE = text
```

```
  NAME="litterbox"
  VALUE=" "
  SIZE = 40>
</FORM>
</BODY>
</HTML>
```

After you click a check box, a message appears in a text box below it, as shown in Figure 18-10.

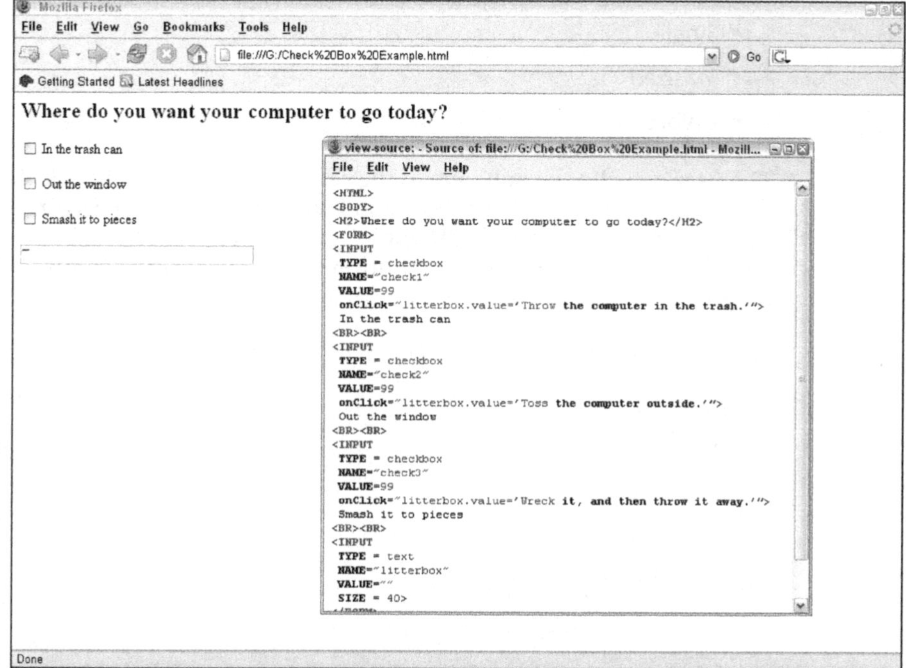

Figure 18-10: Creating three check boxes and one text box.

If you type text to appear next to a check box, you don't need to enclose it in quotation marks. If you do enclose the text inside quotation marks, the quotation marks appear on-screen as well.

Creating a radio button

A radio button works much like a check box, except that you can choose only one radio button at any given time. Radio buttons enable users to answer questions for which only one answer is possible, as in the following example:

```
What is your current marital status?
```

To answer this question, you need radio buttons for the following three responses:

- Single
- Married
- Divorced

The user can choose only one of the responses. If the user clicks the Single radio button, changes his or her mind, and then clicks the Divorced radio button, a dot appears in the Divorced radio button to show that the user chooses it, and the Single radio button becomes empty to show that it's no longer chosen.

To see how to create a radio button, look at the following code:

```
<FORM>
<INPUT
 TYPE=radio                                      →3
 NAME="radioName"                                →4
 VALUE="buttonValue"                             →5
 [CHECKED]                                       →6
 [onBlur="handlerText"]                          →7
 [onClick="handlerText"]
 [onFocus="handlerText"]>                        →9
 textToDisplay                                   →10
 </FORM>
```

The radio button event works like this:

→3 Creates a radio button on-screen.

→4 Assigns a name to represent that radio button.

If you want only one radio button to appear chosen within a group of radio buttons, you must give all radio buttons exactly the same name. When radio buttons share the same name, the computer makes sure that only one radio button can be selected at a time.

→5 Specifies a number or string that the radio button represents if the user chooses it.

→6 Displays the radio button as chosen as it first appears on-screen.

→7-9 A radio button can respond to three different events: `onBlur`, `onClick`, and `onFocus`. After the user clicks a radio button, a message appears in a text box below the button.

→10 The `textToDisplay` variable represents any text that you want to appear next to the radio button.

Listing 18-2 shows how to create three radio buttons.

Listing 18-2: Creating Radio Buttons with HTML Code

```
<HTML>
<BODY>
<H2>Where do you want your computer to go today?</H2>
<FORM>
<INPUT
 TYPE = radio
 NAME="group1"
 VALUE=99
 onClick="litterbox.value='Throw the computer in the
          trash.'">
 In the trash can
<BR><BR>
<INPUT
 TYPE = radio
 NAME="group1"
 VALUE=99
 onClick="litterbox.value='Toss the computer outside.'">
 Out the window
<BR><BR>
<INPUT
 TYPE = radio
 NAME="group1"
 VALUE=99
 onClick="litterbox.value='Wreck it, and then throw it
          away.'">
 Smash it to pieces
<BR><BR>
<INPUT
 TYPE = text
 NAME="litterbox"
 VALUE=""
```

(continued)

Listing 18-2 ***(continued)***

```
 SIZE = 40>
</FORM>
</BODY>
</HTML>
```

Notice that all radio buttons in the preceding example share the same name, which is `"group1"`. That way, the computer makes sure that the user can select only one radio button at a time.

Chapter 19

Making Interactive Web Pages with JavaScript

In This Chapter

- Knowing the basics of JavaScript
- Playing around with functions
- Opening and closing windows

HTML code can produce pretty — but ultimately static — pages that resemble billboards or magazine advertisements. Although these Web pages are functional, many people want to take fuller advantage of the computer and create miniprograms so that people can interact with the Web page by playing games or analyzing their stock portfolios.

So to create more interactive Web pages, programmers created specialized Web page programming languages, such as *JavaScript.* With JavaScript, you can create your own programs just for running on your Web site.

Despite the name similarities, JavaScript programming code bears only a superficial resemblance to Java programming code. JavaScript uses simple commands, and JavaScript programs can run only inside a browser. The Java programming language uses more complicated commands and can create separate applications.

To practice writing JavaScript programs, use a text editor (such as Windows Notepad or the Liberty BASIC editor) and save your files with the HTML file extension. Then open your browser, choose File➪Open, and choose the file that you just saved with the HTML file extension to see how your browser interprets your JavaScript programs.

JavaScript is a full-blown programming language, far too complex to cover completely in this chapter. For more information about JavaScript, pick up a copy of *JavaScript For Dummies,* 4th Edition, by Emily A. Vander Veer (Wiley).

Animating Web pages with Flash

Besides designing Web pages by using HTML codes, many people now use Flash, which lets you create animation to make your Web pages visually appealing. Learning Flash is an entire skill by itself, so if you're serious about learning how to animate Web pages, you should learn more about HTML coding along with learning how to create and develop Flash animation.

Just remember that the simpler your Web pages, the faster they load and the more responsive they appear to the user. The more graphics and Flash animation you add to a Web page, the slower your Web pages appear and the more likely users could be annoyed and leave your Web site before they can see anything. Flash can be a great way to make your Web site look more like a TV program, but use Flash sparingly. When displaying a Flash animation, many Web sites also offer a Skip Flash Movie option so users can jump right to the site without waiting for the Flash animation to appear. For more information about Flash, visit Adobe's Web site (`www.adobe.com`).

Understanding the Basics of JavaScript

To define the start and end of a JavaScript program, you use just two tags, which look similar to HTML tags. Following is an example:

```
<script language = "JavaScript">
</script>
```

You can insert a JavaScript program between the `<BODY>` and `</BODY>` HTML tags, as in the following example:

```
<HTML>
<HEAD>
 <TITLE>Document title</TITLE>
</HEAD>
<BODY>
<script language = "JavaScript">
</script>
</BODY>
</HTML>
```

Because older browsers may not understand JavaScript commands, insert two additional lines immediately after the `<script>` tag and immediately before the `</script>` tag, as follows:

```
<script language = "JavaScript">
<!--
//-->
</script>
```

The middle two lines tell older browsers to treat any JavaScript commands as comments, essentially making the browser ignore JavaScript altogether. Newer browsers that can understand JavaScript simply run the JavaScript commands.

As an alternative to typing JavaScript code directly into an HTML file, you can store your JavaScript code in a separate file. Then to load and run the code in your JavaScript file, you can use the SRC attribute, as in the following example:

```
<script language = "JavaScript" SRC="program.js">
</script>
```

This example tells the computer to load and run the JavaScript program stored in the PROGRAM.JS file.

Displaying text

JavaScript includes a document.write command for printing text on-screen: To see how this command works, look at the following example:

```
document.write("Text to print goes here.")
```

If you want to get fancy, you can include ordinary HTML tags inside the parentheses to format the text. To display text in boldface, for example, just shove in the HTML bold tag, as in the following example:

```
document.write("<B>", "This text appears bold.", "</B>")
```

Objects and JavaScript

JavaScript is based on *objects.* Objects include three characteristics: *properties, methods,* and *events.*

Properties define the appearance of the object, such as its color. Methods define actions that you can make the object perform. One of the most common objects is a document object, and its most common method is the write command. Events are occurrences that the object can respond to, such as a mouse clicking an object.

You can still use JavaScript without knowing much about objects, but knowing how objects work can help you better understand JavaScript. For now, just keep in mind that JavaScript is based on objects, so if you see strange JavaScript commands — such as document.write("Hello, there!") — you can recognize that this command is telling a document object to write something on-screen.

The `document.write` command can also smash strings together by using the plus (+) sign, as follows:

```
document.write("<B>", "This text appears bold.", "</B>" +
          " And this text appears as normal text.")
```

The preceding command creates the following display:

> **This text appears bold.** And this text appears as normal text.

Creating variables

In the `document.write` example in the preceding section, the plus sign (+) links strings and variables that represent strings. In JavaScript, you can declare a variable by using the magical `var` command, as follows:

```
var variablename
```

In JavaScript, you don't need to declare a variable data type; you just declare a variable name. Then you can set a variable to represent a string and use the plus sign (+) to link a string to a variable representing a string, as in the following example:

```
<script language = "JavaScript">                              →1
<!--                                                          →2
var mymessage                                                 →3
mymessage = "A goldfish."                                     →4
document.write("What animal has a near death experience
          every time you flush the toilet? Answer: " +
          mymessage)                                          →5
//-->                                                         →6
</script>                                                     →7
```

This JavaScript program tells the computer to do the following:

- **→1-2** Tell the computer that anything between the `<script>` and the `</script>` tags is a JavaScript program.
- **→3** Creates the variable `mymessage`.
- **→4** Assigns the string `A goldfish` to the `mymessage` variable.
- **→5** Writes the string `What animal has a near death experience every time you flush the toilet? Answer: A goldfish.`
- **→6-7** Tell the computer that the JavaScript program is at an end.

Making dialog boxes

The `document.write` command can come in handy for displaying text on-screen. But JavaScript can go much further than displaying text by creating dialog boxes. JavaScript can create the following types of dialog boxes:

- An alert dialog box
- A confirmation dialog box
- A prompt dialog box

Making an alert dialog box

One type of dialog box that programs use fairly often is an *alert dialog box*. An alert dialog box usually pops up on-screen to alert the user that something important has just happened or is about to happen, as shown in Figure 19-1. To create this alert dialog box, you use the following `alert` command:

```
alert("Nuclear meltdown has occurred. Time to evacuate!")
```

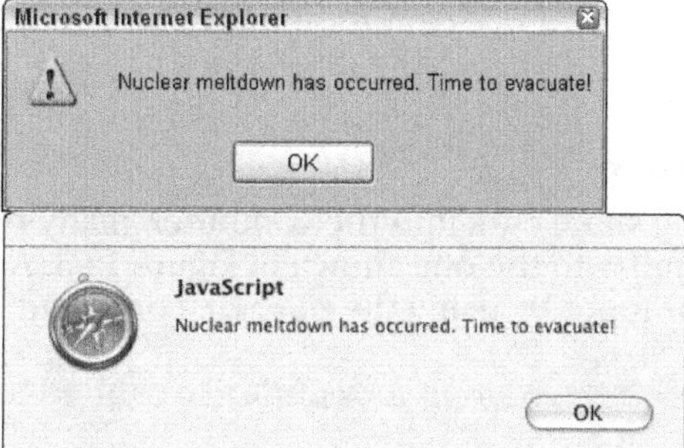

Figure 19-1: An alert dialog box created with the alert JavaScript command as shown in different browsers.

The `alert` command displays a dialog box that stays visible on-screen until the user clicks OK to make it go away.

Making a confirmation dialog box

A *confirmation dialog box* displays a message and gives the user a choice of two buttons — OK and Cancel. If the user clicks OK, the value of the `confirm` command is true. If the user clicks Cancel, the value of the `confirm` command is false. The following program creates a confirmation dialog box that looks like the one shown in Figure 19-2:

```
if (confirm("Do you want to erase your hard drive now?"))
 document.write("Now erasing your hard drive.")
else
 document.write("Then wait until Windows crashes, and that
          will erase your hard drive for you.")
```

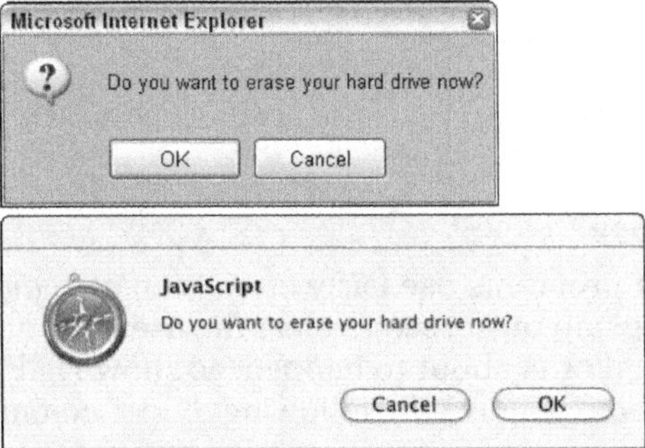

Figure 19-2: A confirmation dialog box offers the user a choice.

If the user clicks OK, the program displays the string `Now erasing your hard drive.` If the user clicks the Cancel button, the program displays the string `Then wait until Windows crashes, and that will erase your hard drive for you.`

Making a prompt dialog box

To prod the user into typing some data into the computer, many programs use a *prompt dialog box,* similar to the one shown in Figure 19-3. A prompt dialog box asks the user for input by using the `prompt` command, as follows:

```
prompt("How many times has your computer crashed on you
          today?")
```

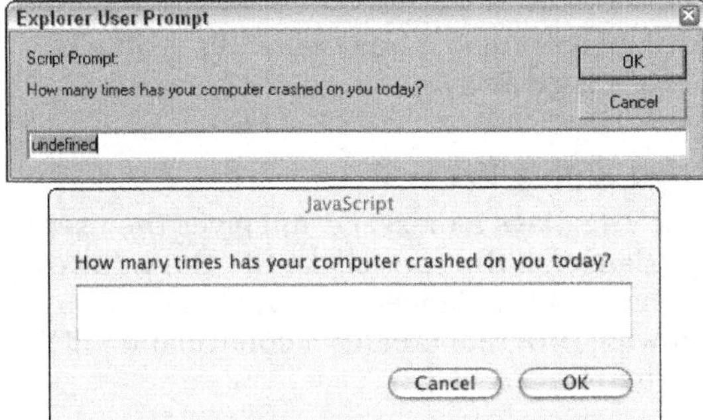

Figure 19-3: A prompt dialog box.

If you want to provide a default value that the user can choose without typing anything, you can add the default value after the message text, as in the following code:

```
prompt("How many times has your computer crashed on you
        today?", 98)
```

Because the prompt dialog box asks the user for input, you need to create a variable to hold the data that the user types into the prompt dialog box. After creating a variable, you need to set the variable equal to the prompt command, as in the following example:

```
<script language = "JavaScript">                    →1
<!--                                                 →2
var userdata                                         →3
userdata = prompt("How many times has your computer
        crashed on you today?", 98)                  →4
document.write("This is what the user typed in = ",
        userdata)                                    →5
//-->                                                →6
</script>                                            →7
```

This JavaScript program tells the computer to do the following:

- **→1-2** Tells the computer that anything within the `<script>` and `</script>` tags is a JavaScript program.
- **→3** Creates the `userdata` variable.
- **→4** Displays a prompt dialog box with the message `How many times has your computer crashed on you today?` The text box displays a default value of `98`. Any data that appears in the text box after the user clicks OK is what the program stores in the `userdata` variable.
- **→5** Prints `This is what the user typed in =` on-screen, following it with the data that the program's storing in the `userdata` variable.
- **→6-7** Tells the computer that the JavaScript program is at an end.

Playing with Functions

Rather than create one massive JavaScript program, you can create subprograms known as *functions*.

A function consists of the following four parts:

- **Keyword:** This part identifies your function as a legitimate JavaScript subprogram.
- **Name:** This part is the name that your JavaScript uses to call the function and make it run. In the following example, the function name is `square`:

  ```
  function square(number) {
   return number * number
  }
  ```

- **A list of arguments (data) that the function requires:** The data can be numbers or strings, but you must separate items by using commas. In the example for the preceding bulleted item, the only data that the function requires is a number.
- **Curly brackets enclosing the function instructions:** The instructions between the curly brackets tell the function how to work. In the preceding example, the function accepts a number, multiplies that number by itself, and returns the value of this multiplication.

  If you don't want the function to return a value, omit the `return` keyword.

A typical function may look like this:

```
function FunctionName(Data) {
 // one or more instructions
}
```

To see how functions can work in a real JavaScript program, type the following code into an editor (such as Windows Notepad) and save it with the HTML file extension:

```
<html>
<body>
<script language = "JavaScript">
<!--
function square (number) {
 return number * number
}
function printbig (headlevel, headtext) {
 document.write("<H", headlevel, ">", headtext, "</H",
          headlevel, ">")
}
var myvalue, longstring
myvalue = prompt ("How many times has your computer
          crashed on you today?", 98)
longstring = " This is how many more times your computer
          will crash = " + square(myvalue)
```

```
printbig (2, longstring)                              →14
//-->
</script>
</body>
</html>
```

This JavaScript program tells the computer to do the following:

→3 Tells the computer that anything within the <script> and </script> tags is a JavaScript program.

→4 Tells the computer to treat everything sandwiched between the <!–and //--> tags as a comment by older browsers that don't understand JavaScript.

→5 Defines the square function, which accepts one chunk of data that the program stores in the number variable.

→6 Tells the square function to multiply the number that the number variable stores and to return the multiplication result to the main JavaScript program.

→7 Marks the end of the JavaScript function square.

→8 Defines the printbig function, which accepts two chunks of data that the program stores in the headlevel and headtext variables.

→9 Creates an HTML tag for defining a heading level and for displaying text in that heading level.

→10 Marks the end of the JavaScript printbig function.

→11 Creates two variables, myvalue and longstring.

→12 Displays a prompt dialog box that asks, How many times has your computer crashed on you today? For a default value, the prompt dialog box displays the number 98. After the user clicks OK, the program stores the submitted value in the myvalue variable.

→13 Calls the square function by using the value that the myvalue variable stores. It takes this result and tacks it onto the end of the string "This is how many more times your computer will crash = ". Then it assigns the entire string, plus the value of square(myvalue), to the longstring variable.

→14 Calls the printbig function and feeds it the number 2 and the data that the longstring variable stores. In this case, the printbig function creates a heading 2 and displays the text that the longstring variable stores as a heading 2 on-screen.

Opening and Closing a Window

Although your browser may normally display only one window at a time, you can open two or more windows on-screen to display different Web pages. (Web sites often open multiple windows to display those annoying pop-up or pop-under advertisements.)

Opening a window

To open a window, sandwich the open command between the <script> and </script> tags, as in the following example:

```
<script language = "JavaScript" SRC="program.js">
<!--
 WindowName = window.open(web page or address)
//-->
</script>
```

You can also use the window.open command with a user interface item such as a button.

You must define the WindowName, which can be any name you want. You also must define what the window displays. If you want the window to display a specific Web page, you must type the filename of that Web page, as in the following example:

```
MyWindow = window.open("index.html")
```

This command opens a new window, MyWindow, and displays the Web page that the index.html file stores. If you want the window to display another Web site, you must type the entire Web site address, as follows:

```
MyWindow = window.open("http://www.dummies.com")
```

Defining a window's appearance

You can define the size and appearance of a window. If you define a window's appearance, you must give the window a second name, following it with any attributes that you want, as in the following example:

```
MyWindow = window.open("index.html", "secondname",
          "toolbar=no, resizable=yes")
```

This command opens a window that displays the index.html Web page. The window doesn't have toolbars, but you can resize the window. You use the second name of the window (in this example, `"secondname"`) if you want to refer to this window from another window, such as through a hyperlink.

Attributes can modify the appearance of a window. For example, you can use attributes to add a toolbar and a menu bar. The following list explains the attributes that you can define for any window that you open:

- `toolbar[=yes|no]|[=1|0]`: Displays a toolbar at the top of the window with buttons such as Back, Forward, and Stop
- `location[=yes|no]|[=1|0]`: Creates a text box displaying the current Web page or Web address
- `directories[=yes|no]|[=1|0]`: Displays directory buttons at the top of the window
- `status[=yes|no]|[=1|0]`: Displays a status bar at the bottom of the window
- `menubar[=yes|no]|[=1|0]`: Displays menus at the top of the window
- `scrollbars[=yes|no]|[=1|0]`: Creates horizontal and vertical scrollbars if the document is larger than the window dimensions
- `resizable[=yes|no]|[=1|0]`: Enables the user to resize the window
- `width=pixels`: Specifies the width of the window, measuring it in pixels
- `height=pixels`: Specifies the height of the window, measuring it in pixels

If you want to open a window but hide the toolbar, for example, you can set the toolbar attribute to either `yes/no` or `0/1`, as in the following example (using `yes/no`):

```
MyWindow = window.open("index.html", "secondname",
            "toolbar=no")
```

Or you can use the following example (with `1/0`) for the same task:

```
MyWindow = window.open("index.html", "secondname",
            "toolbar=0")
```

Closing a window

After you open a window, you may want to close it. To close a window, you must use the `close` command, as in the following example:

```
WindowName.close()
```

This command closes a window that you identify as `WindowName`. If you want to close a window that you call `adWindow`, use the following command:

```
adWindow.close()
```

The name of the window that you use with the `close` command is the same name that you use to open the window. You open a window with the following command:

```
WeirdStuff = window.open("index.html")
```

You close the same window with the following command:

```
WeirdStuff.close()
```

Chapter 20

Using Java Applets on Web Pages

In This Chapter

- Understanding how Java applets work
- Adding a Java applet to a Web page
- Finding free Java applets

Java can create two types of programs: full-blown applications (such as word processors or Web browsers) and smaller applets that can run only when viewed through a browser. This chapter is concerned only with using Java to write applets.

When you write applets in Java, you can add more sophisticated features to your Web pages. If you'd rather not write your own Java applets, you can always use applets that someone else has written for you, as long as you trust that the applet works correctly.

Writing Java applets can get extremely detailed and time-consuming, depending on how much work you want to put into your applet. For specific instructions on how to write programs in Java, pick up a copy of *Beginning Programming with Java For Dummies,* by Barry Burd (Wiley Publishing).

How Java Applets Work

A Java applet is a miniature program written in the Java programming language. Typically, an applet performs a single function such as displaying a clock or a calendar on a web page. Unlike C++ (which compiles programs into machine code), Java applets get converted from source code into a special byte code format.

The source code of a Java program is stored in an ASCII file with the `.java` file extension, such as `Virus.java`. When you compile a Java program into byte code format, you create a separate file with the `.class` file extension, such as `Virus.class`.

Because computers understand only machine code, no computer in the world knows how to run a Java program saved in byte code format. If you want to run a Java program stored in byte code format, you have to use a special (and free) program called a Java Virtual Machine (VM).

To run a Java applet, your computer needs a copy of the Java Virtual Machine (VM). To get the latest copy of the Java VM for your computer, visit Sun's Java site (`www.java.com`).

Many browsers restrict Java programs from running for security reasons. If you want to run Java programs, you might have to lower or alter your browser's security settings, which could also open up your computer to malicious attacks at the same time.

Java programs can run on any computer that has a copy of the Java VM, including computers running Windows, Mac OS, or UNIX. If you compile your Java programs into byte code format, you can run them on a variety of computers and operating systems without any modifications whatsoever.

If you want to write your own Java applets, you have to spend some time studying Java programming. Until you master Java (or instead of mastering Java), you may prefer to use Java applets written by other people.

You can paste other people's ready-made applets into your Web pages. Or if the source code is available, you can modify the applet and recompile it yourself, which often helps you understand the Java code more quickly.

To find a list of Web sites that offer Java applets, visit your favorite Internet search engine, such as Google (`www.google.com`), and search for the string *"Java applet"*. Or you can visit Yahoo! (`http://dir.yahoo.com`) and click the Computers and Internet, Programming and Development, Languages, Java, and Applets links. These links take you to a list of dozens of Web sites where you can download free Java applets and source code.

Java versus JavaScript

Both Java and JavaScript enable you to create interactive Web pages that you can't create with ordinary HTML code. But when should you use Java, and when should you use JavaScript?

JavaScript is easier to learn and use than Java is, so it's much faster for creating interactive Web pages. On the other hand, Java is a much more powerful and flexible programming language that enables you to create features that would be cumbersome, difficult, or impossible to duplicate in JavaScript.

As a general rule, use JavaScript for short, simple tasks and use Java for more complicated tasks. Of course, you can use both JavaScript and Java together on the same Web page to get the best of both worlds.

Limiting the power of Java applets

Java applets are miniature programs, which means that they have the potential to erase files or mess up your computer if someone writes a virus or Trojan horse in them. To prevent malicious Java applets from attacking your computer, Java restricts Java applets from performing certain tasks such as deleting files, reading the contents of a hard drive, renaming files, creating directories, or running any external programs.

Naturally, since Java's introduction, people have found numerous holes in Java's defenses. Although none of these weaknesses have yet allowed a malicious hacker to exploit these holes and threaten the world, these flaws do serve to remind programmers that Java presents opportunities to attack your computer, given enough creativity and persistence on the part of a malicious Java programmer.

Adding a Java Applet to a Web Page

When you have a Java applet compiled into byte code format (with the `.class` file extension), you're ready to use HTML tags to run that Java applet on a Web page. Adding a Java applet to a Web page involves using the `<APPLET>` and `</APPLET>` tags, sandwiched between the `<BODY>` and `</BODY>` tags, as shown here:

```
<APPLET CODE = "JavaAppletName">
Text to display if the Java applet can't run
</APPLET>
```

The `JavaAppletName` variable is the actual name of the Java applet that you want to run. If you want to run a Java applet named `Message.class`, the HTML applet tag looks like this:

```
<APPLET CODE = "Message.class">
Text to display if the Java applet can't run
</APPLET>
```

You can sandwich one or more lines of text between the `<APPLET>` and `</APPLET>` tags. This text appears only if the Java applet can't run within a particular browser. So rather than display a blank image on-screen, the text appears to explain to the user that the Java applet can't run.

Defining the size of a Java applet window

For additional fun, you can define the size of the area that your Java applet appears in by using the `WIDTH` and `HEIGHT` commands, as in the following example:

```
<APPLET CODE = "GrimaceClockApp.class" WIDTH = 300 HEIGHT
          = 180>
Your browser does not support Java or Java is not enabled.
</APPLET>
```

This example defines a width of 300 pixels and a height of 180 pixels for the applet. Figure 20-1 shows the HTML code used to display a Java applet named `GrimaceClockApp.class`.

Aligning the location of a Java applet window

When an applet appears on a Web page, you may want to use the `ALIGN` command to define how text appears next to the applet. You can use the following three `ALIGN` commands:

- `ALIGN=TOP` aligns the text with the top of the applet.
- `ALIGN=MIDDLE` aligns the text in the middle of the applet.
- `ALIGN=BOTTOM` aligns the text with the bottom of the applet.

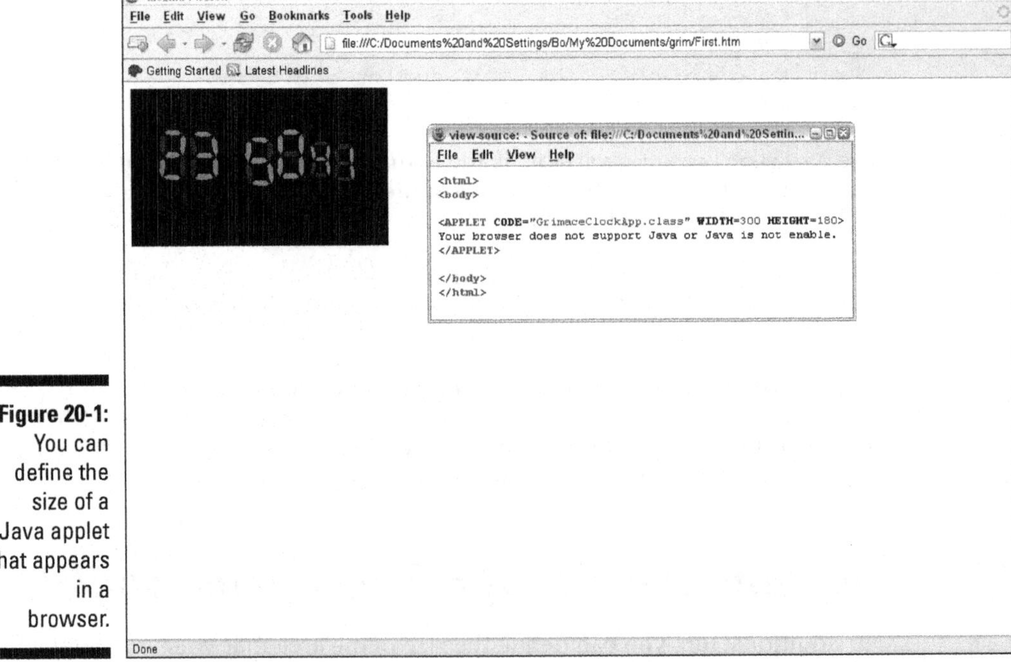

Figure 20-1: You can define the size of a Java applet that appears in a browser.

Figure 20-2 shows how text appears when aligned with an applet in three ways.

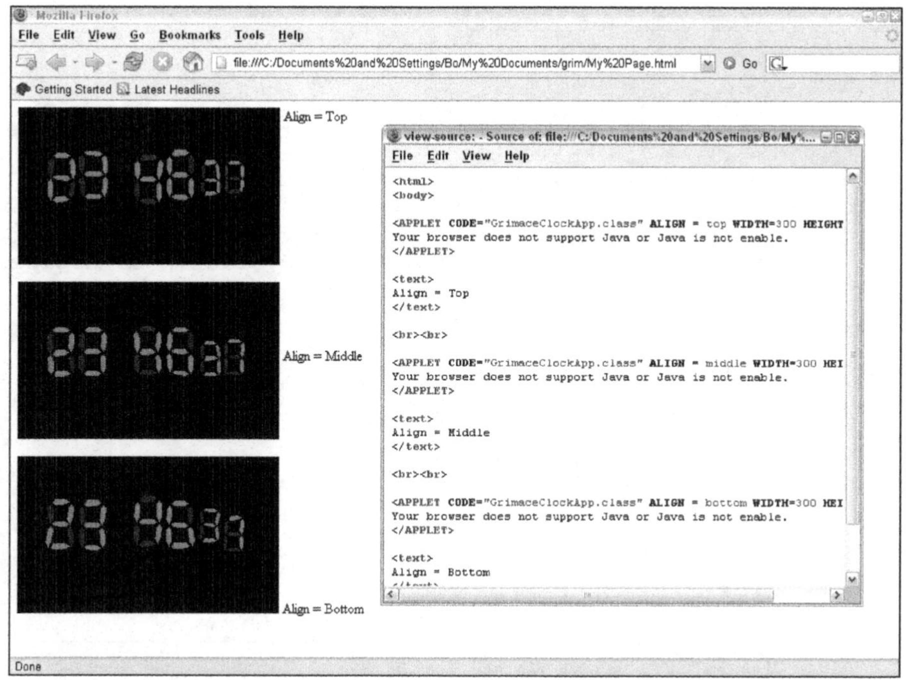

Figure 20-2: Three different ways to align text with a Java applet.

Defining space around a Java applet

To keep your text from appearing too close to an applet on a Web page, you can define the amount of horizontal and vertical space to put between the applet and the text. The following examples use the `HSPACE` and `VSPACE` commands to define the spacing:

```
<APPLET CODE = "Message.class" WIDTH = 250 HEIGHT = 100
        VSPACE = 25 HSPACE = 15>
Text to display if the Java applet can't run
</APPLET>
```

The preceding code defines a vertical space of 25 pixels and a horizontal space of 15 pixels, putting distance between text and the applet. Figure 20-3 shows what appears when you view the following code in your browser:

```
<html>
<body>

<applet code="GrimaceClockApp.class" align = "middle"
        width=250 height=200>
```

```
</applet>

<text>
The value of HSPACE = 0
</text>

<p>
This paragraph appears smashed near the Java applet since
        the value of VSPACE = 0
</p>

<applet code=" GrimaceClockApp.class" align = "middle"
        width=250 height=200 vspace = 45 hspace = 55>
</applet>

<text>
The value of HSPACE = 55
</text>

<p>
This paragraph appears at a distance from the Java applet
        since VSPACE = 45
</p>
</body>
```

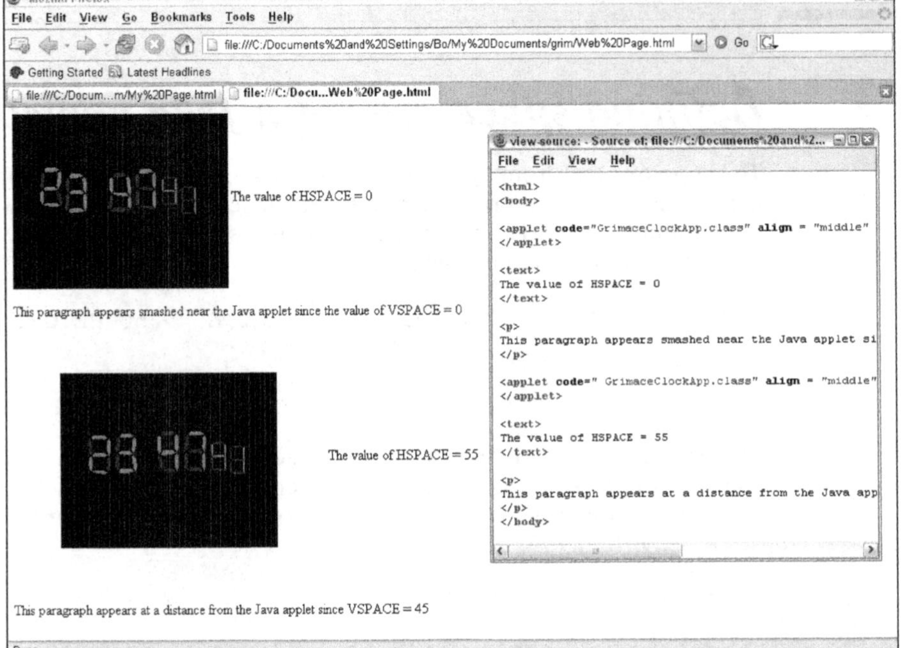

Figure 20-3: The HSPACE and VSPACE commands keep text away from the edges of a Java applet.

Part V
The Part of Tens

In this part . . .

The biggest problem with learning a programming language is knowing what to do with your skill after you obtain it. Most programming books, classes, and schools cheerfully push you out the door, wish you the best of luck, and expect you to find your own way in the programming world.

Instead of abandoning you just as you're learning about programming, this part provides some suggestions for ways to apply your programming skills in directions that most guidance counselors and vocational books likely won't talk about.

As a programmer, you possess a unique skill, so don't settle for an ordinary job working for an ordinary company so you can live an ordinary life. Instead, take a look at this part of the book and look at several exciting, fun, and challenging careers you can pursue. Who knows? With a little bit of programming skill and a lot of creativity, you could create the next programming revolution — or at least have a lot of fun and make a lot of money in the meantime.

Chapter 21

Ten Additional Programming Resources

In This Chapter

- Using Windows compilers
- Finding sources for source code
- Joining a user group
- Browsing Usenet newsgroups
- Playing Core War
- Building battling robots
- Playing with Lego Mindstorms

There will always be a need for programmers to write software for computers, whether those computers are embedded in a rocket to launch a probe to explore the surface of Mars, or just a simple program that people use in their home or office.

If you're serious about programming, take the time to master at least one programming language thoroughly, such as C++. Then take some time to learn additional languages, such as C++ variants (like C# or Java) or completely different languages with names like BASIC.

Then again, why limit yourself to C, C++, Java, or any version of BASIC? You can choose from literally hundreds of programming languages with oddball names such as Modula-2, LISP, LOGO, Scheme, Prolog, Ruby, APL, COBOL, FORTRAN, Ada, and Perl.

Because programming can often get frustrating and downright troublesome, this chapter also includes resources where you can find additional help from real-life people — for example, at computer user groups in your area or Usenet newsgroups on the Internet.

Just remember that no matter what language you use or where you find additional programming help, ultimately your own skills determine how fast you complete a project and how useful it is when it's completed.

Developing Windows Programs

Whether you like it or not, more computers in the world run the Windows operating system than any other operating system, so if you want to write and market software to the largest possible audience, you need to use a compiler that lets you create Windows programs.

The standard language for developing Windows programs is C++ although Microsoft's C# language has been unofficially recognized as the new future programming language of Windows.

Of course, you don't have to learn C++ or C# to write Windows programs; Microsoft also offers additional languages: J# and Visual Basic. J# is Microsoft's version of Java whereas Visual Basic is designed to make Windows programming easier by using the BASIC language rather than C++ or C#.

To encourage people to write Windows programs, Microsoft even gives away free copies of the popular Visual Express programming language compilers. By downloading these free compilers from `http://msdn.microsoft.com/vstudio/express`, you can create full-blown Windows programs by using C++, C#, J#, or Visual Basic.

Although Microsoft's free language compilers may sound appealing, you may still want to consider buying a different compiler, especially if you want cross-platform capabilities. Try these

- Many BASIC programmers are using REALbasic. Unlike Visual Basic, REALbasic offers cross-platform capabilities so you can create programs for Windows, Mac OS X, or Linux.
- Revolution also offers cross-platform capabilities along with offering its own simpler, but powerful, programming language.
- If you're interested in another cross-platform programming language, try writing Java programs by using the open-source NetBeans program.
- Many programmers find Delphi a unique mixture of power and simplicity. Like Visual Basic, Delphi is simple to learn, but like C++, Delphi offers many features for directly accessing the hardware of your computer while also letting you create programs for Windows or Linux.

To help you choose the best compiler for your needs, Table 19-1 lists several popular Windows compilers.

Table 19-1	Popular Windows Compilers	
Compiler Name	*Language Used*	*Web Site*
Visual C++ .NET	C++	`www.microsoft.com`
Visual Basic .NET	BASIC	`www.microsoft.com`
Visual C# .NET	C#	`www.microsoft.com`
REALbasic	BASIC	`www.realbasic.com`
NetBeans	Java	`www.netbeans.org`
Revolution	Transcript	`www.runrev.com`
Delphi	Pascal	`www.borland.com`

Developing Macintosh Programs

The Macintosh easily maintains its reputation as one of the easiest computers in the world to use — and one of the hardest to program. Fortunately, the latest Macintosh programming tools make Macintosh programming much easier.

The main Macintosh programming tool is called Xcode, which comes free with every Macintosh computer. Xcode lets you write programs in C, C++, and a variation of the C language called Objective-C.

If you'd rather use BASIC to program your Macintosh, you can use REALbasic or another BASIC compiler called Future Basic (`www.stazsoftware.com`).

Table 19-2 lists the most popular Macintosh compilers for writing programs for the Mac.

Table 19-2	Popular Macintosh Compilers	
Compiler Name	*Language Used*	*Web Site*
Xcode	C, C++, Objective-C, Java	`www.apple.com`
REALbasic	BASIC	`www.realbasic.com`
NetBeans	Java	`www.netbeans.org`
Revolution	Transcript	`www.runrev.com`
Future Basic	BASIC	`www.stazsoftware.com`

Programming a handheld computer

Microsoft created a stripped-down version of Windows known as *Windows Mobile* for use in handheld and palm-size computers (formerly known as *Windows CE* or *PocketPC computers*). Unfortunately, programs that you write for Windows 98/Me/NT/2000/XP can't run on Windows Mobile. If you want to write programs for Windows Mobile, you must use a special Windows Mobile compiler. Microsoft developed Windows Mobile, so naturally Microsoft offers Windows Mobile programming toolkits so that you can write programs for Windows Mobile computers by using either Visual C++ or Visual Basic.

Two other programming languages for writing Windows Mobile programs are Pocket C (`www.orbworks.com`) and NSBASIC (`www.nsbasic.com`). Pocket C uses a stripped-down version of the C programming language, and NSBASIC uses a stripped-down version of the BASIC programming language. Pocket C and NSBASIC aren't quite as powerful as Visual C++ and Visual Basic, but they still enable you to create commercial-quality programs for a Windows Mobile computer.

Both Pocket C and NSBASIC also come in versions that run under the Palm OS, so you can also write programs for the Palm handheld computer. Because the Palm OS and Windows Mobile are drastically different operating systems, you can't run your programs on both the Palm OS and Windows Mobile without extensive modification.

Developing Linux Programs

Linux offers a wide variety of free language compilers, such as GCC (`http://gcc.gnu.org`), which lets you write Linux programs in C, C++, Objective-C, FORTRAN, Ada, and Java. Table 19-3 lists some popular Linux compilers.

Table 19-3 Popular Linux Compilers

Compiler Name	*Language Used*	*Web Site*
GCC	C, C++, Objective-C, Java	`http://gcc.gnu.org`
NetBeans	Java	`www.netbeans.org`
REALbasic	BASIC	`www.realbasic.com`
Revolution	Transcript	`www.runrev.com`

Using a Database Language

One problem with popular programming languages like C++ and BASIC is that they're designed to create any type of program from a video game to a lottery-picking program. As a result, general-purpose programming languages tend to be good at everything but not very good at anything in particular.

As an alternative to general-purpose programming languages, consider using a database language. A database language is designed solely to help you create programs that rely on storing large amounts of information, such as inventory-management or customer-tracking programs. Some of the advantages of database languages are

- A database application is much faster and easier to create in a database language than a general-purpose language such as C++ or BASIC.
- Database languages can take advantage of all the built-in features of a database program, which would be difficult to write in another programming language such as C++.

Although database programming languages can prove easier to learn and enable you to create fancy applications with minimum programming, they have their own disadvantages:

- Third-party support (such as books or magazines) for database languages may be much harder to find than for popular languages.
- Database languages may be limited to certain operating systems (meaning that porting the program to another operating system may prove virtually impossible).
- You're dependent on a single company for support. If the company that makes your database language goes out of business, your program may prove difficult or next to impossible to update.

Clarion

Clarion (`www.softvelocity.com`) is a programming language specifically designed for creating database applications. Because you compile Clarion programs into machine code, they run much faster than similar database programs such as Microsoft Access or Visual FoxPro. Best of all, Clarion can create programs for Windows and the Web without any modification whatsoever of your original source code.

In addition to letting you create database applications, Clarion includes a C++ and Modula-2 compiler just in case you need to add certain features to your program that the Clarion language itself can't do.

PowerBuilder

PowerBuilder combines the ease of creating a user interface (like Visual Basic) with the power of storing and manipulating data (like a database language). At one time, PowerBuilder was extremely popular for creating database applications, but its popularity declined as other languages like Visual Basic and Delphi added database capabilities.

Still, if you need to create database applications with fancy user interfaces and find Visual Basic or Delphi too complicated to use, consider giving PowerBuilder a try. Like Clarion, PowerBuilder can create only Windows applications. To find out more about PowerBuilder, visit `www.sybase.com/powerbuilder`.

FileMaker

FileMaker is unique in that it's one of the few database programs that can run on both Windows and the Macintosh. By writing programs in FileMaker, you can create programs that you can sell to both Windows and Macintosh users.

Even better, FileMaker has long enjoyed a strong following among developers and users so you can find plenty of books, magazines, and even conferences devoted to using and developing programs in FileMaker. As one of the most popular cross-platform database programs around, FileMaker is a safe bet for developing programs for now and in the future. For more information about FileMaker, visit `www.filemaker.com`.

SQL

One of the most popular database languages is SQL. To teach yourself about SQL, grab a free copy of SQLite (`www.sqlite.org`), which runs on both Windows and Linux and includes C source code for you to study, too. By teaching yourself SQL database programming skills with SQLite, you can increase the chances of getting a job working with any company that needs to store and retrieve data by using any version of SQL.

Shopping by Mail Order

You can buy language compilers directly from the publishers, but unless they're offering a special discounted price, you're better off buying from a mail-order house. Mail-order houses sell products at a discount — and they often don't charge you sales tax.

In addition to offering a wide variety of commercial compilers at discounted prices, mail-order houses often stock a variety of programming tools that you may never find anywhere else, such as special programming editors, code analyzers, language utilities to make programming easier, copy-protection kits, and installation programs.

The following mail-order houses specialize in programming tools:

- **Programmer's Paradise** (`www.pparadise.com`) offers a variety of programming tools for a variety of languages.
- **Xtras.Net** (`www.xtras.net`) specializes in .NET programming tools (Visual Basic and Visual C#) but also provides a variety of other programming tools such as installers and help-file creators.

Getting Your Hands on Source Code

Because one of the best ways to learn anything is to learn from someone else, many programmers voluntarily share their source code so that others can benefit from their work. The Linux operating system is the ultimate example of people sharing source code.

If you can get the source code to another program, you can include its features in your own program, thus saving you time. Many companies sell programming utilities (such as miniature word processors, spreadsheets, or graphics-charting programs) that you can paste together into your own programs. As a bonus, some of these companies also include the source code so that you can modify the program for your needs.

You can often find the source code to small programs scattered around the Internet for free. These small programs typically solve simple problems, but one of those problems may prove to be exactly what you need.

To find source code for your favorite language, use a search engine to search for the string *"C source code"*. This search string likely turns up a long list of useless Web sites and an occasional useful Web site that offers source code that you can download for free.

To help narrow your search for source code, try visiting one of the following Web sites:

- **CodeGuru** (www.codeguru.com) offers source code snippets to a variety of popular languages, including C/C++, Visual Basic, and Java.
- **Planet Source Code** (www.planet-source-code.com) provides source code for a variety of languages including Visual Basic, Perl, SQL, Delphi, C/C++, and Java.
- **DelphiSource** (www.delphisource.com) features source code just for Delphi programmers.
- **Visual Basic Code Source** (www.vbcodesource.com) provides source code for Visual Basic.
- **RB Garage** (www.rbgarage.com) provides source code examples for REALbasic.
- **The Flexible Learning Company** (www.flexiblelearning.com) provides source code examples for all variations of the HyperTalk language, which is the language that Revolution is based on.
- **The JavaScript Source** (http://javascript.internet.com) offers loads of free source code for programming in JavaScript.
- **Cprogramming.com** (www.cprogramming.com) offers lots of source code for C/C++ programmers to use and enjoy.

Joining a Local User Group

Programming can prove lonely and difficult in isolation. If you're lucky (or unlucky, depending on your point of view) enough to live in a big city, you can find a local programming user group to join.

User groups meet regularly — usually weekly or monthly — and enable programmers to share tips and information with one another concerning their favorite languages, such as C/C++, Java, Visual Basic, or Delphi.

Many user groups advertise in local computer magazines and newsletters, which you can often find in your favorite computer store. For another way to find a user group in your area, visit the Web site of your favorite compiler company (such as www.microsoft.com). Company Web sites often list user group meetings in different cities.

Frequenting Usenet Newsgroups

Learning anything can prove much easier if you have some friends to help you out. If you don't have any knowledgeable programming friends nearby, use the next best resource — a Usenet newsgroup.

Newsgroups act as electronic bulletin boards, where anyone can leave a message asking for help. Complete strangers from all around the world can give you advice or information to answer your question. If you browse through newsgroups long enough, you can often respond to other people's messages and give them some help as well.

Nearly every programming language has a newsgroup where loyal programmers gather and swap tips, tricks, and news. Check out the following newsgroups:

- `comp.lang` is a general-purpose programming newsgroup.
- `comp.lang.basic` is a newsgroup for BASIC programming enthusiasts.
- `comp.lang.c` is for C programming fanatics and followers.
- `comp.lang.c++` enables you to learn C++.
- `comp.lang.delphi` enables you to band together with other Delphi programmers.
- `comp.lang.java.help` is a great place for getting help with programming and using Java.
- `comp.lang.basic.realbasic` covers REALbasic programming.

To visit a newsgroup, you have to use a special newsgroup reader. If you use Windows, you can use Outlook Express to browse through newsgroups. As another alternative, you can use Thunderbird (`www.mozilla.com/thunderbird`) or Opera (`www.opera.com`), which is a browser with a built-in newsgroup reader.

This list is just a short sampling of available programming newsgroups. With a little bit of searching, you can find newsgroups for other programming languages and specific compilers such as Visual Basic and C#.

Playing Core Wars

People tend to learn faster and more effectively if they're having fun (which is a lesson that public schools and copycat book publishers still haven't figured out yet). Although writing a program that can calculate a second-order differential equation may improve your programming skills, it may also make you think that programming is extremely boring.

So to keep from getting bored and to see that programming can actually prove to be a lot of fun, you can play one of many programming games available for free (or for a nominal price). The purpose of programming games is to help sharpen your programming skills. If you want to win, you must learn to write the smallest, fastest, and most efficient programs — just as in real life.

The granddaddy of all programming games is *Core Wars*. In the old days, computers didn't use floppy or hard disks. Instead, they stored data on a magnetically charged doughnut-shaped device called *core memory* or just *core* for short.

The idea behind Core Wars is to write a program that you "store" in the core memory of an imaginary mainframe computer. To play Core Wars, each player must write a program by using a simplified version of assembly language, dubbed Red Code. Each program must search for enemy programs and erase them from the computer's core memory. The winner is the player whose program is the last surviving program in core memory.

Although Core Wars is popular, it's not a very visually exciting game to watch. All you see are the various programs stalking one another in core memory and trying to erase the instructions of enemy programs, which often looks no more interesting than watching a visual depiction of defragmenting your hard drive.

For more information about Core Wars, visit one of the following sites:

- `www.corewars.org`
- `www.koth.org`

To exchange messages with other Core Wars fanatics, visit the `news:rec.games.corewar` newsgroup, where you can learn about the latest Core Wars tournaments and start writing your own killer programs.

Programming a Battling Robot

The Core Wars programming game (described in the preceding section) doesn't offer great graphics to hold a player's attention. To satisfy the players' need for visual appeal, rival programming games incorporate more adventurous graphics. And, of course, what can prove any more appealing than war and gladiatorial combat? Instead of sending human gladiators into an arena to fight to the death, however, some programming games provide an imaginary arena where battling robots fight to the death.

Each robot incorporates identical capabilities to move, search, and shoot. But the way that each player programs his or her robot determines the actual actions of each robot. To program a robot, you must write a miniature program by using a simplified version of the C, C++, or Pascal language.

The challenge is not only to write a program that runs correctly, but also to provide your robot with instructions that create an optimum defensive and offensive strategy for surviving, stalking, and killing enemy robots at the same time.

If you write a large program that gives your robot limited choices, your robot will probably get blown up within seconds. Instead, your goal is to write a small program that runs quickly and provides your robot with enough intelligence to avoid damage while pummeling its opponents as often as possible. If you do that, your robot will likely survive any battle.

In addition to providing a more visually appealing way to see whose programming is better, battling robot games also give you a chance to practice writing programs in your favorite language, such as C, C++, or Pascal. After you master how to control a robot by using C or Pascal, you can transfer your robot programming skills to real-life programs.

Most battling robot programs run only on MS-DOS. If that's okay with you, download a free copy of a battling-robots game from one of the following Web sites:

- **The C++ Robots game** is at `www.gamerz.net/c++robots`.
- **The C-Robots and P-Robots game** is at `www.informatik.uni-frankfurt.de/~hbecker/pcroth.html`.

Toying with Lego Mindstorms

Nearly every kid has had the chance to play with Lego building blocks (and plenty of parents have had the chance to step on a Lego building block in their bare feet). Because so many kids love playing with computers, the fine people controlling the Lego empire decided to combine Legos with computers, and the result is something known as *Lego Mindstorms NXT* (`http://mindstorms.lego.com`).

By using Lego Mindstorms NXT, you can use Lego bricks to build a robot and then program it by using a simplified, graphically oriented programming language. Programming a Lego robot involves pasting together blocks of instructions, similar to snapping together Lego building blocks.

For hard-core programmers who'd rather use C/C++ to program their Lego robots, visit the brickOS Web site (`http://legos.sourceforge.net`).

By using a copy of Lego Mindstorms NXT (or any of the free programming toolkits available), you can create your own robots out of Legos and program them to attack one another, chase your dog around the house, or run berserk and protect your house against prowlers. After you practice your programming skills with Lego Mindstorms NXT, you can create almost anything that you want within the safe, friendly environment of Legos.

Chapter 22

Ten Cool Programming Careers

In This Chapter

- Programming computer games
- Animating with computers
- Encrypting data
- Programming for the Internet
- Fighting computer viruses
- Hacking for hire
- Working on an open-source project
- Programming for a specialized market
- Sharing your skills with others
- Selling your own software

Ask most high school or college guidance counselors what you can do with your programming skills, and they're likely to steer you in the direction of sterile job titles such as programmer analyst or data-entry operator. To help stimulate your imagination so that you can get a really cool job playing around with computers all day, this chapter lists some unusual programming jobs that you may want to consider so that you can actually have fun with your life and your job at the same time.

Programming Computer Games for Fun and Profit

Of all the programming topics in the world, none is more popular than game programming. Besides the obvious job of designing computer games (and getting paid to do it), game programming offers a wide variety of related jobs that can prove to be just as much fun as game designing but don't get as much publicity.

Most computer games are team designs. One team may design the game rules; another team does the actual programming; another creates the graphic backgrounds and animation; and still another gets paid to play the latest games to look for bugs and offer suggestions for making the games more exciting (and, hence, more profitable for the publisher).

To get your foot in the door in professional game programming, you obviously must love computer games. If you want to write computer games, you need to learn C/C++ and a little bit of assembly language because games need to be as small and as fast as possible. If you'd rather exercise your graphic skills, you need to learn animation.

To start writing your own games, consider using a game engine — a special program that provides instructions to tell the computer how to move animated objects around on-screen. You then spend your time designing your game, not worrying about the details of controlling animated characters on-screen.

For a free game engine that runs on Windows, the Macintosh, and Linux, download the Crystal Space game engine from the official Crystal Space Web site (`www.crystalspace3d.org`). By using Crystal Space (and other game engines), you can create 3-D triangle mesh sprites with frame animation or transparent and semitransparent textures for creating see-through water surfaces and windows.

If none of this stuff makes any sense to you, imagine trying to create a game and, at the same time, needing to learn all these technical terms and how to program them yourself. That's why many people use game engines to help them make new games. Without a game engine, making a game can prove as complicated as making your own word processor just so that you can write a letter.

To find out more about game programming, visit one of the following Web sites (and start on your new career as a professional game programmer today!):

- **International Game Developer's Association** (`www.igda.org`) is the granddaddy of computer-gaming organizations. It promotes and protects the computer-gaming industry and provides conferences to bring computer gaming professionals together.
- **Game Developer** (`www.gdmag.com`) is a special online magazine devoted exclusively to covering the latest game-programming techniques and game-programming industry news.
- **Game Programmer** (`www.gameprogrammer.com`) is a Web site that provides information and links to the multitude of game-programming resources all across the Internet.

- **DigiPen** (www.digipen.edu) is the site of one of the first schools (with close ties to Nintendo) devoted to training game-programming professionals and awarding them with real college degrees.
- **GameJobs** (www.gamejobs.com) is a site that provides information, tips, and contacts to help you find a job in the computer-gaming industry.

Creating Computer Animation

Computer animation isn't just for creating animated characters to shoot or blow up in video games. Programmers also use computer animation in virtual reality, training simulators, and Hollywood special effects (because blowing up a computer-animated building is easier than building a mock-up of an existing building to blow up).

Computer animation can range from creating lifelike images for TV and movies to creating multimedia presentations for business, to making cartoons and animated films. If you like to draw but want to become more than just an artist, combine your knowledge of graphics with programming and help design new graphics-animation programs, create virtual-reality simulators, or work on the next Hollywood blockbuster's special effects.

To learn more about the wonderfully weird world of computer animation, browse through these Web sites and see what sparks your imagination:

- **Pixar Animation Studios** (www.pixar.com) is a leading Hollywood animation studio responsible for animating movies such as *Toy Story, Finding Nemo, The Incredibles,* and *Cars.*
- **International Animated Film Society** (www.asifa-hollywood.org) grants awards (similar to the Academy Awards) for the best computer-animation short films.
- **Animation Magazine** (www.animationmagazine.net) provides news and information for the entire animation industry.
- **National Centre for Computer Animation** (http://ncca.bournemouth.ac.uk) is the United Kingdom's leading research and training institution for computer animation and digital media.
- **Computer Graphics World Online** (http://cgw.pennnet.com) is a magazine covering all the tools, news, and conferences that professional computer-graphics artists may need to know about.

Making (And Breaking) Encryption

Ever since nations decided to play the high-stakes game of war and send their people into battle for their own political reasons, armies have used secret codes to communicate with their commanders without revealing information to their enemies.

Because war isn't likely to disappear anytime soon, every country in the world continues to develop encryption techniques for creating codes and breaking the codes of others. If the world of James Bond, espionage, and cloak-and-dagger spies appeals to your sense of adventure, consider a career in encryption.

Encryption is the art of converting plain-text information into unreadable garbage (which often resembles tax forms or legal documents) so that no one but your intended recipient can read it. Then by using a secret password or code phrase, the recipient of your encrypted message can unscramble and read it.

The art of encrypting data involves plenty of math (usually focusing on prime numbers). If you plan to pursue a career in encryption, earn some graduate degrees in advanced mathematics and practice your C/C++ programming skills. Then get a job working for the military, a defense contractor, a software encryption publisher, or a security agency such as the National Security Agency (`www.nsa.gov`).

The National Security Agency (open to United States citizens only) is the premier code-making and code-breaking agency in the world, housing the most supercomputers in one location. If you know programming, advanced math, or any foreign language, you can use your abilities to read intercepted messages, track enemy submarine acoustic signatures in the Atlantic Ocean, or search through databases to spot the movements and operations of international terrorists.

If you find encryption fascinating but you'd rather not help your country prepare for war, consider putting your encryption skills to use in the international banking and financial world, where encryption protects electronic transactions worth billions of dollars every day.

For more information about encryption, visit one of the following Web sites. Many of these sites offer C/C++ source code to various encryption algorithms, so you can practice both your programming and encryption skills at the same time.

- **CypherNet** (`www.cyphernet.org`) is a grass-roots organization dedicated to helping individuals use encryption to protect themselves against their own governments.

- **Central Intelligence Agency** (www.cia.gov) is the most famous intelligence agency in the world, responsible for spying on other countries.
- **International PGP Home Page** (www.pgpi.org) is the home of the most famous personal encryption program in the world, Pretty Good Privacy (PGP).
- **RSA** (www.rsasecurity.com), the name of which derives from the first names of its founders, Rivest, Shamir, and Adleman, is the number-one encryption company providing encryption technology for many programs that rely on the Internet.

Internet Programming

Besides Internet companies gobbling up programmers, many old-fashioned companies also need programmers to help them create interactive Web sites. With so much activity revolving around the Internet, the increasing demand for Internet programmers is no surprise.

To get involved in this field, spend some time mastering the intricacies of HTML so that you know the basics of designing Web pages. (A little bit of training in graphic design and layout doesn't hurt either.)

Although HTML can create pretty Web pages, companies really want to take advantage of the Internet to sell products online. To create interactive Web sites, programmers use a variety of languages, including Java, XML, JavaScript, Perl, C#, and Python.

To get a start in Internet programming, teach yourself HTML; start playing around with an Internet programming language (such as JavaScript); sharpen your Windows XP, Mac OS X, or Linux operating system skills; learn more about accessing databases by using SQL; and play with Web servers such as Apache (which often comes free with Linux).

(Coincidentally, Wiley publishes many books about the preceding topics, including Java and Linux. To learn more about these books, visit www.dummies.com.)

Visit one of the following Web sites to see how quickly you can start working (and earning a lot of money) in an Internet programming position:

- **GeekFinder** (www.geekfinder.com) provides plenty of jobs for a wide variety of computer-related jobs all around the world.
- **Web Jobs USA** (www.webjobsusa.com) is dedicated to helping Internet professionals find jobs by using their Web page and Internet-programming skills.
- **Java Jobs** (www.javajobs.com) provides tutorials, training, and Java-related job listings.

Fighting Malware

Malware describes the entire range of malicious software that includes viruses, worms, Trojan horses, spyware, and adware. In the old days, people wrote malware for their own amusement and entertainment. Nowadays, many people are writing malicious programs, such as spyware and adware, for profit.

To help rid the world of pests such as viruses and spyware, you need to study how specific operating systems work, such as Windows or Mac OS X. Anti-malware programmers need to know C/C++, assembly language, and possibly VBA (Visual Basic for Applications), the macro programming language that Microsoft uses in its Office suite. To learn more about different antivirus companies and what type of positions they have available, visit any of the following Web sites:

- **McAfee** (`www.mcafee.com`) publishes the popular VirusScan antivirus program.
- **Sophos** (`www.sophos.com`) publishes the popular Sophos Anti-Virus program.
- **Symantec** (`www.symantec.com`) publishes the popular Norton AntiVirus program.
- **Trend Micro** (`www.trendmicro.com`) publishes the popular PC-cillin antivirus program.
- **Webroot Software** (`www.webroot.com`) publishes the popular Spy Sweeper program for detecting and killing spyware.
- **F-Secure** (`www.f-secure.com`) publishes the well-regarded F-Secure antivirus program.

Hacking for Hire

Hackers are often extremely skilled (or extremely patient) people who enjoy the technical challenge of breaking into computers. Although breaking into computers is technically illegal, your chances of getting caught increase immensely the moment that you start causing damage.

Rather than risk getting thrown in jail because you can't resist playing around with computers, consider the alternative challenge of trying to outwit the hackers themselves. As a computer-security expert, you can work for the government to help track down malicious hackers, or you can work for a corporation and help keep hackers out of a company's computers.

By working as a "good" hacker, you get to face all the technical challenges of hacking while getting paid. Plus you get to experience the thrill of working on the side of law-enforcement agencies to track down hackers around the world.

To learn more about using your hacking skills on the side of law enforcement, visit the following Web sites:

- **Federal Bureau of Investigation** (`www.fbi.gov`) is the agency in charge of United States law enforcement on a national level, including investigating and prosecuting computer hackers.
- **AntiOnline** (`www.antionline.com`) provides news and hacking tools, along with a network of computers on which hackers can safely and legally expand their skills.
- **2600** (`www.2600.com`) is a quarterly hacker magazine that provides hacking-related articles and information.

Participating in an Open-Source Project

To get a job, you need job experience, but you can't get job experience unless you have a job. Given this paradox, the most reliable way to solve this problem is to demonstrate your abilities by working for free.

To get valuable programming experience that impresses big companies, consider participating in an open-source project. The whole idea behind an open-source project is to get programmers to contribute to the development of a single project, such as the Linux operating system or the GNOME user interface for Linux.

Working on an open-source project not only gives you instant credibility (providing that you actually contribute something useful), but also gives you valuable experience in working with a real-life programming project. Whereas other programmers may get shuffled into entry-level positions working on boring projects that nobody really cares about, you get to work on something that can give you pride and a sense of accomplishment.

The prestige of contributing to an open-source project can later help you find a better-paying job, or it can serve as an amusing hobby. Either way, open-source projects give you a chance to prove to the world what you can actually accomplish with your programming skills.

To get involved with an open-source project, visit one of the following Web sites and start programming:

- **Open Source Initiative** (`www.opensource.org`) provides news and information about the value of open source projects.
- **Free Software Foundation** (`www.fsf.org`) offers information about open-source projects in general and the GNU C compiler in particular.
- **Apple Open Source** (`http://developer.apple.com/opensource`) is the place for information about Apple Computer's open-source operating-system projects.
- **Mozilla** (`www.mozilla.org`) is the open-source project for the Firefox browser and the Thunderbird e-mail program.
- **Linux** (`www.linux.org`) is the premier UNIX-clone operating system that worries even Microsoft.

Niche-Market Programming

One problem with programming classes is that they teach you how to write programs, but they don't teach you how to put your skills to practical use. Most companies use computers, so try to combine your knowledge of programming with another field. If you can do that, you'll practically double your job opportunities.

Who's better qualified to design and write medical software than a programmer with a medical background (or a medical professional with a programming background)? Sports fanatics combine programming skills with enthusiasm for sports to design horse-race-handicapping software; health professionals design nutrition and diet software; and lawyers create special legal software.

Practically every field faces unique needs that general-purpose software (such as spreadsheets or databases) can't solve. That's why professionals hire programmers to develop custom software.

Best of all, niche markets are so small that you never need to worry about monolithic companies such as Microsoft competing against you and wiping out your business. In addition, only a handful of programmers can even possibly write programs for certain niche markets — how many programmers have experience in hotel management, for example? — which means that you face less competition and a market practically begging for your software.

Perhaps one of the hottest niche markets is the field of *bioinformatics,* which uses programming languages such as Perl, Python, and Java to analyze DNA structures. Bioinformatics requires knowledge of both molecular biology and programming, which is a rare combination that could translate into a secure, high-paying career. If you'd like to use your programming skill to help find new drugs that could cure diseases, visit `http://bioinformatics.org` to find out more about bioinformatics today.

If you ever want to take advantage of your previous job experience and combine it with your new programming skills, consider developing a program that solves a specific problem in a niche market. Who knows? With your programming skills, you can perhaps find new opportunities in a field that may have seemed like a dead end.

Teaching Others about Computers

When you become an expert in any field, you can teach others your unique skills. In addition to the obvious teaching positions in schools, training others to use popular programs such as Microsoft Word, Red Hat Linux, or C++ programming is a lucrative business.

Training professionals travel around the world, conducting classes for corporations who want to train their workers to use a variety of programs so that they can become more productive. As a trainer, you get to see the world, meet people, and see for yourself how many different ways Holiday Inns can design the inside of a hotel room.

If you like dealing with people, enjoy traveling, and love sharing your knowledge of computers with others, this sort of job may be the perfect position for you.

Selling Your Own Software

There's no cheaper way to go into business for yourself than to develop and sell your own software. Unlike restaurants or bookstores, you don't need a large amount of space or an extensive inventory. You simply write a program and sell it electronically across the Internet.

The most popular way to test-market a program is through shareware distribution: You give away copies of your software and ask that people send you money if they find it useful. To encourage more people to send money, your program must prove useful and work reliably.

Despite the seemingly bizarre business logic of giving away your product and trusting that people actually pay you for it, many shareware authors earn hundreds (and sometimes millions) of dollars for their programs over the years. (One of the most successful shareware programs is WinZip, which you can download at `www.winzip.com`.) Distributing programs as shareware can make you rich or earn you a little bit of extra spending money.

If you ever wanted to start your own business but didn't want to take out a loan, starting a shareware business is the easiest and cheapest solution. All it takes is a good idea, some decent programming skills, and a little bit of marketing know-how to launch your business.

If your program doesn't appeal to the average computer user, try selling it to a niche market instead. In addition to niche markets for stockbrokers, law-enforcement agencies, or restaurant owners, you can also find niche markets that target specific computers, such as the Palm or PocketPC hand-held computers.

You can turn your programming skills into your own business with the right computer program. And if you like programming, what other job lets you stay home all day, play around with your computer, and still get paid for it in a business all your own?

Appendix A

Common Loop and Branching Structures

Common Loop Structures

Liberty BASIC	REALbasic
`WHILE` *condition* *Instructions* `WEND`	`WHILE` *condition* *Instructions* `WEND`
`FOR i =` *Start* `TO` *End* *Instructions* `NEXT i`	`FOR i =` *Start* `TO` *End* *Instructions* `NEXT`
`FOR I =` *Start* `TO` *End* `STEP` *Inc* *Instructions* `NEXT i`	`FOR i =` *Start* `TO` *End* `STEP` *Inc* *Instructions* `NEXT`
	`FOR i =` *Start* `DOWNTO` *End* *Instructions* `NEXT`

C++	Revolution

`while (`*condition*`)`
 `{`
 Instructions
 `}`
	`repeat while` *condition*
	 Instructions
	`end repeat`

`for (`*initial;*
 conditional; incr`)`
 `{`
 Instructions
 `}`
	`repeat with i=`*Start* `to` *End*
	
	 Instructions
	`end repeat`

(continued)

C++	Revolution
	repeat with i=*Start* to *End* step *Incr* *Instructions* end repeat
	repeat with i=*Start* down to *End* *Instructions* end repeat

Common Branching Structures

Liberty BASIC	REALbasic
IF *condition* THEN *Instruction*	

IF *condition* THEN
 Instructions
END IF
	IF *condition* THEN
	 Instructions
	END IF

IF *condition* THEN
 Instructions
ELSE
 Instructions
END IF
	IF *condition* THEN
	 Instructions
	ELSE
	 Instructions
	END IF

	IF *condition1* THEN
	 Instructions
	ELSEIF *condition2* THEN
	 Instructions
	END IF

SELECT CASE *variable* CASE *value1* *Instructions* CASE *value2* *Instructions* END SELECT	SELECT CASE *variable* CASE *value1* *Instructions* CASE value2 *Instructions* END SELECT

Liberty BASIC	***REALbasic***
SELECT CASE *variable* CASE value1, *value2*, *value3* *Instructions* CASE *value4*, *value5*, *value6* *Instructions* END SELECT	SELECT CASE *variable* CASE *value1*, *value2*, *value3* *Instructions* CASE *value4* TO *value5* *Instructions* END SELECT
SELECT CASE CASE (*Variable* [<, >, <=, >=, =, <>] *Value1*) *Instructions1* CASE (*Variable* [<, >, <=, >=, =, <>] *Value2*) *Instructions2* END SELECT	SELECT CASE *variable* CASE IS [<, >, <=, >=, =, <>] *Value1* *Instructions* CASE IS [<, >, <=, >=, =, <>] *Value1* *Instructions* END SELECT

C++	***Revolution***

if (*condition*)
 {
 instructions
 }
	if *condition* then
	 Instructions
	end if

if (*condition*)
 {
 instructions
 }
else
 {
 instructions
 }
	if *condition* then
	 Instructions
	else
	 Instructions
	end if

if (*condition1*)
 {
 instructions
 }
else if (*condition2*)
 {
 instructions
 }	

(continued)

C++	*Revolution*

switch (*variable*)
{
case *value1*:
instructions
break;
case *value2*:
instructions
break;
default
instructions
}
	switch *variable*
	case *value1*:
	instructions
	break;
	case *value2*:
	instructions
	break;
	default
	instructions
	end switch

switch (*variable*)
{
case *value1*:
case *value2*:
case *value3*:
instructions
break;
case *value4*:
case *value5*:
case *value6*:
instructions
break;
default
instructions
}
	switch *variable*
	case *value1*:
	case *value2*:
	case *value3*:
	instructions
	break;
	case *value4*:
	case *value5*:
	case *value6*:
	instructions
	break;
	default
	instructions
	end switch

	switch case (*variable* [<, >, <=, >=, =, <>] *value1*) *instructions* break; case (*variable* [<, >, <=, >=, =, <>] *value2*) *instructions* break; default *instructions* end switch

Appendix B

Free Language Compilers and Interpreters

Alice (`www.alice.org`): A Windows and Macintosh tool to teach programming by using interactive 3-D graphics.

Dev-C++ (`www.bloodshed.net`): Open-source C++ compiler for Windows.

Dev-Pascal (`www.bloodshed.net`): Open-source Pascal compiler for Windows.

Free Pascal (`www.freepascal.org`): Open-source compiler that runs on a variety of processors including Intel, AMD, and PowerPC processors.

Java (`http://java.sun.com`): Cross-platform programming language that can be used to write small Web-based programs or full-fledged applications.

Just BASIC (`www.justbasic.com`): A Windows BASIC compiler from the makers of Liberty BASIC.

Kid's Programming Language (`www.kidsprogramminglanguage.com`): Freeware programming language designed to teach kids how to program.

Perl (`www.perl.com`): An open-source, cross-platform language.

Phrogram (`www.phrogram.com`): A language designed to teach novices how to program, based on Kid's Programming Language.

Python (`www.python.org`): An open-source, cross-platform language.

Turbo C++ for Windows and .NET (`www.turboexplorer.com`): A free C++ compiler for Windows.

Turbo C# for Windows and .NET (`www.turboexplorer.com`): A free C# compiler for Windows.

Turbo Delphi for Windows and .NET (`www.turboexplorer.com`): A free Delphi compiler for creating Windows or .Net programs.

Visual Basic 2005 Express (`http://msdn.microsoft.com/vstudio/express/vb`): A free Visual Basic compiler for Windows.

Visual C++ 2005 Express (`http://msdn.microsoft.com/vstudio/express/visualc`): A free C++ compiler for Windows.

Visual C# 2005 Express (`http://msdn.microsoft.com/vstudio/express/visualcsharp`): A free C# compiler for Windows.

Visual J# 2005 Express (`http://msdn.microsoft.com/vstudio/express/visualJ`): A free J# compiler for Windows. J# is Microsoft's version of Java.

Visual Prolog (`www.visual-prolog.com`): A free edition of Visual Prolog available for home or educational use only.

Xcode (`http://developer.apple.com/tools/xcode`): Apple Computer's free tool for writing C, C++, Objective-C, or Java programs on the Macintosh.

Appendix C

Common Programming Terms

& (ampersand): A symbol commonly used in programming languages for concatenation, which combines two strings together.

*** (asterisk):** A symbol commonly used in programming languages for multiplication.

\ (backward slash): A symbol commonly used in programming languages for integer division.

^ (caret): A symbol commonly used in programming languages for exponentiation.

– (dash): A symbol commonly used in programming languages for subtraction.

/ (forward slash): A symbol commonly used in programming languages for division.

+ (plus): A symbol commonly used in programming languages for addition. Some programming languages use this for concatenation, which combines two strings together.

algorithm: A step-by-step method for solving a problem.

array: A data structure that can hold one or more values that consist of the same data type. Arrays can be static or dynamic. A static array can only hold a fixed number of items. A dynamic array can expand or shrink while the program runs. *See also* zero-based array.

assembler: A special program that converts assembly language commands into equivalent machine code commands. *See also* compiler.

assembly language: A programming language designed for a specific microprocessor such as the Intel family of processors used in most personal computers.

BASIC: A programming language designed especially to teach beginners how to program. BASIC stands for *Beginner's All-Purpose Symbolic Instruction Code. See also* Liberty BASIC *and* Visual Basic.

Big-O notation: A way to measure the efficiency of an algorithm so you can see how fast (or slow) it may run under different conditions.

bioinformatics: A programming specialty that uses computers to analyze DNA structures. Some popular languages used in bioinformatics include Perl, Java, and Python.

bloatware: A slang term for any program that keeps adding so many features that most people never use them and the program winds up gobbling up huge amounts of disk space and memory.

Boolean data type: True or False values.

breakpoint: To designate one or more lines in your program where you want your program to stop running so you can examine or debug a program.

bug: A slang term for an error in a program. Nearly every program includes bugs, although most bugs are more annoying than harmful.

byte code: An intermediate format for storing programming language commands that can run on multiple operating systems using a virtual machine. Java programs are commonly compiled into byte code rather than machine code. *See also* virtual machine.

C: A popular programming language originally designed to work with the UNIX operating system. Variations of the C language include C++ and C#.

C++: An object-oriented version of the C programming language.

C#: A Microsoft-developed language that combines the features of C++ and Java.

class: A description of an object used in object-oriented programming languages. After you define a class, you can define an actual object based on that class so it's possible for two or more objects to be based on the same class.

COBOL: An early programming language designed for creating business applications. It stands for COmmon Business-Oriented Language.

collection: A data structure that resembles an array except that it can store information consisting of different data types, such as integers and strings.

comment: Descriptive text that explains how certain parts of a program work, the name or the original programmer, the date of the program's last modification, or other useful information that can help a programmer understand how a program works.

compiler: A program that translates programming language commands into equivalent machine code commands.

constant: A fixed value in a program that's given a descriptive name such as `TaxRate`.

control structure: A part of a program that provides two or more sets of instructions to follow based on a certain condition. An `IF-THEN` statement is an example of a control structure.

crash: When a program fails and stops working and possibly even stops other programs from working as well, including the operating system.

cross-platform: The ability to run on multiple operating systems such as Linux and Windows.

curly-bracket languages: The family of languages derived from the C programming language, because these languages define the start and end of blocks of code using left and right curly brackets {}. Some members of the curly bracket language family include C, C++, C#, Java, and Perl.

data structure: A technique for storing information for easy organization and retrieval.

data type: A specific range of values. Common data types include integers (whole numbers), single-precision numbers (such as 3.14), and strings (such as "Hello").

debug: To examine a program for errors that may keep the program from working.

debugger: A program designed to examine another program for problems or bugs that keep the program from working properly.

Delphi: A Windows RAD programming tool based on the Pascal programming language. *See also* RAD.

Dev-C++: An open-source C++ compiler for Windows.

disassembler: A special program that can convert a compiled program into equivalent assembly language code, which is commonly used by hackers and security researchers to break copy-protection or understand how viruses work. Disassembling programs compiled into byte code format can often retrieve the original source code language such as Java or Visual Basic.NET.

distributions: A specific version of an operating system such as Linux. Under Linux, some popular distributions include Red Hat, SUSE, and Ubuntu Linux.

editor: A program for writing and modifying commands written in a programming language such as BASIC or C++.

encapsulation: Isolating data and subprograms (called *methods*) in an object in an object-oriented programming language.

endless loop: When a program keeps repeating the same instructions over and over again, thus hanging up or freezing the program.

event-driven programming: A type of programming that responds to the user's actions as opposed to following a specific order. Most RAD programming tools, such as Visual Basic or REALbasic, use event-driven programming.

executable file: The compiled, machine code version of a program.

FORTRAN: Early programming language designed for mathematical calculations, which stands for FORmula TRANslator.

function: A subprogram that accepts data and returns a single value. Most programming languages include a collection of functions for calculating mathematical results such as logarithms or cosine.

GUI: An acronym that stands for graphical user interface, which defines windows, buttons, and pull-down menus to help the user give commands.

HTML: An acronym for HyperText Markup Language, which is the special programming language used to define the appearance of Web pages.

IDE: An acronym for integrated development environment. An IDE typically includes an editor, a compiler, and a debugger.

inheritance: The ability to copy part of another object without making a physical second copy.

installer: A special program designed to copy another program on to a computer.

integer: A whole number such as 4 or 109.

interpreter: A program that translates and stores program language commands in the computer's memory. To run, an interpreter must have the source code of a program. *See also* source code.

Java: An object-oriented programming language developed by Sun Microsystems.

JavaScript: An interpreted language used to make Web pages interactive. Despite its name, JavaScript has little in common with the Java programming language.

Liberty BASIC: A shareware BASIC compiler for Windows.

Linux: An open-source, UNIX-based operating system. *See also* distributions.

machine code: The binary language of all computers, which consists of 0s and 1s.

macro languages: Special programming languages used within a specific program such as Microsoft Word or Microsoft Excel. Macro languages let you customize the behavior of a specific program.

method: A subprogram stored inside of an object in an object-oriented programming language.

.NET: A Microsoft created framework designed to allow multiple languages to share data and work together. Rather than compile a language into machine code, languages such as C# and Visual Basic.NET compile programs into byte format that can only run on any computer that includes the .NET framework files.

Objective-C: An object-oriented version of the C programming language commonly used to write programs for the Macintosh.

object-oriented programming: A technique for designing programs divided into isolated parts or objects. Objects typically contain data and mini-programs that manipulate that data.

open source: The sharing of source code that lets anyone examine and modify a program without licensing or restrictions. Linux is one of the most popular open-source programs.

operating system: A program that controls the computer. Some popular operating systems are Microsoft Windows, UNIX, Linux, and Mac OS.

optimization: The process of rewriting a program to make it faster, uses less memory, or take up less hard drive space.

parameter: Data sent or passed to a subprogram.

parameter list: A list that defines the names and data types of all information that a subprogram expects to receive.

Pascal: A programming language designed to teach beginners structured programming, which is the practice of organizing and designing a program to make it easy to read and modify. Pascal is the language used in Delphi. *See also* Delphi.

Perl: An acronym that stands for *Practical Extraction and Report Language*, which is an interpreted language designed for text manipulation.

polymorphism: Used in object-oriented programming to allow two or more objects to use the same method name.

portable: When a program can be transferred and run on different operating systems. C, C++, and Java programs are considered portable because you can often run them on Windows, Linux, and Mac OS computers with little or no modifications.

procedure: A type of subprogram that can optionally accept data and perform a single task. *See also* function.

proprietary code: Source code that is kept private and unavailable for the public to examine or modify.

Python: An object-oriented, interpreted language often compared to Perl.

queue: A data structure that stores data in a line or queue, where the first item stored is the next item to be removed, known as FIFO (*First In, First Out*). *See also* stack.

RAD: An acronym for *rapid application development,* which describes the ability to draw the user interface of a program and then write commands in a programming language to make the user interface work.

Revolution: A programming tool based on Apple Computer's HyperCard program, which lets you organize a program into cards and stacks.

searching: The process of looking for data.

showstopper: A bug that keeps a program from working at all.

sorting: The process of rearranging data. Some common sorting algorithms include quicksort, insertion sort, and bubble sort.

source code: The commands, written in a programming language, stored in one or more files. The source code of any program shows you exactly how that program works.

spaghetti programming: The practice of writing a program with no organization or plan so eventually the organization of the program looks as convoluted as trying to untangle a plate full of spaghetti.

stack: A type of data structure where the last item stored is the first item removed, known as LIFO (*Last In, First Out*). Stacks are named because they resemble a stack of dishes commonly found in cafeterias where the top dish is the first dish people take off the stack. *See also* queue.

stepping: The process of examining a program, line by line, to look for bugs. Stepping is often used with breakpoints and watches. *See also* breakpoint *and* watch.

string: Any data identified inside quotation marks. Strings typically contain letters, symbols, and numbers (such as "My name is R2-D2").

structured programming: A technique for designing and dividing a program into small parts that are easy to read, understand, and modify.

subprogram: A small program that makes up a larger program. Most large programs are divided into hundreds, thousands, or even millions of separate subprograms. *See also* procedure *and* function.

type-safe language: A language that forces programmers to define the data type stored in every variable to prevent the program from manipulating unexpected data. For example, if you created a variable called `FirstName`, a type-safe language would force you to define the only acceptable type of data that `FirstName` variable could hold, such as a string.

UNIX: A popular operating system designed to run on multiple computers and allow multiple users to use a single computer at the same time. Two popular operating systems derived from UNIX include Linux and Mac OS.

user interface: What the user sees when a program runs, such as windows, pull-down menus, and buttons.

variable: A temporary place to hold a value. To make storing and retrieving data easier, most programmers give variables descriptive names such as `Age` or `Phone_Number`.

virtual machine: A program that can run commands stored in byte code format. To run Java programs, your computer needs the Java virtual machine program.

Visual Basic: A Windows BASIC compiler from Microsoft. Visual Basic was one of the first and most popular RAD tools.

watch: To examine the contents of a variable while a program is running. This can help you identify where and when a program may not be working properly.

Windows: Generic term for the Microsoft Windows operating system.

Xcode: Free programming tools developed by Apple Computers to help people write programs for the Macintosh.

zero-based array: An array that numbers the first item with the number 0 (zero) as opposed to the number 1 (one). Languages that use zero-based arrays include nearly all languages related to the C language such as C++ and Java.

Appendix D

Installing the CD Compilers

The only way to learn programming is by writing your own programs, and to write programs, you need a language compiler. To help you get started, this book's CD includes four different language compilers so you can install them and practice writing programs on your own computer:

- **Liberty BASIC:** A shareware program for writing Windows programs using BASIC. `www.libertybasic.com` (Windows only)
- **REALbasic:** A demo that allows you to create Windows, Macintosh, and Linux programs by drawing your user interface and then writing BASIC code to make it work. The Windows and Macintosh versions are trial versions, but the Linux version is completely free. `www.realbasic.com` (Windows, Macintosh, and Linux)
- **Dev-C++:** A freeware and open-source C++ compiler that allows you to see how a compiler works and write C/C++ programs for Windows. `www.bloodshed.net/devcpp.html` (Windows only)
- **Runtime Revolution:** A cross-platform trial program that lets you write programs for Windows, Macintosh, and Linux. `www.runrev.com` (Windows, Macintosh, and Linux)
- **Galaxy:** An editor and debugger designed to make writing Revolution programs much easier. `www.daniels-mara.com` (Windows, Macintosh, and Linux)
- **Valentina:** A database toolkit designed to help create database programs in REALbasic and Revolution. `www.paradigmasoft.com` (Windows and Macintosh).

System Requirements

Make sure that your computer meets the minimum system requirements that I give in the following list. If your computer doesn't match up to most of these requirements, you may experience problems in using the contents of the CD.

- A computer with a 1GHz processor such as an Athlon, Pentium 4, G4, G5, or Intel Core Solo or Intel Core Duo.
- Microsoft Windows 98 or later, Mac OS 10.2 or later, or Linux kernel 2.4 or later.
- At least 256MB total RAM on your computer.
- A CD-ROM drive.
- A monitor capable of displaying at least 256 colors or grayscale.

If you need more information on the basics, check out *PCs For Dummies,* 10th Edition, by Dan Gookin; *Macs For Dummies,* 9th Edition, by Edward C. Baig; *Mac OS X For Dummies,* 2nd Edition, by Bob LeVitus; or *Windows XP,* 2nd Edition, by Andy Rathbone (all from Wiley Publishing).

Using the CD

To install the items from the CD to your hard drive, follow these steps.

1. **Insert the CD into your computer's CD-ROM drive.**

   The license agreement appears.

   Note to Windows users: The interface won't launch if you have autorun disabled. In that case, choose Start⇨Run. In the dialog box that appears, type **D:\start.exe**. (Replace D with the proper letter if your CD-ROM drive uses a different letter. If you don't know the letter, see how your CD-ROM drive is listed under My Computer.) Click OK.

   Note to Mac Users: The CD icon appears on your desktop. Double-click the icon to open the CD and then double-click the Start icon.

2. **Read through the license agreement and then click the Accept button if you want to use the CD. After you click Accept, the License Agreement window won't appear again.**

   The CD interface appears. The interface allows you to install the programs and run the demos with just a click of a button (or two).

If you're running Windows, you can install the following compilers from the CD:

- Liberty BASIC
- REALbasic
- Dev-C++
- Runtime Revolution

If you're running Mac OS X, you can install the following compilers from the CD:

- REALbasic
- Runtime Revolution

Apple provides a free C++ compiler called Xcode. To get the latest version of Xcode, visit `http://developer.apple.com/macosx`.

If You Have Problems (Of the CD Kind)

If you can't install the language compilers that come with this CD, try screaming at the top of your lungs about how stupid and unreliable computers can be. After you finish vocalizing your frustrations out loud, you can calmly try to resolve your problem by following some of these troubleshooting tips.

First, make sure your computer meets the system requirements listed earlier. The older your computer, the more likely it is you'll have problems. The most common problem with older computers is not having enough memory.

Second, try one or more of the following methods and then try using the software again:

- **Turn off any antivirus software that's on your computer.** Installers sometimes mimic virus activity and may make your computer incorrectly believe that a virus is infecting it.
- **Close all running programs.** The more programs you're running, the less memory is available to other programs. Installers also typically update files and programs; if you keep other programs running, installation may not work correctly.
- **Have your local computer store add more RAM to your computer.** This course is, admittedly, a drastic and somewhat expensive step. If you have a Windows 98 PC or a Mac OS computer with a PowerPC chip, however, adding more memory can really help the speed of your computer and enable more programs to run at the same time.

If you have trouble with the CD-ROM, please call the Wiley Product Technical Support phone number at (800) 762-2974. Outside the United States, call 1(317) 572-3994. You can also contact Wiley Product Technical Support at `www.wiley.com/techsupport`. John Wiley & Sons will provide technical support only for installation and other general quality control items. For technical support on the applications themselves, consult the program's vendor or author.

To place additional orders or to request information about other Wiley products, please call (877) 762-2974.

Index

• G •

• L •

• M •

• N •

• O •

• P •

• Q •

• R •

• V •

• W •

• Z •

SPORTS, FITNESS, PARENTING, RELIGION & SPIRITUALITY

0-7645-5146-9

0-7645-5418-2

Also available:

- Adoption For Dummies 0-7645-5488-3
- Basketball For Dummies 0-7645-5248-1
- The Bible For Dummies 0-7645-5296-1
- Buddhism For Dummies 0-7645-5359-3
- Catholicism For Dummies 0-7645-5391-7
- Hockey For Dummies 0-7645-5228-7
- Judaism For Dummies 0-7645-5299-6
- Martial Arts For Dummies 0-7645-5358-5
- Pilates For Dummies 0-7645-5397-6
- Religion For Dummies 0-7645-5264-3
- Teaching Kids to Read For Dummies 0-7645-4043-2
- Weight Training For Dummies 0-7645-5168-X
- Yoga For Dummies 0-7645-5117-5

TRAVEL

0-7645-5438-7

0-7645-5453-0

Also available:

- Alaska For Dummies 0-7645-1761-9
- Arizona For Dummies 0-7645-6938-4
- Cancún and the Yucatán For Dummies 0-7645-2437-2
- Cruise Vacations For Dummies 0-7645-6941-4
- Europe For Dummies 0-7645-5456-5
- Ireland For Dummies 0-7645-5455-7
- Las Vegas For Dummies 0-7645-5448-4
- London For Dummies 0-7645-4277-X
- New York City For Dummies 0-7645-6945-7
- Paris For Dummies 0-7645-5494-8
- RV Vacations For Dummies 0-7645-5443-3
- Walt Disney World & Orlando For Dummi 0-7645-6943-0

GRAPHICS, DESIGN & WEB DEVELOPMENT

0-7645-4345-8

0-7645-5589-8

Also available:

- Adobe Acrobat 6 PDF For Dummies 0-7645-3760-1
- Building a Web Site For Dummies 0-7645-7144-3
- Dreamweaver MX 2004 For Dummies 0-7645-4342-3
- FrontPage 2003 For Dummies 0-7645-3882-9
- HTML 4 For Dummies 0-7645-1995-6
- Illustrator CS For Dummies 0-7645-4084-X
- Macromedia Flash MX 2004 For Dummi 0-7645-4358-X
- Photoshop 7 All-in-One Desk Reference For Dummies 0-7645-1667-1
- Photoshop CS Timesaving Technique For Dummies 0-7645-6782-9
- PHP 5 For Dummies 0-7645-4166-8
- PowerPoint 2003 For Dummies 0-7645-3908-6
- QuarkXPress 6 For Dummies 0-7645-2593-X

NETWORKING, SECURITY, PROGRAMMING & DATABASES

0-7645-6852-3

0-7645-5784-X

Also available:

- A+ Certification For Dummies 0-7645-4187-0
- Access 2003 All-in-One Desk Reference For Dummies 0-7645-3988-4
- Beginning Programming For Dummies 0-7645-4997-9
- C For Dummies 0-7645-7068-4
- Firewalls For Dummies 0-7645-4048-3
- Home Networking For Dummies 0-7645-42796
- Network Security For Dummies 0-7645-1679-5
- Networking For Dummies 0-7645-1677-9
- TCP/IP For Dummies 0-7645-1760-0
- VBA For Dummies 0-7645-3989-2
- Wireless All In-One Desk Reference For Dummies 0-7645-7496-5
- Wireless Home Networking For Dumm 0-7645-3910-8

CPSIA information can be obtained
at www.ICGtesting.com
Printed in the USA
LVOW03*0120280516
490346LV00023B/286/P